T0214906

Deep Learning with Swift for TensorFlow

Differentiable Programming with Swift

Rahul Bhalley

Apress®

Deep Learning with Swift for TensorFlow: Differentiable Programming with Swift

Rahul Bhalley
Ludhiana, India

ISBN-13 (pbk): 978-1-4842-6329-7   ISBN-13 (electronic): 978-1-4842-6330-3
https://doi.org/10.1007/978-1-4842-6330-3

Copyright © 2021 by Rahul Bhalley

This work is subject to copyright. All rights are reserved by the Publisher, whether the whole or part of the material is concerned, specifically the rights of translation, reprinting, reuse of illustrations, recitation, broadcasting, reproduction on microfilms or in any other physical way, and transmission or information storage and retrieval, electronic adaptation, computer software, or by similar or dissimilar methodology now known or hereafter developed.

Trademarked names, logos, and images may appear in this book. Rather than use a trademark symbol with every occurrence of a trademarked name, logo, or image we use the names, logos, and images only in an editorial fashion and to the benefit of the trademark owner, with no intention of infringement of the trademark.

The use in this publication of trade names, trademarks, service marks, and similar terms, even if they are not identified as such, is not to be taken as an expression of opinion as to whether or not they are subject to proprietary rights.

While the advice and information in this book are believed to be true and accurate at the date of publication, neither the authors nor the editors nor the publisher can accept any legal responsibility for any errors or omissions that may be made. The publisher makes no warranty, express or implied, with respect to the material contained herein.

Managing Director, Apress Media LLC: Welmoed Spahr
Acquisitions Editor: Aaron Black
Development Editor: James Markham
Coordinating Editor: Jessica Vakili

Distributed to the book trade worldwide by Springer Science+Business Media New York,1 NY Plazar, New York, NY 10014. Phone 1-800-SPRINGER, fax (201) 348-4505, e-mail orders-ny@ springer-sbm.com, or visit www.springeronline.com. Apress Media, LLC is a California LLC and the sole member (owner) is Springer Science + Business Media Finance Inc (SSBM Finance Inc). SSBM Finance Inc is a **Delaware** corporation.

For information on translations, please e-mail booktranslations@springernature.com; for reprint, paperback, or audio rights, please e-mail bookpermissions@springernature.com.

Apress titles may be purchased in bulk for academic, corporate, or promotional use. eBook versions and licenses are also available for most titles. For more information, reference our Print and eBook Bulk Sales web page at http://www.apress.com/bulk-sales.

Any source code or other supplementary material referenced by the author in this book is available to readers on GitHub via the book's product page, located at www.apress.com/978-1-4842-6329-7. For more detailed information, please visit http://www.apress.com/source-code.

Printed on acid-free paper

Table of Contents

About the Author

Rahul Bhalley is an independent machine intelligence researcher. He was the co-founder of a short-lived deep learning startup in 2018. He has published research papers in areas such as speech processing and generative modeling. He actively contributes to open source projects related to deep learning on GitHub. He has also worked with Apple's Swift and shares Google's vision of making it easy for others to understand deep learning with Swift.

About the Technical Reviewer

Vishwesh Ravi Shrimali graduated from BITS Pilani in 2018, where he studied mechanical engineering. Since then, he has worked with Big Vision LLC on deep learning and computer vision and was involved in creating official OpenCV AI courses. Currently, he is working at Mercedes-Benz Research and Development India Pvt. Ltd. He has a keen interest in programming and AI and has applied that interest in mechanical engineering projects. He has also written multiple blogs on OpenCV and deep learning on Learn OpenCV, a leading blog on computer vision. He has also coauthored *Machine Learning for OpenCV* (second edition) by Packt. When he is not writing blogs or working on projects, he likes to go on long walks or play his acoustic guitar.

Preface

As a programmer and student pursuing graduation, I had a lot of trouble understanding deep learning by myself when I started this journey back in 2015. So I decided to write a deep learning programming book that might help people in a similar situation as mine to easily understand deep learning. I have tried to keep the explanation of difficult deep learning concepts simple throughout the book.

But why Swift for deep learning? Swift is a powerful general-purpose differentiable programming language. Swift is a well-researched programming language and the code written in it seems like reading English sentences, making it easy for newcomers to learn programming and even deep learning. Furthermore, Swift is optimized for performance, so researchers can write all deep learning algorithms in a single language with simple syntax.

And what about Python's wide ecosystem of various libraries? With the Python interoperability feature of Swift for TensorFlow (S4TF), you can use Python libraries within Swift!

The intended audience of this book is as follows:

1. Newcomers to programming and/or deep learning, expert programmers, and deep learning researchers

2. People who desire to work in user space instead of framework space with the same programming language in deep learning without compromising the speed

For newcomers, I hope this book serves as a good starting point to learn programming and deep learning. And for researchers, I hope this book will make the adoption of Swift for TensorFlow for deep learning research easy.

CHAPTER 1

Machine Learning Basics

We're unquestionably in the business of forging the gods.[1]

—*Pamela McCorduck*

Nowadays, artificial intelligence (AI) is one of the most fascinating fields of computer science in addition to quantum computing (Preskill, 2018) and blockchain (Nakamoto, 2008). Hype since the mid-2000s in the industrial community has led to large amounts of investments for AI startups. Globally leading technology companies such as Apple, Google, Amazon, Facebook, and Microsoft, just to name a few, are quickly acquiring talented AI startups from all over the world to accelerate AI research and, in turn, improve their own products.

Consider a portable device like Apple Watch. It uses machine intelligence to analyze your real-time motion sensory data to track your steps, standing hours, swimming reps, sleep time, and more. It also calculates your heart rate from temporal blood color variations underneath your wrist's skin, alerts you about your heartbeat irregularities, performs electrocardiography (ECG), measures oxygen consumption in blood (VO max) during exercise, and much more. On the other hand, devices like

---

[1]Quoted from (McCorduck, 2004).

© Rahul Bhalley 2021
R. Bhalley, *Deep Learning with Swift for TensorFlow*,
https://doi.org/10.1007/978-1-4842-6330-3_1

iPhone and iPad use the LIDAR information from camera sensors to create depth map of surrounding instantly. This information is then combined with machine intelligence to deliver computational photography features such as bokeh effect with adjustable strength, immersive augmented reality (AR) features such as reflection and lighting of surrounding on AR objects, object occlusions when humans enter in the scene, and much more. Personal voice assistant like Siri understands your speech allowing you to do various tasks such as controlling your home accessories, playing music on HomePod, calling and texting people, and more. The machine intelligence technology becomes possible due to fast graphics processing unit (GPU). Nowadays GPU on portable devices are fast enough to process user's data without having to send it to the cloud servers. This approach helps in keeping the user's data private and hence secure from undesirable exposure and usage (Sharma and Bhalley, 2016). In fact, all the features mentioned above are made available with on-device machine intelligence.

It might surprise you that AI is not a new technology. It actually dates back to the 1940s, and it was not considered useful and cool at all. It had many ups and downs. The AI technology arose to popularity for mainly three times. It had different names over these eras, and now we popularly know it as deep learning. Between the 1940s-1960s, AI was known as "cybernetics"; around the 1980s–1990s, it was known as "connectionism"; and since 2006, we know AI as "deep learning."

At some point in the past, there was also a misconception, believed by many researchers, that if all the rules of the way everything in the universe works were programmed in a computing machine, then it would automatically become intelligent. But this idea is strongly challenged by the current state of AI because we now know there are simpler ways to make machines mimic human-like intelligence.

In earlier days of AI research, the data was sparsely available. The computational machines were also slow. These were one of the main factors that drowned the popularity of AI systems. But now we have the Internet, and a very large fraction of the population on Earth interacts with one another which generates humongous amounts of data quickly which are stored in servers of respective companies. (Raina et al., 2009) figured out a way to run the deep learning algorithms with faster speed. The combination of large datasets and high-performance computing (HPC) has led researchers to quickly advance the state-of-the-art deep learning algorithms. And this book is focused on introducing you to these advanced algorithms starting from the simpler concepts.

In this chapter, we will introduce the basic concepts of machine learning which remain valid for its successor, the deep learning field. Chapter 2 focuses on the mathematics required to clearly understand the deep learning algorithms. Because deep learning is an empirical subject, understanding only mathematical equations for deep learning algorithms is of no use if we cannot program them ourselves. Moreover, the computers were built to test theorems of mathematics by performing numerical computation (Turing, 1936). Chapter 3 introduces a powerful, compiled, and fast programming language for deep learning called Swift for TensorFlow which extends Apple's Swift language (which is already capable of differentiable programming) to include deep learning–specific features with the TensorFlow library. TensorFlow is a deep learning–specific library and deserves the whole Chapter 4 dedicated to its introduction. Then we dive into the basics of neural networks in Chapter 5. Finally, we will program some advanced computer vision algorithms in Chapter 6.

But let us first differentiate between the terms artificial intelligence, machine learning, and deep learning because these are sometimes used interchangeably. Artificial intelligence, also called machine intelligence, represents a set of algorithms which can be used to make machines intelligent. AI systems usually contain hard-coded rules that a program follows to make some sense out of the data (Russell & Norvig, 2002), for instance, finding a noun in a sentence using hard-coded English grammar rules, preventing a robot from falling into a pit using if and else conditions, and so on. These systems are considered weakly intelligent nowadays. Another term is machine learning (ML) which unlike AI algorithms uses data to draw insights from it (Bishop, 2006), for instance, classifying an image using non-parametric algorithms like k-nearest neighbors, classifying a text using decision tree methods, and so on. ML uses data to learn and is also known to perform weaker than deep learning. Finally, the current state-of-the-art AI is deep learning. Deep learning (DL) also uses data for learning but in a hierarchical fashion (LeCun et al., 2015) taking inspiration from the brain. DL algorithms can learn the mapping of very complicated datasets easily without compromising accuracy, but they instead perform better than machine learning algorithms. If you'd draw a Venn diagram, shown in Figure 1-1, you'd see deep learning is a subset of machine learning, whereas the artificial intelligence field is a superset of both these fields.

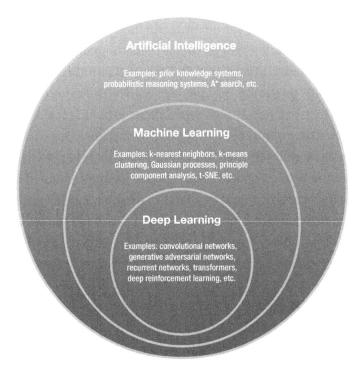

Figure 1-1. *A Venn diagram representing the overlap (not precisely scaled) between artificial intelligence, machine learning, and deep learning algorithms. Each set gives a few examples of algorithms belonging to that field.*

Now we can begin our journey with deep learning starting with simple machine learning concepts.

1.1 Machine Learning

A machine learning algorithm learns to perform some task by learning itself from the data while improving its performance. The widely accepted definition (Mitchell et al., 1997) of machine learning is as follows: "A computer program is said to learn from experience E with respect to some class of task T and performance measure P if its performance at task T, as measured by P, improves with experience E." The idea is to write a computer program that can update its state via some performance measure to perform the desired task with good performance by experiencing the available data. No human intervention should be required to make this program learn.

Based on this definition, there are three fundamental ideas that help us in making machines learn, namely, experience, task, and performance measure. Each of these ideas is discussed in this section. In Section 1.4, we will see how these ideas are expressed mathematically such that a learning computer program can be written. Following Section 1.4, you will realize that this simple definition forms the basis for how machines learn and that each paradigm of machine learning discussed in the book can be implicitly expressed in terms of this definition.

Before we proceed further, it's important to clarify that a machine learning algorithm is made up of various basic components. Its learning component is called a model which is simply a mathematical function. Now let us move on to understand these fundamental ideas.

1.1.1 Experience

The *experience* is multiple observations made by a model to learn to perform a task. These observations are samples from an available dataset. During learning, a model is always required to observe the data.

5

The data can be in various forms such as image, video, audio, text, tactile, and others. Each *sample*, also known as *example*, from data can be expressed in terms of its *features*. For example, features of an image sample are its pixels where each pixel consists of red, green, and blue color values. The different brightness value of all these colors together represents a single color in the visible range of the spectrum (which our eyes can perceive) of electromagnetic radiations.

In addition to the features, each sample sometimes might also contain a corresponding *label* vector, also known as *target* vector, which represents the class to which the sample belongs. For instance, a fish image sample might have a corresponding label vector that represents a fish. The label is usually expressed in *one-hot encoding* (also called 1-*of-k coding* where k is the number of classes), a representation where only a single index in a whole vector has a value of one and all others are set to zero. Each index is assumed to represent a certain class, and the index whose value is one is assumed to represent the class to which the sample belongs. For instance, assume the [1 0 0] vector represents a dog, whereas [0 1 0] and [0 0 1] vectors represent a fish and a bird, respectively. This means that all the image samples of birds have a corresponding label vector [0 0 1] and likewise dog and fish image samples will have their own labels.

The features of samples we have listed previously are raw features, that is, these are not handpicked by humans. Sometimes, in machine learning, feature selection plays an important role in the performance of the model. For instance, a high-resolution image will be slower to process than its low-resolution counterpart for a task like face recognition. Because deep learning can work directly on raw data with great performance, we won't discuss feature selection in particular. But we will go through some preprocessing techniques as the need arises in code listings to get the data in correct format. We refer the interested readers to (Theodoridis and Koutroumbas, 2009) textbook to read about feature selection.

In deep learning, we may require to preprocess the data. *Preprocessing* is a sequence of functions applied on raw samples to transform them into a desired specific form. This desired form is usually decided based on the design of the model and the task at hand. For instance, a raw audio waveform sampled at 16 KHz has 16,384 samples per second expressed as a vector. For even a short audio recording, say 5 seconds, this vector's dimension size will become very large, that is, an 81,920 elements long vector! This will take longer to process by our model. This is where preprocessing becomes helpful. We can then preprocess each raw audio waveform sample with the fast Fourier transform (Heideman et al., 1985) function to transform it into a spectrogram representation. Now this image can be processed much faster than the previous lengthy raw audio waveform. There are different ways to preprocess the data, and the choice depends on the model design and the task at hand. We will cover some preprocessing steps in the book for different kinds of data, non-exhaustively, wherever the need occurs.

1.1.2 Task

The *task* is an act of processing the sample features by the model to return the correct label for the sample. There are fundamentally two tasks for which machine learning models are designed, namely, regression and classification. There are more interesting tasks which we will introduce and program in later chapters and are simply the extension of these two basic tasks.

For instance, for a fish image, the model should return the [0 1 0] vector. Because here the image is being mapped to its label, this task is commonly known as image classification. This serves as a simple example for a classification task.

A good example of a regression task is object detection. We might want to detect the location of an object, say ball, in an image. Here, features are image pixels, and the labels are the coordinates of an object in the image. These coordinates represent a bounding box for the object, that is, the location where the object is present in a given image. Here, our goal is to train a model that takes image features as input and predicts the correct bonding box coordinates for an object. Because the prediction output is real-valued, object detection is considered as a regression task.

1.1.3 Performance Measure

Once we have designed a model to perform a task, the next step is to make it learn and evaluate its performance on the given task. For evaluation, a performance measure (or metric) of some form is used. A performance metric can take various forms such as accuracy, F1 score, precision and recall, and others, to describe how well the model performs a task. Note that the same performance metric should be used to evaluate the model during both training and testing phases.

As a rule of thumb, one must try to select a single-number performance metric whenever possible. In our previous image classification example, one can easily use accuracy as a performance metric. *Accuracy* is defined as a fraction of the total number of images (or other samples) classified correctly by the model. As shown next, a multiple-number performance metric can also be used, but it makes it harder to decide which model performs best from a set of trained models.

Let us consider two image classifiers C_1 and C_2 whose task is to predict if an image contains a car or not. As shown in Table 1-1, if classifier C_1 has 0.92 accuracy and classifier C_2 has 0.99 accuracy, then it is obvious that C_2 performs better than C_1.

Table 1-1. *The accuracies of classifiers C_1 and C_2 on an image recognition task.*

Classifier	Accuracy
C_1	92%
C_2	99%

Now let us consider precision and recall for these two classifiers which is a two-number evaluation metric. *Precision* and *recall* are defined as a fraction of *all* and *car* images in the test or validation set that the classifier correctly labeled as cars, respectively. For our arbitrary classifiers, these metric values are shown in Table 1-2.

Table 1-2. *The precision and recall of classifiers C_1 and C_2 on an image recognition task.*

Classifier	Precision	Recall
C_1	98%	95%
C_2	95%	90%

Now it seems unclear which model has a superior performance. We can instead turn precision and recall into a single-number metric. There are multiple ways to achieve this such as mean or F_1 score. Here, we will find its F_1 score. *F_1 score*, also called *F-measure* and *F-score*, is actually a harmonic mean between precision and recall and is calculated with the following formula:

$$F_1 = \frac{2}{\dfrac{1}{\text{Precision}} + \dfrac{1}{\text{Recall}}} \tag{1.1}$$

Table 1-3 shows the F_1 score for each classifier by putting their precision and recall values in Equation 1.1.

From Table 1-3, by simply looking at the F_1 scores, we can easily conclude that classifier C_2 performs better than C_1. In practice, having a single-number metric for evaluation can be extremely helpful in determining the superiority of the trained models and accelerate your research or deployment process.

Table 1-3. *The precision, recall, and F_1 score of classifiers C_1 and C_2 on an image recognition task.*

Classifier	Precision	Recall	F1 score
C_1	98%	85%	91%
C_2	95%	90%	92.4%

Having discussed the fundamental ideas of machine learning, we will now shift our focus toward different machine learning paradigms.

1.2 Machine Learning Paradigms

Machine learning is usually classified into four categories based on the kind of dataset experience a model is allowed as follows: supervised learning (SL), unsupervised learning (UL), semi-supervised learning (SSL), and reinforcement learning (RL). We briefly discuss each of these machine learning paradigms.

1.2.1 Supervised Learning

During training, when a model makes use of labeled data samples for learning to perform a task, then this type of machine learning is known as *supervised learning*. It is called "supervised" because each sample belonging to the dataset has a corresponding label. In supervised learning, during training, the goal of the machine learning model is to map from samples to their corresponding targets. During inference, the supervised model must predict the correct labels for any given samples including samples unseen during training.

We have already gone through an idea of an image classification task previously which is an example of SL. For example, you can search photos by typing the class (or category) of object present in the photo in Apple's Photos app. Another interesting SL task is automatic speech recognition (ASR) where a sequence of audio waveforms is transcribed by the model into a textual sequence representing the words spoken in the audio recording. For instance, Siri, Google Assistant, Cortana, and other personal voice assistants on portable devices all use speech recognition to convert your spoken words into text. At the time of writing, SL is the most successful and widely used machine learning in production.

1.2.2 Unsupervised Learning

Unsupervised learning is a type of machine learning where a model is allowed to observe only sample features and not the labels. UL usually aims at learning some useful representation of a dataset in the hidden features of model. This learned representation can later be used to perform any desired task with this model. UL is of great interest to the deep learning community at the time of this writing.

As an example, UL can be used to reduce the dimensionality of high-dimensional data samples which, as we discussed earlier, can help in processing the data samples faster through the model. Another example is density estimation where the goal is to estimate the probability density of a dataset. After density estimation, the model can produce samples similar to those belonging to the dataset it was trained on. UL algorithms can be used to perform various interesting tasks as we shall see later.

It's very important to note that UL is called "unsupervised" because of the fact that labels aren't present in the dataset but we still require labels to be fed to the loss function (which is the fundamental requirement of maximum likelihood estimation discussed in Section 1.3) along with the prediction in order to train the model. In this situation we assume some appropriate labels for the samples ourselves. For example, in generative adversarial networks

(Goodfellow et al., 2014), the label for datapoint generated from a generator is given a fake label (or 0), whereas a datapoint sampled from a dataset is given a real label (or 1). Another example is auto-encoder (Vincent et al., 2008) where labels are the corresponding sample images themselves.

1.2.3 Semi-supervised Learning

Semi-supervised learning is concerned with training a model from a small set of labeled samples and the predictions (using the contemporarily semi-trained model) for unlabeled samples as *pseudo-targets* (also called *soft targets*) during training. From the perspective of the kind of data experienced during training, SSL is halfway between supervised and unsupervised learning because it observes both labeled and unlabeled samples. SSL is particularly useful when we have a large dataset containing only a handful of labeled samples (because they're laborious and hence costly to obtain) and a large number of unlabeled samples. Interestingly, an SSL technique for training the model can considerably boost its performance.

We do not cover semi-supervised learning in the book. For rigorous understanding of semi-supervised learning, we refer the interested readers to (Chapelle et al., 2006) textbook.

1.2.4 Reinforcement Learning

Reinforcement learning is based on reward obtained by the agent interacting with the environment to maximize its cumulative reward (weighted average sequence of rewards, also known as return) over a number of trials (called episodes) to achieve its goal. RL is a paradigm of machine learning that involves a sequence of decision-making processes.

The agent acts on the world by taking some action, say it moves forward. Following this, the environment's state gets updated, and a reward is returned (or given) back to the agent by the environment.

The reward is either positive or negative and can be, respectively, regarded as a good or bad response to the agent from the world in accordance to the behavioral science viewpoint. We are more interested in return instead of the current step reward because the goal of the agent is to maximize the return over the course of each episode. Here, an episode is a sequence of interactions between an agent and its environment from a start to an end. Examples of an episode are as follows: a gameplay by the agent where the game ends when a certain condition is met and an agent trying to stay alive in harsh environmental conditions until it dies due to some accident. See Figure 1-2 for a diagrammatic view of an interaction between the agent and its environment.

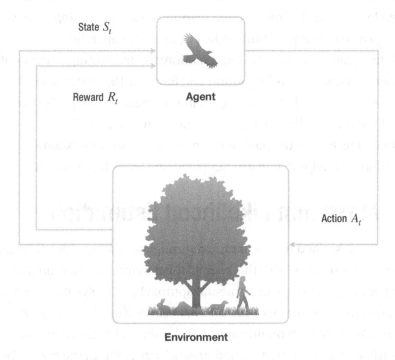

Figure 1-2. *An interaction between a reinforcement learning agent and the environment.*

The agent perceives the previous state of the environment S_{t-1} and takes an action A_t on the environment whose state S_t changes and is returned to the agent. The agent also receives a scalar reward R_t from the environment describing how good is the current state for the agent. Although the state of the environment changes when the agent acts, it may also change by itself. In multi-agent reinforcement learning, there might also be other agents maximizing their own returns.

Reinforcement learning is a very interesting machine learning field and is being studied aggressively at the time of this writing. It is also considered to be more close to the way humans (or other mammals) learn by making behavioral modifications, that is, reinforcing an action based on the reward. A recent work (Minh et al., 2015) showed that a combination of deep learning and reinforcement learning called *deep reinforcement learning* can even surpass human-level gameplay capabilities.

Unfortunately, we don't discuss reinforcement learning in the book. Interested readers may refer (Sutton and Barto, 2018) textbook for the fundamentals of this field. For deep reinforcement learning advances, we suggest the works (Mnih et al., 2015; Schulman et al., 2017).

Now let us look at the basic idea known as maximum likelihood estimation that helps in constructing machine learning algorithms.

1.3 Maximum Likelihood Estimation

The setting described here is assumed throughout the machine learning literature. Constrained with this setting, the parameters of a model are estimated. There are two fundamental approaches to solve the parameters estimation problem, namely, *maximum likelihood estimation* and *Bayesian inference*. We will focus on maximum likelihood estimation because this is what we'll use to train neural networks throughout the book. The readers interested in Bayesian inference are suggested to read Chapter 2 of (Bishop, 1995) textbook. And for detailed notes on the origination of the maximum likelihood function, please refer (Akaike, 1973).

To solve a machine learning problem, we require a dataset $\mathbb{D}$ containing a set of N datapoints (or samples), that is, $\mathbb{D} = \left\{ \left(\mathbf{x}^{(i)}, t^{(i)} \right) \right\}_{i=1}^{N}$. Assume that each datapoint is identical and sampled independently from a joint data-generating distribution $P_d(\mathbf{x}, t)$ which is a probability density function (PDF) meaning that data sample $\mathbf{x}$ and corresponding target t are continuous random variables. Note that the distribution of target random variable t is actually dependent on the task performed by the model, that is, the target's distribution is, respectively, continuous and discrete for regression and classification tasks. We will also call $P_d(\mathbf{x}, t)$ as a *data probability density function* (or data PDF). We only have access to the dataset $\mathbb{D}$ sampled from the data PDF and not the distribution itself. Therefore, we cannot access more datapoints than what are available to us.

Because the dataset $\mathbb{D}$ is sampled from the data PDF, it statistically describes the data PDF itself. Our goal in parametric machine learning is to approximate the mapping of the data PDF by estimating the parameters of a parameterized probability density function $P_m(\mathbf{x}, y|\theta)$ (or simply $P_m(\mathbf{x}, y)$) of our own choice which we will call a *model probability density function* (or model PDF), and we will also frequently refer to it simply as a *model* throughout the book. Here, θ represents parameters, and the random variables $\mathbf{x}$ and $\mathbf{y}$ are the data sample and the corresponding predicted value given $\mathbf{x}$ as input. We will actually minimize the distance, also called loss or error, between prediction variable $\mathbf{y}$ and target variable $\mathbf{t}$ by updating the parameter values using the maximum likelihood function.

The model and data PDFs are completely different distributions such that their samples are also statistically different. But we want the predictions $\mathbf{y}$ from the model PDF to resemble corresponding targets $\mathbf{t}$ from the data PDF for a given data sample $\mathbf{x}$. As pointed out earlier, we don't have access to the parameters of the data PDF so we cannot simply copy its parameter values to those of the model function. But we do have dataset $\mathcal{X}$ at our disposal which we can exploit to approximate the data PDF because it's its statistical description.

Now we will describe *maximum likelihood estimation* to approximate the data PDF with our parameterized model PDF. Because the datapoints in $\mathcal{X}$ are independent and identically distributed, their joint probability is given by

$$P_m\left(\mathbb{D}|\theta\right) = \prod_{i=1}^{N} P_m\left(\mathbf{x}^{(i)}, \mathbf{t}^{(i)}|\theta\right) = \mathcal{L}\left(\theta|\mathbb{D}\right) \tag{1.2}$$

Here, $P_m(\mathbb{D}|\theta)$ is the conditional model PDF and is read as "joint probability of a dataset given the parameters." The function $\mathscr{L}(\theta|\mathbb{D})$ is a *likelihood function* of parameters θ for a given fixed and finite dataset $\mathbb{D}$. You may also interpret this function as "likely a good approximation of the data PDF from which the dataset $\mathbb{D}$ is sampled." To reduce the clutter, we will implicitly assume the parameters conditioning in both the model and log-likelihood function. We will use the Bayes theorem to convert joint data probability distribution into a conditional distribution we care about.

$$\mathcal{L} = \prod_{i=1}^{N} P_m\left(\mathbf{x}^{(i)}, \mathbf{t}^{(i)}\right) = \prod_{i=1}^{N} P_m\left(\mathbf{t}^{(i)}|\mathbf{x}^{(i)}\right) P_m\left(\mathbf{x}^{(i)}\right) \tag{1.3}$$

The data PDF is approximated by maximizing the likelihood function which requires updating the parameter values of the model PDF. More specifically, the parameters are updated by an iterative method as briefly described in Section 1.4 and at great length in Section 5.1. Numerically, it is more convenient to first take the negative logarithm of the likelihood and then minimize it. This is equivalent to maximizing the likelihood function.

$$L = -\ln\mathcal{L} = -\sum_{i=1}^{N} \ln P_m\left(\mathbf{t}^{(i)}|\mathbf{x}^{(i)}\right) - \sum_{i=1}^{N} \ln P_m\left(\mathbf{x}^{(i)}\right) \tag{1.4}$$

The logarithm function plays a very important role here. It turns the products into summations which helps in stabilizing the numerical computation. This is because the products of values closer to zero are much smaller values which may get rounded off due to limited-precision representational capacity of computational devices. This is why machine learning frequently uses the logarithm function.

The negative log-likelihood function can be regarded as a *loss* or *error function* denoted by L(.). Our goal is to minimize the loss function by updating its parameter values such that our parameterized model PDF approximates the data PDF using the available fixed and finite data samples from the data PDF. Note that the second term in this equation doesn't contribute in the parameters estimation of the model PDF because it doesn't depend on the model's parameters and is simply a negative additive term which can be ignored for maximizing the likelihood function. The loss function can now be simply described by the following equation:

$$L = -\sum_{i=1}^{N} \ln P_m\left(\mathbf{t}^{(i)} \middle| \mathbf{x}^{(i)}\right)$$
(1.5)

Minimizing the loss function is equivalent to minimizing the negative log-likelihood function which further can be considered as maximizing the log-likelihood function, hence the term *maximum likelihood estimation*. Here, our model PDF represents a conditional distribution of targets given the data samples $P_m(\mathbf{t}|\mathbf{x})$. We shall see later that a neural network is a framework for modeling this conditional distribution. And also based on the distribution of the target random variable, different loss functions arise using this equation.

As a sidenote, hypothetically speaking, if the likelihood function perfectly approximates the data PDF, then the available dataset $\mathcal{X}$ and other identical datasets can be sampled from it. But in practice, it is not possible to perfectly approximate the data PDF, but we can instead closely approximate it. This is all what we do in machine learning.

Now let us look at the elements of a machine learning algorithm and make the vague definition of machine learning given by (Mitchell et al., 1997) mathematically concrete.

1.4 Elements of a Machine Learning Algorithm

In this section, we describe the fundamental elements of a machine learning algorithm that apply to all paradigms of machine learning briefly discussed in Section 1.2. There are four crucial components of a machine learning algorithm, namely, data, model, loss function, and optimization. Optionally, one can also use regularization techniques to improve the generalization of the model and balance the bias and variance trade-off (see Section 1.5).

Remember that in machine learning, our primary goal is to train a model that should perform well on unseen data because our training dataset will not contain the data generated by users in the future.

1.4.1 Data

The data present in the dataset serves as an experience for the machine learning model. When the model is first initialized with random parameter values, it has no knowledge of how to perform well on the certain task. This knowledge is gained by iteratively exposing the model to data (usually in small sample counts, also known as *mini-batches*). As the model experiences more samples, it gradually learns to perform the task more accurately.

A *dataset* is simply a structured, usually a tabular (or matrix), arrangement of datapoints. Table 1-4 shows an arbitrary example of a dataset. This dataset contains some characteristics (or features) of people where each row contains the features for a single person. Each row contains the height (in centimeters), age (in years), and weight (in kilograms) values for a certain person. Note that features and their corresponding targets can be tensor values of any dimensions (0 dimensions, i.e., scalar variables, here).

Table 1-4. *Dataset of people with their heights, ages, and weights represented by x_1, x_2, and t scalars, respectively.*

Height (x_1)	Age (x_2)	Weight (t)
151.7	25	47.8
139.7	20	36.4
136.5	18	31.8
156.8	28	53.0

Given the dataset, we must decide the features and targets for a task. In other words, selection of the correct features for a task is dependent solely upon our decision. For instance, we can use this dataset to perform a regression task of predicting the weight given the height and age of a person. In this setting, our *feature vector* **x** contains height x_1 and age x_2, that is, **x** = [x_1 x_2], for each person (called sample), whereas the target t is the weight of a person. For example, **x** = [136.5 18] and $t = 31.8$ are the feature vector and target scalar for the third person in the given dataset.

In machine learning literature, datapoint input to the model is also known as *example* or *sample,* and its features are also known as *attributes.* For instance, features of a car can be color, tire size, top speed, and so on. Another example can be a drug whose features may include chemical formula, proportion of each chemical element, and so on. The target, also known as *label* or *hard target* (when differentiating from soft target), is the desired output corresponding to a given sample. For instance, given the features of an image (pixel values), the target can be a chair, table, and so on, represented as a vector. Also note that all targets always remain the same for a given sample in a dataset. In rare cases, we generate *soft targets* for unlabeled samples in semi-supervised learning, whereas the targets are *always* assumed immutable in supervised learning.

1.4.1.1 Design Matrix

The most popular way of representing a dataset is design matrix as described in Table 1-4. *Design matrix* is a collection of samples and targets where each row contains a single sample (and each of its columns contains a feature describing it) and its corresponding target. The target values are used for supervised learning tasks. It is *only* the sample that contains the features and not the target. The target is the desired output we expect for our model to predict for a given sample's features.

1.4.1.2 Independent and Identical Samples

A good dataset should statistically represent the overall distribution of samples in a data-generating probability density function. Remember that we never have access to this PDF but the dataset only. Since a dataset statistically represents a probability distribution, there are always some patterns in the way samples are distributed. And the machine learning algorithms aim to discover such patterns in datasets to perform the desired tasks. We can only intuitively judge the patterns easily in low dimensions (at most three dimensions) by staring at a set of samples, but machine learning algorithms can understand the patterns in higher dimensions (even billions). For instance, we can say "If the height of a person lies in range [110,160], then their weight will lie in range [30,80]" and so on. But if we add features such as workout time, nutrition intake, and so on, then the sample has much more complex detailed patterns which can become difficult for us to process collectively, but the machine learning algorithm can analyze it for us and even more accurately.

For any machine learning algorithm to perform well on the task, we need two constraints on the dataset for discovering patterns between samples. First, the value of each sample should be independent of another sample, that is, samples should not be correlated, although the individual features in each sample should be correlated. Second, the samples should be identical, that is, their corresponding features should be similar and exhibit some patterns over the distribution.

That being said, an imaginary dataset of photographs of nature conforming to such constraints might contain images of rivers, vehicles, skies, underwater lives, plants, humans, animals, and so on, where each sample is a photograph and its features are pixel values as a combination of red, green, and blue colors. This suffices the identical requirement because, for instance, the landscape image will always contain the sky and the ground. Furthermore, this nature dataset also conforms to the independent constraint because none of the images affect the other image's feature (pixel) values. One great example of such dataset is ImageNet (Russakovsky, et al., 2015).

1.4.1.3 Dataset Splits

Now that we know what a dataset is and how it is represented, the next step is to use it to learn its hierarchical representation in a model. But before model training, the dataset must be split into multiple subsets. It is a very important step to follow before training a machine learning model for reasons discussed in the following.

In practice, the model typically has a large number of parameters and easily overfits the whole dataset. By *overfitting*, we mean that the model performs very well on the dataset but performs poorly on the unseen examples which it will certainly encounter in the real world. Another term is *underfitting* which means that the model doesn't perform well on either the dataset it was trained on or the unseen dataset. Balancing between both underfitting and overfitting is a problem that plagues the whole machine learning landscape and is also known as the *bias and variance trade-off* (see Section 1.5).

We split our whole dataset into mainly three subsets, namely, training set, test set, and validation set. If the complete dataset contains examples which are i.i.d, then each subset will contain i.i.d examples also. Each of these subsets plays a crucial role in building a good machine learning model and are explained as follows.

The *training set* contains the examples and targets used to tune the model's learnable parameters. The model is trained to minimize the error between the predicted output and the desired target value for a given input features sample, iteratively. As a prerequisite for the model to perform well on unseen examples, it should initially perform well on the training set which it is allowed to experience during the training process.

The *test set* contains the examples which the model is not allowed to experience during the training process. It is *only* used for testing the performance of the model. In the real world, the test set is curated to contain examples from the dataset which are usually difficult to perform well on. This is done so as to choose a better machine learning model. The test set might also contain examples which are likely to be experienced by the machine learning model in reality. We are usually more concerned with the real-world data we might expect from users, for instance, photographs taken by a smartphone than the cartoon character images. So our test set should contain smartphone-clicked photographs. The end result we want is our model to produce good predictions on unseen examples that are closer to true targets. If a given model performs well on unseen examples, it is said to have a good *generalization* property – otherwise, bad.

The *validation set*, also known as the *development set*, is used to select over a set of possible hyper-parameter configurations, model architectures, and so on for a machine learning algorithm. Unlike the test set, the validation set is used during the training process to evaluate the model's performance. But reusing the same validation set can lead the machine learning algorithm to overfit it. To overcome this problem, researchers sometimes use multiple cross-validation sets. Then the machine learning algorithm is evaluated on multiple validation sets one by one to evaluate its accuracy on unseen examples.

As a rule of thumb, the dataset should be split into 70% training set and 30% test and validation sets. But if the dataset has a large number of samples, then you might not require to follow this criteria. The approach should be to split the dataset such that it represents a good estimate of misclassified examples in terms of accuracy. For more details, we refer the reader to (Ng, 2018) for guidelines on designing the machine learning workflow, mainly for supervised learning tasks for industrial applications, whereas in this book our aim is to introduce you to advanced deep learning algorithms and program them.

1.4.2 Models

We discussed about the dataset in the previous section. The goal is to utilize the dataset in a machine learning algorithm that learns to make predictions on the unseen samples. To accomplish this, we need a machine learning model.

In machine learning, the *model* is a mathematical function with learnable coefficients. In this context, the coefficients of the function are termed as *parameters*. Before training, the machine learning model is initialized with small random parameter values. These parameters are slowly changed during the *optimization phase*, also known as the *training phase*. The aim is to have a machine learning model that performs well on the unseen examples. During the *inference phase*, the machine learning model is used in real-world applications where it encounters the examples not seen during the training phase.

There are two kinds of models that are widely used to approximate the data probability density function, namely, parametric and non-parametric models. We briefly discuss each of these models in the following text.

1.4.2.1 Non-parametric Models

Non-parametric models use a whole dataset to predict the label for a given test sample's features. They use a kernel function that measures the similarity between samples. This function is iteratively called for all training examples and a test example. The choice of kernel function varies between different kernel methods. For instance, the radial basis kernel method uses the radial basis function; k-nearest neighbor regression and classification methods use functions such as Manhattan, Euclidean distance, and others. The kernel function can also be easily extended to give rise to a neural network.

Deeper explanation of non-parametric models lies outside the scope of this book. We refer you to (Bishop, 2006) and (Murphy, 2012) textbooks in this literature.

1.4.2.2 Parametric Models

A *parametric model* is a function that contains tunable coefficients (also known as parameters). The parametric model learns by updating its parameter values to perform a task. Unlike non-parametric models, which always use the whole dataset to make predictions, the parametric model learns the representation of a dataset once and makes prediction using the knowledge present in its parameters. It is difficult to interpret the knowledge present in parametric models and this is an active area of research. Please refer (Carter et al., 2019; Olah et al., 2017, 2018) for in-depth visualization of neural network's features. Non-parametric models merge the training and testing concepts. The parametric models are sometimes slow to train but fast for inference, that is, they are good candidates for real-time deployment for users of either on-device or on-cloud services.

The main focus of this book are parametric models introduced in Chapter 5. In Section 1.1, we didn't discuss how a model learns. In the following text, we will explain the learning (or training) process.

1.4.3 Loss Function

The *loss function* computes the distance between prediction and target values. It measures how good the model is at predicting the correct output for a given input by finding the distance between prediction and target values where the notion of distance is defined by various loss functions (see Section 5.5) based on the prediction distribution. Note that the loss function is also called the *error function, cost function,* and *objective function* in other textbooks. In this book, we prefer the term loss function.

During training, the loss function guides the learnable parameters of the model toward the values such that the model predicts the desired outputs for the corresponding inputs. Note that the loss function is not to be used as a performance metric for the evaluation of the model.

For a regression task, the most common choice of loss function is sum of squared errors defined by the following equation:

$$L(\mathcal{X};\theta) = \frac{1}{2}\sum_{i=1}^{N}\left(y^{(i)} - t^{(i)}\right)^{2},$$

(1.6)

where $L(\mathcal{X};\theta)$ is the loss function, $y^{(i)}$ is the predicted value for an input sample $x^{(i)}$, $t^{(i)}$ is its corresponding target value, and θ are learnable parameters. In total, there are N number of samples in the dataset. The square in this loss function ensures that the overall loss remains non-negative. The fraction term in the loss function has its own importance in that it simplifies the derivative of the loss function as follows:

$$\nabla_{\theta}L = \frac{dL}{dy^{(i)}} = y^{(i)} - t^{(i)}$$

(1.7)

Note that, once our model is trained, we denote the learnable parameters as θ^* and the loss function as $L(\mathcal{X}; \theta^*)$ or simply $L(\theta^*)$ leaving it abstract for which subset of the dataset is the loss function being used.

Now that we have our dataset for experience and model for learning the task, the last component of a machine learning algorithm is an optimizer (and, optionally, regularizer) which is used to make the model learn from data and is discussed next.

1.4.4 Optimizer

Optimization, also known as *training*, is a process of updating the learnable parameters of a model using the loss function to minimize the error between targets and predictions. During training, we optimize our machine learning model which is a two-step process, namely, calculation of the gradient of the error with respect to each learnable parameter of the model and updating the parameter values.

In the first step, we compute the gradient of the loss function with respect to each learnable parameter of the machine learning model. To accomplish this task, we use an efficient algorithm called *error backpropagation* (Rumelhart et al., 1986) (also known as *backpropagation*, or simply *backprop*). This algorithm is simply a successive application of the chain rule of calculus (see Section 2.3) to compute the gradients. A more general algorithm to compute gradients is automatic differentiation (see Section 3.3) of which error backpropagation is a special case.

In the second step, we update the parameters of the model using the gradient information obtained in the first step of optimization. Since the gradient of the loss function gives a direction in which its output increases the most, we iteratively update the parameters with small steps in the direction negative to the gradient because our goal is to minimize the loss function. The learning algorithm used for this parameter update step of optimization is called *gradient descent* as described by the following equation:

$$\theta_{(\tau+1)} \leftarrow \theta_{(\tau)} - \eta \nabla_{\theta(\tau)} L \qquad (1.8)$$

Here, τ denotes the time step of the optimization process, $\theta_{(\tau)}$ denotes the value of a parameter at time step τ, and similarly $\theta_{(\tau+1)}$ is for the parameter values at time step $\tau + 1$. The term $\nabla_{\theta(\tau)}L$ denotes the gradient computed in the preceding text with algorithmic differentiation at time step τ with respect to the weight parameter $\theta_{(\tau)}$. Since the gradient values are usually large, we must take small steps with a hyper-parameter, denoted by term η, known as *step size* (or *learning rate*), to minimize the loss function where $\eta \in (0,1]$. To take small steps, the learning rate is multiplied by the negative gradient of the loss function with respect to each parameter of the model. The optimization is a sequential iterative process, and at each step of iteration, the parameter $\theta_{(\tau)}$ is added with a small step update of $-\eta \nabla_{\theta(\tau)}L$ toward lowering the error between predictions and targets.

In a nutshell, a *single training step* involves alternately forward propagating the input features signal and then backward propagating the error signal computed and emitted by the loss function. The backward propagation computes the gradient which is then utilized to update the parameters of the model. This vanilla gradient descent technique might not always give best results. But there exist various modifications to it for more robust optimization as described at length in Section 5.6.

Note that the models can suffer from overfitting and underfitting problems discussed in Section 1.5. The model is no longer useful if it reaches one of these states for any dataset's splits. To overcome these problems, usually different machine learning models with varying capacities are trained on the same dataset. Another solution is to use regularization techniques while training the model as briefly discussed next and at length in Section 5.7.

1.4.5 Regularizer

Although regularization maybe considered as an optional element of a machine learning algorithm, it plays an important role in training a much more generalized model. *Regularization* is any modification made to the data, model, loss function, or optimizer so as to reduce the model's generalization error (i.e., the model should have low bias and variance).

Here, we describe the widely used regularization term for the loss function known as L^2 *norm penalty*, or *ridge regression* (Hoerl & Kennard, 1970), which modifies the loss function as follows:

$$L(\mathbf{x};\theta) = \frac{1}{2}\sum_{i=1}^{N}\left(y^{(i)} - t^{(i)}\right)^2 + \frac{\lambda}{2}\|\theta\|_2^2 \tag{1.9}$$

where $\|\theta\|_2$ computes the L^2 norm of parameters and λ denotes the weighting of the regularization term which is usually set equal to 1. Training the model with this new loss function helps in reducing the generalization error we care about, that is, the model will perform better on unseen samples.

In Section 5.7, we will discuss various other regularization techniques. For now, let us shift our attention from training models to the concept of bias and variance.

1.5   Bias and Variance Trade-Off

Bias and variance are the characteristics of the model performance on different datasets. *Bias* is concerned with model performance on training set, whereas *variance* is concerned with model performance on validation sets. We desire to find a model that has low bias and variance. But, in practice, we usually trade one for the other. Furthermore, bias and variance trade-off not only affects the traditional machine learning methods but plagues the whole machine learning landscape.

Before discussing bias and variance trade-off, let us introduce the term generalization. The model is said to have a good *generalization* property if it performs very well on the unseen datapoints. We aim to find such model in machine learning.

There are mainly three cases related to bias and variance of a model. Although the fourth case (not mentioned but inferable from other three cases) might be desirable, it is *not* possible statistically, even in theory; otherwise, we might never require to train models.

In the first case, when the model performs well on the training set but poorly on multiple validation sets, it is said to have *low bias and high variance*, respectively. This means the model has a sufficient number of parameters to perform well on the training set, but it overfits the training set (because the number of parameters is more than the requirement to discover the underlying data PDF) or *memorized* the mapping of the training set and has not approximated the underlying data-generating PDF. This is because if it has approximated the data distribution, it should also be able to perform well on the validation sets because, like the training set, validation sets also statistically represent the data PDF.

In the second case, when the model performs well on both training and multiple validation sets, it is said to have *low bias and low variance*, respectively. Here, the model has approximated the underlying data PDF from which all datasets were sampled for both training and testing purposes. In practice, we strive to search for this model.

In the third case, when the model does not perform well on both training and multiple validation sets, it is said to have *high bias and high variance*, respectively. Here, the model does not have a sufficient number of parameters to approximate the training set and, therefore, doesn't also perform well on multiple validation sets. Because the model has low capacity and does not perform well even on the training set, it is said to *underfit*.

1.6 Why Deep Learning?

We discuss various issues with traditional machine learning methods which can be easily tackled with the deep learning approach. This motivates us to study and explore deep learning methods as we shall see in the following.

1.6.1 Curse of Dimensionality

In practice, we usually have samples of dimensions sometimes up to even thousands or even millions. Processing such samples with traditional machine learning methods such as the k-nearest neighbor regressor or classifier, decision trees, and others becomes very inefficient or sometimes even intractable.

Consider a problem of designing a machine learning algorithm that aims to approximate the mapping of an available dataset. Now assume that the available data sample x has a dimension of 1 and is a scalar variable, that is, $x \in \mathbb{R}$. We can start by partitioning the input one-dimensional vector space by a definite integral interval. And doing so, we actually divide the input vector space into M such one-dimensional cells (see Figure 1-3 (a)). We can plot each data sample from the training set on this line. We require to have at least one training point in each cell to make good predictions. Since we have label information for each sample, when we require to predict the label for a new unseen sample, we can simply plot it on this line and assign it to that label which has a maximum count in that cell, for a classification task. In the case of regression, we can take the average of all real-valued labels of training points and assign that value to this test sample.

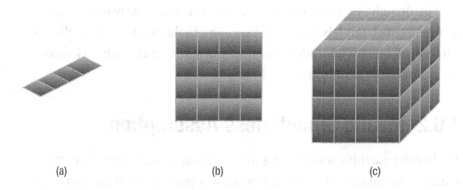

(a)   (b)   (c)

Figure 1-3. *The curse of dimensionally for (a) one-, (b) two-, and (c) three-dimensional datapoints. There is an exponential requirement M^d of samples for predicting the label of a new sample where M = 4 is the number of sections along each dimension and d is the number of dimensions.*

Working in one-dimensional input space seems very easy. But when we jump to higher-dimensional spaces, we start to see the problem arising quickly. Now assume a two-dimensional input vector space for variable $\mathbf{x} \in \mathbb{R}^2$ composed of variables x_1 and x_2 representing x and y axes, respectively. Each training point can now be plotted as a point in the matrix. We can again divide each of the x and y axes for x_1 and x_2 variables into M sections which gives us M^2 cells (see Figure 1-3 (b)). We can again simply predict the label for this test sample using the process described previously. As we move to a third-dimensional vector space $\mathbf{x} \in \mathbb{R}^3$, where x, y, and z axes are represented by x_1, x_2, and x_3 variables, respectively, then we get M^3 sections (see Figure 1-3 (c)) for which we again need at least one training sample in each cell, that is, at least M^3 labeled samples. Following this trend of increasing dimensions, we can see that the number of labeled samples required in a training set increases exponentially with a linear increase in dimensions. We require a total of M^d samples at least to approximate the dataset mapping where d is the dimension of the sample features space. This exponential relation between dimensions and number of samples required is known as *curse of dimensionality* (Bellman, 2015).

Fortunately, we can tackle the curse of dimensionality with deep neural network models as we shall see later in the book. Now we discuss another problem with traditional machine learning algorithms known as the smoothness assumption.

1.6.2 Invalid Smoothness Assumption

Traditional machine learning algorithms assume that a minor change in the input variable's value doesn't bring abrupt changes in the predicted output variable's value. This is known as the *smoothness assumption*. This means that for any two similar input values (for instance, similar-looking images), the predicted label should always be same as the true label. Intuitively, this also holds true for our vision system because we can tell the difference when two images are similar or not. This assumption is helpful when we have sparse training data that doesn't fill up all the cells; then we can simply interpolate the input value closer to the available training sample and assign the same label to our test sample.

This view has been largely assumed valid for non-linear methods also until the work by (Szegedy et al., 2013). The authors showed that we can intentionally construct input images which look similar but are classified wrongly by deep neural networks. Geometrically, we can say that this assumption is valid but only for linear models, whereas for non-linear models, this doesn't hold true. But since we are interested in processing high-dimensional data because it carries important information and due to the weak representational capacity of traditional machine learning methods, we cannot achieve good accuracy. This motivates us to adopt deep learning methods.

Next, we look at some of the advantages offered by deep learning over traditional machine learning methods.

1.6.3 Deep Learning Advantages

As we have discussed earlier, traditional machine learning methods have various problems. This hinders us from analyzing high-dimensional data. There are various advantages of deep learning methods over traditional machine learning methods as discussed here.

Unlike traditional machine learning methods, deep learning is known to give highly accurate results, sometimes even surpassing human-level performance on some tasks. The idea of deep learning is loosely inspired by the way the brain's neural system processes raw data directly obtained from our world. Analogous to the fact that our sensory organs like eyes and ears preprocess the data before sending to the brain, we also sometimes preprocess the data before using it with a deep learning model, but this preprocessing uses entirely a different sequence of functions. But note that there are many things we do not know about the brain itself. Deep learning methods use raw data as input samples and process them to learn abstract information in internal hierarchical high-dimensional spaces. We do not need to select important features for the model. Because the selection process is opinionated among humans, some will find a certain set of features important for the task, while others will prefer some other set of features. Deep learning solves this *feature handcrafting problem* by simply processing the raw data itself. Models in deep learning have multiple layers of neuron-like functions where each layer usually has a different dimension. The high-dimensional input enters the model and gets transformed into different dimensions in different layers until the last layer where the prediction output is generated. Assume a task of image classification. Here, the initial layers (closer to the input) might learn fine-scale details from the image dataset like edges, color gradients, and so on, whereas the intermediate layers (known as hidden layers) might learn more coarse-scale details like shapes such as circle, rectangle, and so on; the layers closer to last layer (known as the prediction layer) might learn the features like eyeball, body shape, and so on; and then finally the prediction layer will predict the label for a given image sample. These models in deep learning are known by many names such as deep learning models, artificial neural networks, deep neural networks, or simply neural networks, and the list of names goes on. Chapter 5 is dedicated to the introduction of neural networks and various successful techniques to train them.

We also notice that traditional methods are sometimes intractable from the random access memory (RAM) and computational speed viewpoint when we have a large number of samples and each of them is representable in large dimensions. Deep learning models exploit the fact that parallel processing is way faster than sequential processing. These models process the features of samples in parallel. Although machine learning was revived in 2006 (Bengio et al., 2007; Hinton et al., 2006; Ranzato et al., 2007), around 2009, it became clear that graphics processing units (GPUs) can speed up deep learning models (Raina et al., 2009) up to even 10 or 20 times faster than central processing unit (CPU) devices for training and inference processes. Since then, companies like Nvidia have put extreme efforts[2] into building faster GPUs with ever-evolving architectural design considerations. Google has also put efforts in building faster parallel processing devices which they call tensor processing units (TPUs). TPUs are available on the cloud and even edge devices. At the time of this writing, famous platforms as a service (PaaS) such as Google Colaboratory and Kaggle offer free access to GPU and TPU devices on the cloud for deep learning. This has helped in immensely accelerating the deep learning research. All the codes written in this book are executable on the Google Colaboratory platform.

Deep learning methods can be considered as successors to traditional machine learning methods because of their various interesting

---

[2]Nvidia Tesla V100 Performance Guide, 2018. Available at `www.nvidia.com/content/dam/en-zz/Solutions/Data-Center/tesla-product-literature/v100-application-performance-guide.pdf`

advantages. Nearly every idea and concept discussed in this chapter for traditional methods (except non-parametric methods) ports without nearly any modifications to the deep learning framework. Fundamentally, the definition remains the same for deep learning: an idea of maximum likelihood estimation is well suited because deep learning models are essentially parametric models, deep learning also requires all the elements of learning algorithms as discussed in Section 1.4, and every type of machine learning can be performed (and much better) with deep learning methods. We will dive deeply into deep learning starting from Chapter 5 with simple neural networks.

1.7 Summary

This chapter introduced the fundamental concepts related to machine learning. We discussed various paradigms of machine learning and introduced the concept of maximum likelihood estimation that helps in training the machine learning models. Then we dived into various fundamental elements of a machine learning algorithm. We also introduced the idea of bias and variance to understand the generalization property of a model. Finally, we shed some light on the advantages of deep learning methods over traditional machine learning methods.

We will study deep learning starting from basic concepts in the following chapters. But before going that far, in the next chapter, we will study various topics from different branches of mathematics which are essential to understand deep learning.

CHAPTER 2

Essential Math

Nothing takes place in the world whose meaning is not that of some maximum or minimum.

—*Leonhard Euler*

This chapter introduces mathematics essential to understand the basics of neural networks. We emphasize you to not skip this chapter if your mathematical concepts are rusty. You may use this chapter as reference when studying later chapters.

In Section 2.1, we introduce linear algebra which is used to make predictions with the neural network and compute the gradients of the loss function with respect to the neural network which makes learning possible. Efficient implementation of linear algebraic operations, like basic linear algebra subroutines (BLAS), also allows the fast computation on modern hardware accelerators such as GPUs using parallel processing. Linear algebra also plays an important role in designing the architecture of the neural network. The neural network can be considered as a probabilistic framework for approximating probability distribution of the available dataset (Section 1.3) which requires the understanding of probability theory discussed in Section 2.2. Unlike deterministic programming, a probabilistic approach to the neural network makes it robust in processing the input data whose values may vary in a continuous space. In Section 2.3, we introduce differential calculus to calculate the gradient of the neural network's loss function which helps in determining how to train the neural network.

© Rahul Bhalley 2021
R. Bhalley, *Deep Learning with Swift for TensorFlow*,
https://doi.org/10.1007/978-1-4842-6330-3_2

2.1 Linear Algebra

This section introduces different matrices and vectors, important unary and binary matrix operations, and norms. These data structures are generalized under the concept of tensor, discussed in Section 4.1.

2.1.1 Matrices and Vectors

There are various types of matrices and vectors, but we restrict ourselves to those important in the deep learning field. We start by introducing different matrices, and then we discuss some important vectors.

When all the attributes of a *square matrix* (having the same number of rows and columns) along the main diagonal are ones, the matrix is termed as an *identity matrix* and is denoted by $\mathbf{I}_n$, where $\mathbf{I}_n \in \mathbb{R}^{n \times n}$, having n rows and columns, and is called an n-order *identity matrix*. For instance, an identity matrix of order 5 is written as follows:

$$\begin{bmatrix} 1 & 0 & 0 & 0 & 0 \\ 0 & 1 & 0 & 0 & 0 \\ 0 & 0 & 1 & 0 & 0 \\ 0 & 0 & 0 & 1 & 0 \\ 0 & 0 & 0 & 0 & 1 \end{bmatrix} \tag{2.1}$$

We can also find an inverse matrix of a given matrix denoted by $\mathbf{A}^{-1}$ where $\mathbf{A}$ is an invertible matrix. An inverse matrix is defined by the following equation:

$$\mathbf{A}^{-1}\mathbf{A} = \mathbf{I}_n \tag{2.2}$$

where $\mathbf{I}_n$ is an n-order identity matrix. Note that the matrix $\mathbf{A}$ must be invertible for producing its inverse matrix $\mathbf{A}^{-1}$.

A diagonal matrix **D** is defined as a matrix with all the elements zero except the ones where $i = j$. For instance, the following is a diagonal matrix:

$$\begin{bmatrix} 2.5 & 0 & 0 & 0 & 0 \\ 0 & 8 & 0 & 0 & 0 \\ 0 & 0 & -3 & 0 & 0 \\ 0 & 0 & 0 & 4 & 0 \\ 0 & 0 & 0 & 0 & 5 \end{bmatrix} \quad (2.3)$$

We can get all the attributes of a matrix along the main diagonal as a vector by using the diag(.) operator. If our matrix is **D,** then diag(**D**) returns a vector **x** containing elements along the main diagonal of **D** as follows:

$$\mathbf{x} = \begin{bmatrix} 2.5 \\ 8 \\ -3 \\ 4 \\ 5 \end{bmatrix} \quad (2.4)$$

When we transpose a matrix **S** and obtain the same matrix, then this kind of matrix is termed as a *symmetric matrix*. Formally, a symmetric matrix is a matrix whose transpose returns the same matrix, that is, $S^T = S$:

$$\mathbf{S} = \begin{bmatrix} 0 & 8 & 5 & 6 & 2 \\ 8 & 4 & 3 & 7 & 9 \\ 5 & 3 & 7 & 1 & 1 \\ 6 & 7 & 1 & 3 & 6 \\ 2 & 9 & 1 & 6 & 5 \end{bmatrix} \quad (2.5)$$

In the preceding equation, matrix **S** is symmetric because it's equal to its own transpose.

We now introduce some vectors significant in deep learning. Assume two vectors $\mathbf{u}, \mathbf{v} \in \mathbf{R}^n$ such that $\mathbf{u}^T\mathbf{v} = 0$, given that both vectors are non-zero vectors, are known as *orthogonal vectors*. When the Euclidean norm of a vector is one, then it is termed as a *unit vector*, that is, $\|\mathbf{u}\|_2 = 1$. Now let us assume that both vectors $\mathbf{u}$ and $\mathbf{v}$ are also unit vectors; then both these vectors are called *orthonormal vectors*. Formally, when two unit vectors are orthogonal in nature, then they are simply called *orthonormal vectors*.

2.1.2 Unary Matrix Operations

We introduce some unary operators that are applicable on matrices. The transpose is one of the commonly used unary operations on a matrix in neural networks. The *transpose* of matrix $\mathbf{B}$ gives a new matrix $\mathbf{A}$ with its row elements interchanged by its own column elements using the following rule:

$$A_{i,j} = B_{j,i} \forall i \neq j \tag{2.6}$$

For instance, assume a transpose on the following non-symmetric matrix with a different number of rows and columns:

$$\mathbf{S} = \begin{bmatrix} -2 & 0 & 5 \\ 4 & 5 & 9 \end{bmatrix} \tag{2.7}$$

$$\mathbf{S}^T = \begin{bmatrix} -2 & 4 \\ 0 & 2 \\ 5 & 9 \end{bmatrix} \tag{2.8}$$

It can be clearly seen that rows have been interchanged with their corresponding columns, that is, matrix $\mathbf{S} \in \mathbb{R}^{2 \times 3}$, while its transpose $\mathbf{S}^T \in \mathbb{R}^{3 \times 2}$. Another operator termed the diagonal operator, denoted by diag(.), discussed earlier is also an example of a unary operator. If the need arises to calculate the sum of all the main diagonal entries, then we use the *trace operator* denoted by Tr(.). Mathematically, it is described by the following equation:

$$Tr(\mathbf{D}) = \sum_i D_{i,i} \tag{2.9}$$

Applying the trace operator on the diagonal matrix **D** we considered earlier gives the following:

$$\mathbf{D} = \begin{bmatrix} 2.5 & 0 & 0 & 0 & 0 \\ 0 & 8 & 0 & 0 & 0 \\ 0 & 0 & -3 & 0 & 0 \\ 0 & 0 & 0 & 4 & 0 \\ 0 & 0 & 0 & 0 & 5 \end{bmatrix}, \mathbf{x} = \begin{bmatrix} 2.5 \\ 8 \\ -3 \\ 4 \\ 5 \end{bmatrix}, s = \sum_i x_i = 16.5 \tag{2.10}$$

By summing the elements along the main diagonal of matrix **D**, we get the sum equal to 16.5.

2.1.3 Binary Matrix Operations

We introduce some important binary operations on matrices for two particular cases: one operand is a matrix and the other is a scalar and both operands are matrices. This categorization simplifies the understanding of binary operations on matrices.

A few of the simplest operations on matrices are operations between a matrix and a scalar. Assume a scalar s and matrix $\mathbf{A} \in \mathbb{R}^{m \times n}$ which results in another matrix of the same shape, $\mathbf{B} \in \mathbb{R}^{m \times n}$, when some operator acts between operands s and $\mathbf{A}$. Here, the operator can be any of the elementary operators such as addition, subtraction, multiplication, or division. When any of these operators is applied between s and $\mathbf{A}$, then an operation occurs between s and every element of $\mathbf{A}$, individually. For instance, an addition operation can be written as follows:

$$s + \mathbf{A} = s + A_{i,j} \qquad (2.11)$$

Assume a multiplication operator between matrix $\mathbf{A} \in \mathbb{R}^{2 \times 2}$ and a scalar $s = 3$:

$$\mathbf{A} = \begin{bmatrix} 1 & 5 \\ 4 & 9 \end{bmatrix} \qquad (2.12)$$

$$s\mathbf{A} = 3 \begin{bmatrix} 1 & 5 \\ 4 & 9 \end{bmatrix} = \begin{bmatrix} 3.1 & 3.5 \\ 3.4 & 3.9 \end{bmatrix} = \begin{bmatrix} 3 & 15 \\ 12 & 27 \end{bmatrix} \qquad (2.13)$$

Here, we denote multiplication between scalars with a dot for simplicity. Notice that a scalar s gets multiplied by each element of matrix $\mathbf{A}$.

Having discussed operations between a scalar and a matrix, we now introduce one of the most important operations between two matrices known as *matrix multiplication*. It is the fundamental operation which allows the efficient working of neural networks on modern parallel processing hardware accelerators.

Let us assume two matrices $\mathbf{X} \in \mathbb{R}^{m \times n}$ and $\mathbf{Y} \in \mathbb{R}^{n \times o}$ which when multiplied together produce a new matrix $\mathbf{Z} \in \mathbb{R}^{m \times o}$. The matrix multiplication of $\mathbf{X}$ and $\mathbf{Y}$ is simply written as $\mathbf{Z} = \mathbf{XY}$. These matrices must satisfy some conditions for the multiplication between them to be valid. We require that the count of columns of $\mathbf{X}$ must equal the count of rows of $\mathbf{Y}$ which after multiplication results in a matrix $\mathbf{Z}$ having the count of rows and columns equal to those of $\mathbf{X}$ and $\mathbf{Y}$, respectively. Formally, the product between two matrices is defined as follows:

$$Z_{i,j} = \sum_{k} X_{i,k} Y_{k,j} \qquad (2.14)$$

Here, i, j, and k are indexes starting from one up to their dimension size–defining variables m, n, and o, respectively. Let us assume $m = 2$, $n = 3$, and $o = 2$ for matrices $\mathbf{X}$ and $\mathbf{Y}$. By applying matrix multiplication between them, we get $\mathbf{Z} \in \mathbb{R}^{2 \times 2}$ as follows:

$$\mathbf{X} = \begin{bmatrix} 1 & 6 & 2 \\ 3 & 1 & 4 \end{bmatrix}, \mathbf{Y} = \begin{bmatrix} 5 & 1 \\ 2 & 2 \\ 3 & 2 \end{bmatrix} \tag{2.15}$$

$$\mathbf{Z} = \begin{bmatrix} 1.5+6.2+2.3 & 1.1+6.2+2.2 \\ 3.5+1.2+4.3 & 3.1+1.2+4.2 \end{bmatrix} = \begin{bmatrix} 23 & 17 \\ 29 & 13 \end{bmatrix} \tag{2.16}$$

The preceding example shows that matrix multiplication between $\mathbf{X} \in \mathbb{R}^{2 \times 3}$ and $\mathbf{Y} \in \mathbb{R}^{3 \times 2}$ returns $\mathbf{Z} \in \mathbb{R}^{2 \times 2}$. Also notice that matrix multiplication $\mathbf{YX}$ is not possible because it does not satisfy the dimension size requirement for matrix multiplication. Therefore, matrix multiplication is not a commutative operation.

Note that matrix multiplication is simply the repeated application of the dot product between rows of the left matrix and columns of the right matrix. This is why it is very common to find a function named dot in some libraries like NumPy, while others like Swift for TensorFlow name it matMul.

There also exists another kind of product between matrices called *element-wise* or *Hadamard* product represented by $\mathbf{P} = \mathbf{Q} \odot \mathbf{R}$, but in Swift for TensorFlow, we use the * operator for the same. Here, we require that both $\mathbf{Q}$ and $\mathbf{R}$ must have the same shape, and the Hadamard operation results in a $\mathbf{P}$ matrix of the same shape as either $\mathbf{Q}$ or $\mathbf{R}$. It is given by the following equation:

$$P_{i,j} = Q_{i,j} \cdot R_{i,j} \tag{2.17}$$

An instance of an element-wise product is given in the following:

$$\mathbf{Q} = \begin{bmatrix} 1 & 3 \\ 2 & 4 \end{bmatrix}, \mathbf{R} = \begin{bmatrix} 6 & 9 \\ 4 & 1 \end{bmatrix} \tag{2.18}$$

$$\mathbf{P} = \mathbf{Q} \odot \mathbf{R} = \begin{bmatrix} 1.6 & 3.9 \\ 2.4 & 4.1 \end{bmatrix} = \begin{bmatrix} 6 & 27 \\ 8 & 4 \end{bmatrix} \tag{2.19}$$

The Hadamard product generates the matrix $\mathbf{P}$ with the same shape as $\mathbf{Q}$ and $\mathbf{R}$.

2.1.4 Norms

Sometimes there might arise a need to measure the size of a vector in deep learning. To accomplish this task, a function called norm is used. *Norm* measures the distance of the vector from the origin in the p-dimensional vector space. The norm of a vector is denoted by L^p or $\|x\|_p$ and is computed using the following formula:

$$\|x\|_p = \left(\sum_i |x_i|^p \right)^{\frac{1}{p}} \tag{2.20}$$

where p must satisfy the condition $p \geq 1$.

Some norms are so commonplace in deep learning that they have their own names. The *Euclidean norm* or L^2 *norm* is such an example where $p = 2$, and it measures the Euclidean distance of a vector from the origin. Another kind of norm of interest is the L^1 *norm* where $p = 1$. It also measures the distance from the origin, but it is more helpful in situations where the differentiation between zero and very small non-zero values matters. If we add a small non-negative value e to each of the elements of the vector, then the L^2 norm increases proportionally to the square of itself, but the L^1 norm is preferred over L^2 when very small changes have high significance.

We discuss two more norms before moving on to probability theory in the next section: max norm and Frobenius norm. The *max norm* denoted as L^∞ is simply the absolute value of largest magnitude of an element in a vector, and it is written as follows:

$$\|x\|_\infty = \max_i |x_i|$$ (2.21)

Finally, we can also measure the distance of a matrix from the origin using the *Frobenius norm*. It is analogous to the L^2 norm of a vector. But it is rarely used and is written as follows:

$$\|\mathbf{A}\|_F = \sqrt{\sum_{i,j} A_{i,j}^2}$$ (2.22)

Now let us familiarize ourselves with another important branch of mathematics concerned with neural networks called probability theory.

2.2 Probability Theory

Deep learning is all about making decisions on unseen datapoints since the real world is highly uncertain. For instance, some uncertainty lies in determining the occurrence of events such as "that you will wake up tomorrow at 5 AM" or "if this music concert will be good." These are uncertain events in the sense that they may or may not occur; therefore, their probability of occurrence lies in the range [0,1]. In contrast, some events are completely certain to happen, for instance, "the sun will rise tomorrow" or "the water is composed of hydrogen and oxygen," so their probability is 1. The events which never occur, for instance, "castor oil is more viscous than water" or "plants do not grow in soil," have probability equal to 0. Probability theory plays a crucial role in framing deep learning problems.

Probability is a mathematical framework for quantifying the uncertain events using a real number lying within the range [0,1]. If an event *e* has a high probability of occurrence, then its probability is quantified by a real number closer to 1, whereas a least probable event has probability closer to 0. Formally, *probability* of an event *e*, denoted by $P(e)$, is defined as the ratio of the number of times the event *e* occurs to the total number of trials *T* when the experiments were performed for infinite times, $T \to \infty$. Another important term in probability is a *random variable* which is defined as a variable that can take a specific value from a defined set of valid values where each value has some probability of being sampled from a given probability distribution. Here, **e** is a random variable; and, mathematically, the probability of occurrence of an event *e* is written as follows:

$$P(\mathbf{e} = e) = \frac{n}{T}. \tag{2.23}$$

Here, *e* is the event or the value the random variable **e** takes on, and *n* is the times event *e* occurred when an experiment was performed for $T \to \infty$ times. Note that sometimes we simply write $P(e)$ which is equivalent to writing $P(\mathbf{e} = e)$. Also don't confuse bold small alphabet notation in probability theory with vector notation in linear algebra. This notation is used here for convenience.

We will now use a simple example to explain the basics of probability theory in an accessible way. The following example, shown in Figure 2-1, has been adapted from the textbook of (Bishop, 2006) textbook. Let us assume a random variable which we will call the time period of day denoted by $\mathbf{t} = \{m, a, e, b\}$, read as "**t** is a set of values *m, a, e,* and *b*," where *m, a, e,* and *b* represent morning, afternoon, evening, and bedtime, respectively. Based on the value sampled from **t**, we can decide the action to take denoted by set $\mathbf{a} = \{s, p, r, w\}$ where *s, p, r,* and *w* simply denote study, play, rest, and workout, respectively. Figure 2-1 shows a diagrammatic representation of random variables **t** and **a**.

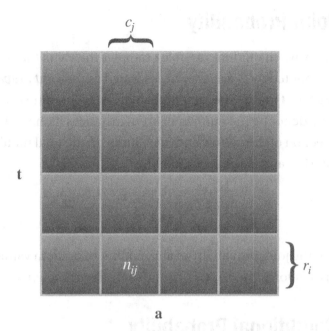

Figure 2-1. *A grid describing the probability of joint and conditional occurrence of events from sets t = {m, a, e, b} and a = {s, p, r, w}*

In Figure 2-1, each row represents the ith index value sampled from an event set {m, a, e, b} that $\mathbf{t}$ can take on, while each column represents the jth index value sampled from event set {s, p, r, w} that $\mathbf{a}$ can take on. The terms r_i and c_j denote the number of event instances t_i and a_j, respectively. Here, i = 1,..., M and j = 1,..., N are the indexes along rows and columns, respectively, and $M = N = 4$. We denote the probability of occurrence of an event t_i by $P(\mathbf{t} = t_i)$ which is simply given by the following equation:

$$P\left(\mathbf{t}=t_{i}\right)=\frac{r_{i}}{T}. \tag{2.24}$$

Here, T is the total number of experiments performed. Similarly, the probability of occurrence of an event a_j is given by

$$P\left(\mathbf{a}=\mathbf{a}_{j}\right)=\frac{a_{j}}{T}. \tag{2.25}$$

47

2.2.1 Joint Probability

The probability when random variable **t** samples the value t_i and **a** samples the value a_j, denoted by $P(\mathbf{a} = a_j, \mathbf{t} = t_i)$, is termed as the *joint probability* of random variables **t** and **a**. The joint probability of event t_i and a_j is given by the ratio of n_{ij}, denoting the number of event instances in the cell present at the intersection of the ith row and jth column, to the total number of instances or trials and is written as follows:

$$P\left(\mathbf{a} = a_j, \mathbf{t} = t_i\right) = \frac{n_{ij}}{T}. \qquad (2.26)$$

Note that the joint probability of any number of random variables is symmetric; therefore, $P(\mathbf{a} = a_j, \mathbf{t} = t_i)$ is the same as writing $P(\mathbf{t} = t_i, \mathbf{a} = a_j)$.

2.2.2 Conditional Probability

In situations when we have to find the probability of an event given that another event has already occurred and that these two events are related, then this kind of probability is termed as *conditional probability*. Following our example, let us assume that **t** has occurred and taken the value t_i; and given this, we have to find the probability of **a** taking the value a_j. This is denoted by $P(\mathbf{a} = a_j | \mathbf{t} = t_i)$, read as "probability of occurrence of event a_j given that event t_i has already occurred," and is given by the ratio of the number of instances in the cell at the (i, j)th index, denoted by n_{ij}, to the number of total event instances in row i given by r_i. Formally, this is given by the following equation:

$$P\left(\mathbf{a} = a_j | \mathbf{t} = t_i\right) = \frac{n_{ij}}{r_i}. \qquad (2.27)$$

Similarly, the conditional probability of occurrence of event t_i given that a_j has occurred is given by the ratio of n_{ij} to the total number of events in column j given by c_j. Formally, $P(\mathbf{t} = t_i | \mathbf{a} = a_j)$ is described by the following equation:

$$P\left(\mathbf{t} = t_i \middle| \mathbf{a} = \mathbf{a}_j\right) = \frac{n_{ij}}{c_j}. \tag{2.28}$$

2.2.3 Elementary Rules

Now we are sufficiently equipped with the knowledge of different kinds of probabilities using which we will derive the two fundamental rules of probability theory, namely, sum and product rules. First, see in Figure 2-1 that $r_i = \sum_j n_{ij}$ because the total number of events in r_i is simply just the sum of all the events in each cell of that row. Using Equations 2.24 and 2.26, we get

$$P\left(\mathbf{t} = t_i\right) = \sum_j P\left(\mathbf{t} = t_i, \mathbf{a} = a_j\right) = \frac{r_i}{T} \tag{2.29}$$

which is termed as the *sum of probability*. It is also called the *marginal probability* since it is obtained by marginalizing or summing out all the variables except the one desired here, that is, $\mathbf{t}$. Similarly, we can write $P(\mathbf{a} = a_j)$ as

$$P\left(\mathbf{a} = a_j\right) = \sum_i P\left(\mathbf{t} = t_i, \mathbf{a} = a_j\right) = \frac{c_j}{T} \tag{2.30}$$

by marginalizing out the random variable $\mathbf{t}$. Next, we will derive the product rule of probability using the already discussed conditional probability. Using Equations 2.26, 2.28, and 2.30, we get

$$P\left(\mathbf{t}=t_i, \mathbf{a}=a_j\right) = \frac{n_{ij}}{T} = \frac{n_{ij}}{c_j} \cdot \frac{c_j}{T} \qquad (2.31)$$

$$P\left(\mathbf{t}=t_i, \ \mathbf{a}=a_j\right) = P\left(\mathbf{t}=t_i \middle| \mathbf{a}=a_j\right) P\left(\mathbf{a}=a_j\right). \qquad (2.32)$$

This is called the *product rule* of probability. Note that it simply decomposes the joint probability of two random variables into the product of their marginal and conditional probabilities.

By now, we have been very exact about the notations, but it complicates the larger equations and deteriorates their eligibility. We now choose a simpler notation to represent such probability equations. Let us denote the probability distribution over random variables $\mathbf{t}$ and $\mathbf{a}$ as $P(\mathbf{t})$ and $P(\mathbf{a})$, respectively, while $P(t_i)$ and $P(a_j)$ denotes the probability distribution evaluated at values t_i and a_j that $\mathbf{t}$ and $\mathbf{a}$ take on, respectively. Now we can rewrite Equations 2.30 and 2.32 more compactly as follows:

$$P(\mathbf{a}) = \sum_i P(\mathbf{t}, \mathbf{a}) \qquad (2.33)$$

$$P(\mathbf{t}, \mathbf{a}) = P(\mathbf{t} | \mathbf{a}) P(\mathbf{a}) \qquad (2.34)$$

Here, Equations 2.33 and 2.34 represent the sum and product rules of probability, respectively. We will now introduce the concept of the chain rule of probability in the following text.

2.2.4 Chain Rule

Now we know that a joint probability of two random variables can be decomposed into the product of their conditional and marginal probabilities. But "what if we desire to decompose a probability over more than two random variables?" This is where the chain rule of probability comes to rescue. The *chain rule of probability* is simply defined as the repeated application of the product rule on joint probabilities over as many random variables. As a consequence, the joint probability is decomposed into the product of marginal and conditional probabilities of all the random variables.

Let us assume four random variables, namely, x_1, x_2, x_3, and x_4. We can write their joint probability as $P(x_1, x_2, x_3, x_4)$ which can be further decomposed using the product rule as described by the following equations:

$$P(x_1, x_2, x_3, x_4) = P(x_4 | x_1, x_2, x_3) P(x_1, x_2, x_3) \qquad (2.35)$$

$$P(x_1, x_2, x_3) = P(x_3 | x_1, x_2) P(x_1, x_2) \qquad (2.36)$$

$$P(x_1, x_2) = P(x_2 | x_1) P(x_1) \qquad (2.37)$$

Using Equations 2.36 and 2.37, Equation 2.35 can be rewritten in its decomposed form as follows:

$$P(x_1, x_2, x_3, x_4) = P(x_1) P(x_2 | x_1) P(x_3 | x_1, x_2) P(x_4 | x_1, x_2, x_3) \qquad (2.38)$$

The general formula of the chain rule of probability can be written as follows:

$$P(x_1, \ldots, x_n) = \prod_{i=1}^{n} P(x_i | x_i, \ldots, x_n). \qquad (2.39)$$

Keep in mind that $P(x|x) = P(x)$. The preceding example demonstrating the chain rule might seem a bit complicated; so let us assume a simpler version which is simplified by the choice of names of random variables, namely, a, b, c, and d.

We will now decompose this probability distribution over these random variables, denoted by $P(\mathbf{a}, \mathbf{b}, \mathbf{c}, \mathbf{d})$, step by step in the following equations:

$$P(\mathbf{a}, \mathbf{b}, \mathbf{c}, \mathbf{d}) = P(\mathbf{a}|\mathbf{b}, \mathbf{c}, \mathbf{d})P(\mathbf{b}, \mathbf{c}, \mathbf{d}) \tag{2.40}$$

$$P(\mathbf{b}, \mathbf{c}, \mathbf{d}) = P(\mathbf{b}|\mathbf{c}, \mathbf{d})P(\mathbf{c}, \mathbf{d}) \tag{2.41}$$

$$P(\mathbf{c}, \mathbf{d}) = P(\mathbf{c}|\mathbf{d})P(\mathbf{d}) \tag{2.42}$$

Substituting Equation 2.42 in 2.41 and then 2.41 in 2.40, we get

$$P(\mathbf{a}, \mathbf{b}, \mathbf{c}, \mathbf{d}) = P(\mathbf{a}|\mathbf{b}, \mathbf{c}, \mathbf{d})P(\mathbf{b}|\mathbf{c}, \mathbf{d})P(\mathbf{c}|\mathbf{d})P(\mathbf{d}). \tag{2.43}$$

Notice that there is symmetry in decomposed Equations 2.38 and 2.43. In simple terms, the chain rule of probability helps us in describing the joint probability over any number of random variables as the product between their conditional and marginal probabilities and is more generally obtained by Equation 2.39.

2.2.5 Bayes Rule

We can also derive a relation between the conditional probabilities of two random variables by exploiting the fact that joint probability is symmetric. We can rewrite the joint probability over random variables $\mathbf{x}$ and $\mathbf{y}$ as

$$p(\mathbf{x}, \mathbf{y}) = P(\mathbf{y}, \mathbf{x}). \tag{2.44}$$

Using the product rule, we get

$$P(\mathbf{x}|\mathbf{y}) = \frac{P(\mathbf{y}|\mathbf{x})P(\mathbf{x})}{P(\mathbf{y})}. \tag{2.45}$$

Here, Equation 2.45 is known as the Bayes rule which relates the conditional probabilities via the symmetric property of joint probability.

2.3 Differential Calculus

The branch of calculus is divided into two subbranches, namely,
differential and integral calculus. Since neural network training requires
computing partial derivatives, studying differential calculus is important
and forms the subject of this section. We are not concerned with integral
calculus. We start by introducing the concept of function and then explain
differential calculus. This section is inspired from Chapter 5 of (Deisenroth
et al., 2020) textbook.

2.3.1 Function

At the heart of calculus lives the concept of function. A mathematical
function, denoted by $f: \mathbb{A} \rightarrow \mathbb{B}$, is a mapping from set $\mathbb{A}$ to set $\mathbb{B}$ associating
each element of $\mathbb{A}$ to a unique element of $\mathbb{B}$. Assume variables $x \in \mathbb{A}$ and
$y \in \mathbb{B}$; then $y = f(x)$ is a function f mapping an individual element $x \in \mathbb{A}$ to
a unique element $y \in \mathbb{B}$. In other words, the function $f(.)$ transforms the
input x and returns the output y.

2.3.1.1 Univariate Function

When the input variable x to the function $f(.)$ is a scalar and the function
returns a scalar output y, then this function is known as a *univariate*
(or *scalar*) *function*, depicted in Figure 2-2. In other words, a univariate
function is simply a mapping from scalar real numbers to scalar real
numbers, $f: \mathbb{R} \rightarrow \mathbb{R}$.

Figure 2-2. *A scalar function f(.) mapping from $x \in \mathbb{R}$ to $y \in \mathbb{R}$*

Consider a scalar function $g : \mathbb{B} \to C$ mapping from set $\mathbb{B}$ to set C and taking the output of function $f(.)$ as its input, that is, $z = g(y) = g(f(x))$. This can be visualized as a sequential chaining of multiple functions, and g in this is also known as the *composite function*, visualized in Figure 2-3. We can also write the composite function as $g{\circ}f(x)$ where the $\circ$ operator represents the composition of $g(.)$ and $f(.)$ functions. Note that the chaining of functions can exist up to as many functions as desired. We will see later that neural networks are simply composite vector functions.

Figure 2-3. *A composite scalar function g ∘ f(x) mapping*

2.3.1.2 Multivariate Function

The univariate function described earlier is the simplest form of a function. But in deep learning, we will require to deal with functions of higher-dimensional input variables. We can extend this definition to a function whose input contains multiple variables, and this function is called a *multivariate function* (shown in Figure 2-4) defined as $f : \mathbb{R}^m \to \mathbb{R}$ where input variable $\mathbf{x} \in \mathbb{R}^m$ (row vector). A real-world example is speed $s(d, t)$ which is a function of two variables, namely, distance $d \in \mathbb{R}$ and time $t \in \mathbb{R}$, defined as $s(d, t) = d/t$, where $s : \mathbb{R}^2 \to \mathbb{R}$. We can represent these two input variables as a two-dimensional row vector $\mathbf{x} = [d\ t]$ variable. Another example is summation operator $\Sigma_i x_i$ that returns a sum of all scalar elements of a vector $\mathbf{x}$.

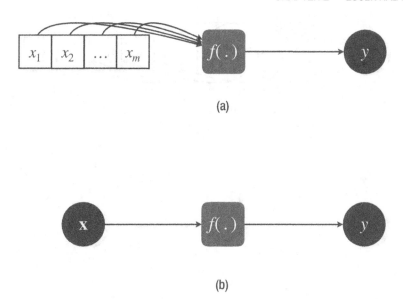

(a)

(b)

Figure 2-4. *A multivariate function f(.) mapping from* ***x*** *∈ ℝ^m to y ∈ ℝ shown explicitly in (a) and compactly in (b)*

2.3.1.3 Vector Function

The *vector function* **f** : ℝ^m → ℝ^n is simply an extended version of the multivariate function f: ℝ^m → ℝ. In the vector function, we have a collection of n multivariate functions **f** = [f_1 ... f_n] in a row vector where y_i = f_i(**x**) and i = 1,...,n. When each multivariate function in the **f** row vector is applied on input vector variable **x**, it returns a scalar y_i = f_i(**x**). We then stack these outputs along the n columns to create a vector **y** = **f**(**x**) ∈ ℝ^n. In other words, applying the vector function **f** on input vector variable **x** ∈ ℝ^m produces an output vector variable **y** ∈ ℝ^n (see Figure 2-5), thus mapping m- to n-dimensional vector space. Note that it is considered more appropriate for a vector to be a column vector but we consider all vectors (otherwise mentioned) to be row vectors. This consideration is for the convenience of how datasets are arranged (see subsection 1.4.1), processed and how we perform differentiation of our neural network functions as we shall see later.

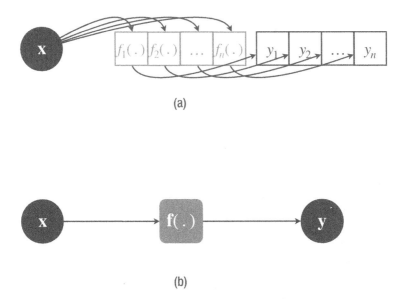

Figure 2-5. *A vector function **f**(.) mapping from **x** ∈ ℝ^m to*
y *∈ ℝ^n shown explicitly in (a) and compactly in (b)*

2.3.1.4 Matrix Function

We can also define higher-dimensional functions such as a *matrix function*,
defined as mapping from vector to matrix $\mathbf{F} : \mathbb{R}^m \rightarrow \mathbb{R}^{n \times o}$ or mapping
from matrix to matrix $\mathbf{F} : \mathbb{R}^{m \times n} \rightarrow \mathbb{R}^{o \times p}$, shown in Figure 2-6. We take a
look at vector to matrix mapping in the matrix function which is simply a
collection of n vector functions $\mathbf{f} = [\mathbf{f}_1 \dots \mathbf{f}_n]$ in a column vector where
$\mathbf{f}_j : \mathbb{R}^m \rightarrow \mathbb{R}^o$ and $j = 1,\dots,n$. When each vector function in the $\mathbf{f}$ column vector
is applied on input vector variable $\mathbf{x} \in \mathbb{R}^m$, it returns a vector
$\mathbf{y}_j = \mathbf{f}_j(\mathbf{x}) \in \mathbb{R}^o$. We then stack these outputs along the q rows to create a
matrix $\mathbf{Y} = \mathbf{F}(\mathbf{x}) \in \mathbb{R}^{n \times o}$.

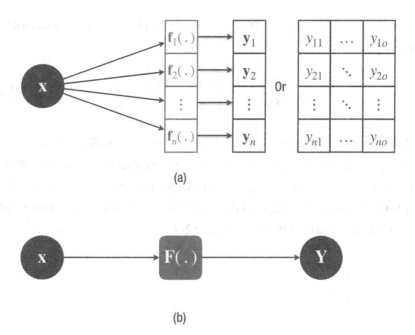

(a)

(b)

Figure 2-6. *A matrix function F(.) mapping from $x \in \mathbb{R}^m$ to $Y \in \mathbb{R}^{n \times o}$*

The following text explains the differentiation of functions we've described in the preceding text. We won't discuss tensor functions because all differentiation in neural networks can be described in vector functions themselves. But we'll differentiate matrix functions to demonstrate a neat trick used in algorithmic differentiation (AD) (Section 3.3) of the Swift language (Section 3.4) to make derivative computation easy.

2.3.2 Differentiation of Univariate Function

We introduce the concept of the difference quotient before starting with the derivative of a function. The *difference quotient* is defined as an amount of change in the output function value when the input changes by a small value. This approach to differentiation is known as *numerical differentiation*:

$$\frac{\delta y}{\delta x} := \frac{f(x+\delta x)-f(x)}{\delta x}. \tag{2.46}$$

Here, δ is a Greek letter *delta* used to represent a small value. In the preceding equation, $\delta y = f(x + \delta x) - f(x)$ is the change in output function value when there is a small change in input δx. When $\delta x = 0$, then $\delta y = 0$. This ratio represents the slope of the secant line (a line that cuts the graph in two or more parts) as shown in Figure 2-7.

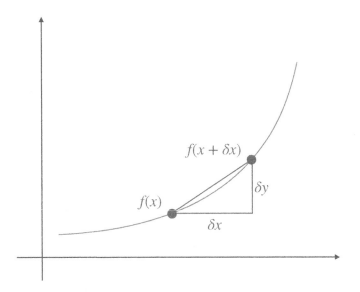

Figure 2-7. *A secant line from $(x, f(x))$ to $(x + \delta x, f(x + \delta x))$ for a univariate function*

When this noticeable small change in input value becomes negligibly small, that is, it approaches 0, denoted as $\delta x \rightarrow 0$, we get a *slope* of the tangent line at x. The tangent line is a line parallel to the curve at a point x and represents the slope of the curve at $f(x)$. The derivative exists if f the function $f(.)$ is differentiable. For a function to be *differentiable*, it must be continuous at every point in the input space, a limit must exist at the point of differentiation, and the limit must also exist at the left and right of a given point approaching it. If a function satisfies these three requirements, it is considered differentiable. Remember that all the functions we deal with in neural network literature are differentiable. The derivative of a function $f(.)$ is defined as

$$\frac{dy}{dx} := \lim_{h \to 0} \frac{f(x+h) - f(x)}{h}. \tag{2.47}$$

Here, $h > 0$ and is a very very small positive number. The tangent of a function $f(.)$ at point x is a *derivative* $f'(x)$ and points to the direction of *steepest ascent* of output function value. We have denoted the derivative of $f(.)$ at x as $f'(x)$. If input to a function is a constant number, the derivative is 0 because a constant value cannot vary.

Some differentiable functions such as sigmoid, softmax, ReLU, and others are so commonplace in neural networks that we usually prefer to remember their derivative functions instead of again finding them. These listed functions are called activation functions and are discussed at length in Section 5.4.

2.3.2.1 Rules of Differentiation

Sometimes we require to compute derivatives of composite or multiple functions combined together using elementary arithmetic operations. Here, we follow the four rules of differentiation described in the following. The following general rules are applicable to univariate functions:

1. **Sum rule:** $(f(x) + g(x))' = f'(x) + g'(x)$

2. **Product rule:** $(f(x)g(x))' = f'(x)g(x) + f(x)g'(x)$

3. **Chain rule:** $(f(g(x)))' = f'(g(x))g'(x)$

4. **Quotient rule:** $\left(\dfrac{f(x)}{g(x)}\right)' = \dfrac{f'(x)g(x) - f(x)g'(x)}{(g(x))^2}$

2.3.3 Differentiation of Multivariate Function

We discussed the differentiation for the univariate function earlier. But in situations when we have to deal with a function of multiple input variables, known as a multivariate function, the concept of partial differentiation is utilized. In partial differentiation, the derivative of the function is computed for each variable individually while treating other variables constant, and the partial derivative of every constant input variable is zero. The partial derivative of a multivariate function $f(.)$ with respect to some input variable x_1 is written as follows:

$$\frac{\partial f(\mathbf{x})}{\partial x_1} = \lim_{h \to 0} \frac{f(x_1 + h, \ldots, x_m) - f(x_1)}{h} \tag{2.48}$$

Here, $\partial f(\mathbf{x})/\partial x_1$ is the partial derivative of $f(.)$ with respect to x_1 meaning that other variables are kept constant during the computation of this partial derivative. This process of calculating partial derivatives of function $f(.)$ is repeated for each input variable in row vector $\mathbf{x} \in \mathbb{R}^m$. We then accumulate these partial derivatives in a row vector and call it the *gradient* of a multivariate function $f(.)$ defined as follows:

$$\nabla_x f = \frac{df(\mathbf{x})}{dx} = \left[\lim_{h \to 0} \frac{f(x_1 + h, \ldots, x_m) - f(x_1)}{h} \cdots \lim_{h \to 0} \frac{f(x_1, \ldots, x_m + h) - f(x_m)}{h} \right] \tag{2.49}$$

Because the gradient is a derivative of the multivariate function, we can write $df(\mathbf{x})/d\mathbf{x}$, whereas $\partial f(\mathbf{x})/\partial x_i$ denotes the partial derivative of $f(.)$ with respect to a single input variable x_i. Sometimes we also use grad

$f(.)$ instead of nabla notation $\nabla_x f$ to denote gradient. We can rewrite the preceding equation in a much more compact manner as follows:

$$\nabla_x f = \left[\frac{\partial f(\mathbf{x})}{\partial x_1} \cdots \frac{\partial f(\mathbf{x})}{\partial x_m} \right] \tag{2.50}$$

Later, for convenience, we will assume gradient $\nabla_x f \in \mathbb{R}^{1 \times m}$ as a matrix instead of a vector. And as we shall see later, for vector functions (densely connected neural networks, for instance), this gradient's row dimension size will increase such that it will become a matrix containing partial derivatives of a vector function.

2.3.3.1 Rules of Partial Differentiation

The rules for calculating partial derivatives of higher-dimensional functions can be easily obtained by extending the previously discussed rules for univariate functions as follows:

1. **Sum rule:** $\dfrac{\partial}{\partial x}\big(f(\mathbf{x}) + g(\mathbf{x})\big) = \dfrac{\partial f(\mathbf{x})}{\partial x} + \dfrac{\partial g(\mathbf{x})}{\partial x}$

2. **Product rule:** $\dfrac{\partial}{\partial x}\big(f(\mathbf{x})g(\mathbf{x})\big) = \dfrac{\partial f}{\partial x}g(\mathbf{x}) + f(\mathbf{x})\dfrac{\partial g}{\partial x}$

3. **Chain rule:** $\dfrac{\partial}{\partial x}(f \circ g)(\mathbf{x}) = \dfrac{\partial}{\partial x}\big(f(g(\mathbf{x}))\big) = \dfrac{\partial f}{\partial g}\dfrac{\partial g}{\partial x}$

We have eliminated the quotient rule for partial derivatives because in neural networks, we will be mostly dealing with these three rules. Notice that the rules are analogous to those for derivatives. Just keep in mind that the order of functions during partial differentiation is of high significance because now matrices and vectors are involved and some operations on these data structures (multiplication, for instance) are not commutative, in contrast to scalar functions.

Next, we introduce differentiation of the vector function which is critical for training neural networks.

2.3.4 Differentiation of Vector Function

We have already discussed the vector function previously. Let us consider a vector function $\mathbf{f}: \mathbb{R}^m \to \mathbb{R}^n$ mapping from m- to n-dimensional vector space. As already described earlier, we have a row vector $\mathbf{f} = [f_1 \dots f_n]$ containing multivariate functions mapping $f_i: \mathbb{R}^m \to \mathbb{R}$. The derivative of the vector function can be written as follows using the limit definition:

$$\nabla_x \mathbf{f} = \begin{bmatrix} \lim_{h \to 0} \dfrac{f_1(x_1 + h, \dots, x_m) - f_1(x_1)}{h} & \dots & \lim_{h \to 0} \dfrac{f_1(x_1, \dots, x_m + h) - f_1(x_m)}{h} \\ \dots & \ddots & \dots \\ \lim_{h \to 0} \dfrac{f_n(x_1 + h, \dots, x_m) - f_n(x_1)}{h} & \dots & \lim_{h \to 0} \dfrac{f_n(x_1, \dots, x_m + h) - f_n(x_m)}{h} \end{bmatrix} \quad (2.51)$$

Here, the $\nabla_x \mathbf{f} \in \mathbb{R}^{n \times m}$ matrix is accumulated with the first-order partial derivatives of vector function $\mathbf{f}(\mathbf{x})$ and is termed as *Jacobian*. Note that higher-dimensional tensors containing derivatives of matrix or other higher-dimensional functions are also called Jacobian; akin to tensor, Jacobian is also a generalized name for a tensor storing partial derivatives. We can rewrite the Jacobian matrix $\nabla_x \mathbf{f}$ as follows:

$$\mathbf{J_f} = \nabla_x \mathbf{f} = \begin{bmatrix} \dfrac{\partial f_1(\mathbf{x})}{\partial x_1} & \dots & \dfrac{\partial f_1(\mathbf{x})}{\partial x_m} \\ \dots & \ddots & \dots \\ \dfrac{\partial f_n(\mathbf{x})}{\partial x_1} & \dots & \dfrac{\partial f_n(\mathbf{x})}{\partial x_m} \end{bmatrix} \quad (2.52)$$

Here, $\mathbf{J_f}$ is another way to represent Jacobian $\nabla_x \mathbf{f}$ of function $\mathbf{f}(\mathbf{x})$. Notice that each row is a gradient of multivariate function $f_i(\mathbf{x})$. As we discussed earlier, Jacobian can be considered as accumulation of multiple multivariate functions' gradients, each stacked in a different row, giving us a matrix of partial derivatives. In other words, the derivative of a multivariate function is a special case of Jacobian when there is only one function in a function row vector.

Next, we introduce differentiation of the matrix function and a simple trick for easy calculation.

2.3.5 Differentiation of Matrix Function

Here, we consider a simple case where we calculate the derivative of output matrix variable $Y \in \mathbb{R}^{n \times o}$ with respect to input vector variable $x \in \mathbb{R}^m$ where $F : \mathbb{R}^m \to \mathbb{R}^{n \times o}$. Here, we set $n = 3$, $o = 4$, and $m = 2$. This describes a function mapping from a m-dimensional vector space to a $n \times o$-dimensional matrix space, that is, $F : \mathbb{R}^2 \to \mathbb{R}^{3 \times 4}$. We know that a Jacobian storing partial derivatives of the output matrix with respect to the input vector will be a tensor $J_F \in \mathbb{R}^{(3 \times 4) \times 2}$. We demonstrate two approaches to calculate this Jacobian.

The first approach, shown in Figure 2-8, to Jacobian is straightforward. Here, we simply calculate the partial derivatives of Y with respect to each scalar input variable of vector x. These partial derivatives are $\partial Y / \partial x_1$ and $\partial Y / \partial x_2$. Now we collate all these partial derivatives in a Jacobian tensor of shape $(3 \times 4) \times 2$.

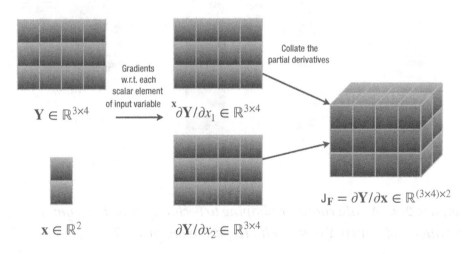

Figure 2-8. A straightforward approach to compute gradients of matrix $Y \in \mathbb{R}^{3 \times 4}$ with respect to vector $x \in \mathbb{R}^2$

The second approach, shown in Figure 2-9, to Jacobian calculation is also straightforward but requires a minor modification to the previous process. In the first step, we flatten the output matrix into a *no*- or 12-dimensional vector, that is, $\bar{\mathbf{y}} \in \mathbb{R}^{12}$. In the second step, we calculate the partial derivatives of this new output vector $\mathbf{y}$ with respect to input vector $\mathbf{x}$ which results in two partial derivatives $\partial \mathbf{y}/\partial x_1$ and $\partial \mathbf{y}/\partial x_2$, each belonging to the $\mathbb{R}^{12}$ vector space. We collect these in a Jacobian matrix of shape *no* × *m* or 12 × 2. Finally, in the third step, we reshape it back to a $(n \times o) \times m$- or $(3 \times 4) \times 2$–dimensional Jacobian tensor which now contains the partial derivatives of output matrix $\mathbf{Y}$ with respect to input vector $\mathbf{x}$.

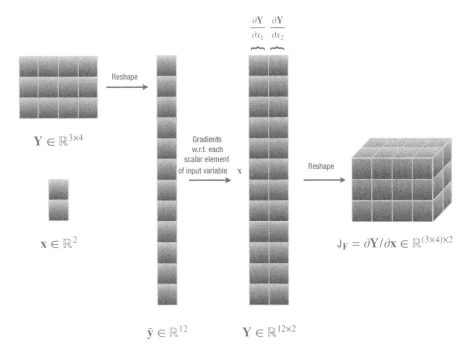

Figure 2-9. *An alternative reshaping to vector approach to compute gradients of matrix $Y \in \mathbb{R}^{3\times4}$ with respect to vector $x \in \mathbb{R}^2$*

The TensorFlow library in Swift for TensorFlow, introduced in Chapter 4, adopts the second approach involving reshaping tensors to compute Jacobian tensors because of its simplicity and efficiency. This also makes it easy to compute partial derivatives of chained composite functions in algorithmic differentiation (Section 3.3) using the chain rule via Jacobian-vector products (JVP) and vector-Jacobian products (VJP) in forward-mode and reverse-mode algorithmic differentiation, respectively. We will describe these terms in the next chapter.

Note that the second approach might seem susceptible to errors because reordering of tensors could seem to destroy the path to calculate the expected final correct output, that is, Jacobian here, but fortunately it does not. To understand this, we turn back to linear algebra for a little help. This approach becomes possible due to the fact that tensor spaces are *isomorphic* by nature, that is, any space can be transformed to another using linear algebraic operations such as matrix multiplication. And this transformation can be again reverted back leading us to the original tensor space. So matrices can be reshaped to vectors and vice versa, and the same approach is also applicable to higher dimensional data structures.

2.4 Summary

Mathematics is essential to understand deep neural networks. In this chapter, we discussed various topics from three subfields of mathematics, namely, linear algebra, probability theory, and differential calculus. Each of these helps in designing and training machine learning models, as we shall see in later chapters. We suggest you to use this chapter as a reference if you get lost in higher-level abstraction either when trying to understand neural networks or programming them.

The next chapter is concerned with differentiable programming with the Swift programming language. We will make extensive use of the differentiation concept to describe algorithmic differentiation and describe Swift's APIs to easily compute the derivatives of functions and data types.

CHAPTER 3

Differentiable Programming

Swift is a syntactic sugar for LLVM compiler.

—Chris Lattner

In this chapter, we start by inspiring you to adopt the Swift language for deep learning by comparing (Section 3.1) its powerful capabilities to the Python language. We also introduce an extended language called "Swift for TensorFlow" (Section 3.2) for general-purpose programming and for learning and researching the deep learning field. The algorithm crucial for automatically computing the derivatives of composite functions (by abstracting away the complexity from users) called algorithmic differentiation is introduced and discussed in detail in section 3.3. Then Swift language's various fundamental and advanced powerful features are introduced (section 3.4). Because contemporarily Python language is heavily used for numerical computation purposes we show how Swift for TensorFlow can easily access (section 3.5) Python's builtins and libraries. Finally, we close this chapter with a summary (section 3.6).

This chapter is highly inspired from "Differentiable Programming Manifesto" (Wei et al., 2018) which laid the foundation of the first-class differentiation feature support for Swift making it an even more general-purpose programming language.

© Rahul Bhalley 2021
R. Bhalley, *Deep Learning with Swift for TensorFlow*,
https://doi.org/10.1007/978-1-4842-6330-3_3

3.1 Swift is Everywhere

Contemporarily, the important numbers crunching libraries used by research communities in data science (Buitinck et al., 2013; Harris et al., 2020), machine learning (Abadi et al., 2016; Chollet et al., 2015; Paszke et al., 2017, 2019), quantum computing (Aleksandrowicz et al., 2019), quantum machine learning (Bergholm et al., 2018), computational neuroscience (Taylor et al., 2018), and others are written in Python. Although Python is very important right now but it is not a good general-purpose programming language (i.e., usable in various parts of a software development stack), it has many serious drawbacks such as slow performance, poor memory management, no multithreading support because of GIL,[1] no serious debugging tools because it's an interpreted language, highly dynamic type system, no true support for mobile development, and so on. Exploring a Python language alternative for, particularly, machine learning, the community has put some efforts into the Julia language (Bezanson et al., 2012, 2017) in various research areas of differentiable programming. But Julia also has some serious downsides such as nonintuitive (if you're already a C++ or Python programmer), complex, and untidy syntax, bloating features list, weird variable scoping, unsafe and highly dynamic type system like Python with allowed redeclaration of same named variables, no support for mobile development, and so on. Because of these and other drawbacks, Python and Julia remain unfit for various research areas concerned with numerical computation.

The machine learning libraries are usually programmed in extended C++ language such as CUDA (Zeller, 2011) for allowing execution on hardware accelerators. Python simply interfaces with the C++ codebase making the low-level code abstract so as to allow you to program deep learning applications with easy Python syntax. As a consequence of this,

---

[1]GIL stands for "Global Interpreter Lock."

the trained machine learning models have to be loaded into C++ for low-latency deployment in production. This gap between your program and low-level C++ code is huge and hinders you from making changes to the codebase easily for your program-specific optimizations. Swift for TensorFlow aims to be the only language required to easily program low-level optimization while also providing you access to high-level APIs, therefore eliminating this gap between your code and the actual machine learning codebase.

We know that Swift is a statically typed language, but it also allows dynamic typing. For instance, although protocols (see Subsection 3.4.6) are not types but rules that a conforming type must follow, you can still use the protocol as a type of an entity whose actual custom type is determined during runtime. But Python has no notion of types except for the object class which is fully dynamic. This poses a problem for machine learning applications because instead knowing the type of instances allows the compiler to report compile-time errors which makes the researchers, practitioners, and learners equally highly productive. This is where Swift for TensorFlow shines! But Python doesn't check any errors until they are encountered during execution. Since machine learning training is time consuming and encountering an error in a certain statement which is not executed until some condition is passed can crash the program and the training might need to be restarted, this makes machine learning programming extremely unproductive.

Unlike Python, Swift is a general-purpose, fast, and compiled language based on the LLVM compiler and has native support for debugging through the LLDB debugger. Swift also supports automatic reference counting, and you almost never need to worry about memory management. Python's GIL prevents the usage of your device's multiple cores effectively and, therefore, doesn't allow multithreading. But you can easily write multithreaded programs with Swift. As already noted, Python doesn't allow app development, whereas nowadays all the apps running on Apple devices are written in the Swift language.

Swift is an open source language and runs flawlessly not only on macOS but also on Linux and Windows operating systems. Swift is used to build apps for Apple devices. Swift also works pretty well on the frontend and server backend for building user interfaces (UIs) with SwiftUI[2] and handling databases with library like Vapor,[3] respectively. Swift can also be used for handling Amazon Web Services (AWS) Lambda runtime.[4] And now Swift's compiler also supports first-class differentiable programming which makes it easy to write parameters-optimization algorithms. *Differentiable programming* is a programming paradigm in which derivatives of types and functions are computed using algorithmic differentiation.

Nearly any portion of the software stack can be developed solely in Swift easily. In less than a decade of its incarnation Swift has quickly become a general purpose programming language. Now we will look at the Swift for TensorFlow language which extends the original Swift language for easily writing deep learning algorithms. Basically, Swift for TensorFlow introduces the TensorFlow library and various deep learning specific features not present in Swift.

3.2 Swift for TensorFlow

Swift for TensorFlow (S4TF) makes it easy to prototype a machine learning project. While it is also possible to deploy S4TF models, we won't be touching that sphere. Since S4TF has newcomer- and experienced programmer–friendly syntax, the learning curve can be short. S4TF can also be used as a first language to learn programming and even machine learning. And S4TF has many powerful features that Python users will find interesting.

---

[2]`https://developer.apple.com/xcode/swiftui/`
[3]`https://vapor.codes`
[4]`https://swift.org/blog/aws-lambda-runtime/`

In addition to running deep learning programs on CPUs, S4TF can also execute them on hardware accelerators such as GPUs or TPUs. At the time of this writing, S4TF uses the XLA compiler in its own X10 library for TensorFlow. This allows you to execute your algorithms on hardware accelerators such as GPUs or TPUs with very minor modification to your code as we shall see when we'll train our machine learning algorithms in later chapters. But in the future, TensorFlow will be built with the MLIR (Lattner and Pienaar, 2019; Lattner et al., 2020) compiler where MLIR stands for "Machine Learning Intermediate Representation." MLIR will be the standard for machine learning libraries. MLIR will allow device-agnostic execution of machine learning code, that is, any new hardware accelerator will be easily supported.

S4TF works well not only in the Xcode integrated development environment (IDE) but also on Google Colaboratory and locally on Jupyter Notebook in browsers on macOS, Linux, and Windows operating systems. But building apps in the Xcode is beneficial because it allows intelligent context-aware code completion, highly controlled debugging, breakpoints, creating and performing tests, fixing program warnings and errors even before source code is compiled, and much more. It even allows you to view disk read or write data transfer statistics, network data sent or received, and most importantly memory consumption in real time. New features keep getting added to Xcode every year presented during Apple's Worldwide Developers Conference (WWDC) to make developers more productive. These Xcode capabilities used for developing amazing Apple platform apps also help develop better machine learning applications.

I originally planned to write all the deep learning programs presented in this book in Xcode, but many users already in the deep learning field use Python on Linux, so they might not be using macOS. For their convenience, I've used the Google Colaboratory platform to build and train all deep learning models presented in the book. So you can simply fire up your favorite browser and start experimenting with code examples right away. Those of you who own Macs may execute the same code in the Xcode.

In S4TF, you can simply import the prebuilt and even installed Python libraries and use them as you would in your Python program. This is known as *Python interoperability* (detailed discussion in Section 3.5). Since Swift's syntax is very similar to Python, calling those functions is seamless and feels as if you're writing in Python. A fun fact: you can import Python's any deep learning library (for instance, PyTorch) and define and train machine learning models in it right in S4TF! You can also import Python's visualization libraries for plotting purposes. Python interoperability helps in using very much-loved Python libraries by researchers and practitioners while still using other powerful features of S4TF.

In the future, iOS, iPadOS, macOS, watchOS, and tvOS developers will be able to write machine learning apps entirely with S4TF in pure Swift without requiring any high-level libraries like Core ML, Natural Language, and so on, provided by Apple. This way, you will be able to flexibly program (by defining and training new neural layers using new optimizers, loss functions, etc.) and distribute apps deploying the recently researched machine learning algorithms right away on-device. These on-device highly custom engineered models will also maintain your users' data privacy. Hopefully, one day you'll also be able to run your models on Neural Engine for fast on-device data processing. Interestingly, you can already build macOS apps in Xcode using the current S4TF toolchains. All the programs written in the book use the S4TF version 0.11.

The next section describes the technique to compute derivatives of neural networks in detail. This section is not a dependency to understand Swift (Section 3.4), but we emphasize you to read it at least once so that you can efficiently use this technology in other fields besides machine learning.

3.3 Algorithmic Differentiation

Here, we discuss *algorithmic differentiation* (AD), also called *automatic differentiation*, to automatically compute the derivative of a function. First, we discuss various programming approaches (Subsection 3.3.1) to compute derivatives. Then we describe two modes of AD (Subsection 3.3.2). Finally, we show how AD is implemented (Subsection 3.3.3).

Note that AD is not specifically used in machine learning but has been applied in various fields such as computational fluid dynamics (Bischof et al., 2007; Müller and Cusdin, 2005; Thomas et al., 2010), optimal control (Walther, 2007), and engineering design optimization (Casanova et al., 2000; Forth and Evans, 2002). (Baydin et al., 2017) review AD at a greater length.

3.3.1 Programming Approaches

There are mainly four approaches to determine the derivative of a function, namely, manual differentiation, numerical differentiation, symbolic differentiation, and algorithmic differentiation. We briefly look at the first three differentiation techniques. And because Swift implements the differentiation feature using the algorithmic differentiation technique, we take a deeper technical dive into it. Understanding algorithmic differentiation is not a prerequisite to use differentiation APIs, but knowing about it might help you write better differentiable programs.

3.3.1.1 Manual, Numerical, and Symbolic Differentiations

Manual differentiation is a very simple but time-consuming approach to program differentiation. It has been used in the past by machine learning researchers to find the derivative of the loss function and plug it into an optimization algorithm such as L-BFGS (Zhu et al., 1994) or stochastic gradient descent (SGD) (Bottou, 1998). Here, the person writes the derivative expression of a function on pen and paper and then programs the derivative function on the computer.

Numerical differentiation is concerned with finite-difference approximation of the derivative, discussed at length in Section 2.3. Although it is easy to implement, its simplicity comes with drawbacks such as inaccurate approximation because values may get rounded off due to machine precision limits (Jerrell, 1997) and taking $O(m)$ evaluations to computing the gradient $\nabla_x f = \begin{bmatrix} \dfrac{\partial f}{\partial x_1} & \cdots & \dfrac{\partial f}{\partial x_m} \end{bmatrix}$ for multivariate function $f : \mathbb{R}^m \to \mathbb{R}$ where $x \in \mathbb{R}^m$ is an input vector. The evaluation time of the gradient, Jacobian, and Hessian matters because deep learning algorithms make extensive use of vector and matrix differential calculus.

Symbolic differentiation is another approach to compute derivatives. In *symbolic differentiation*, the program manipulates the function expression to obtain its derivative expression (Grabmeier and Kaltofen, 2003). We can then simply evaluate the derivative of the function at a point using the newly derived derivative expression. The transformation of function expression into its derivative expression is carried out by using the rules of differentiation discussed in Subsections 2.3.2 and 2.3.3.

Although symbolic differentiation eliminates the limitations and weaknesses of manual and numerical differentiations, derivative expressions suffer from a problem of "expression swell" (Corliss, 1988) which makes them complicated and cryptic to read and understand. Moreover, manual and symbolic differentiations hinder the expressivity of differentiable programs because they don't allow differentiable functions to include control flow statements. To overcome these obstacles, we resort to the algorithmic differentiation technique.

3.3.1.2 Algorithmic Differentiation

Algorithmic differentiation is based on the fact that any numerical computation is made up of a finite set of elementary operations whose derivatives are known (Verma, 2000; Griewank and Walther, 2008). By applying the chain rule of differentiation, one can compute these functions' derivatives and, therefore, obtain the derivative of the whole expression. These elementary operations include binary and unary arithmetic operations and transcendental functions such as logarithmic, exponential, and trigonometric functions.

AD can differentiate through even control flows such as conditional branches, loops, control transfer statements, and recursion. This is possible because, in the end, any numeric program (even including control transfer statements), when executed, will always produce a numeric execution trace with input, intermediate, and output values which are the only things required to compute derivatives using the chain rule of differentiation.

3.3.2 Accumulation Modes

AD can be achieved through two approaches, namely, forward mode and reverse mode. You write the primal program which when executed produces an execution trace (also known as *forward primal/execution trace*). Then forward and reverse modes of AD use it to generate a corresponding *forward tangent* and a *reverse adjoint trace*, respectively, which represents the numeric program's derivative counterpart. The generated trace takes the input value and returns the derivative function's output. Note that you use either of the modes of AD to compute the derivative of the numeric program and not both of them together.

We consider a case of a multivariate composite function $f(x_1, x_2) = \sin(x_1) + \log_2(x_2)$, whose computational graph is shown in Figure 3-1, where our goal is to compute the partial derivatives of output with respect to input variables. The following text explains both of these approaches.

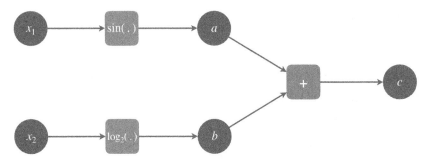

Figure 3-1. *The computational graph of a multivariate function*
$f(x_1, x_2) = sin(x_1) + log_2(x_2)$

Since AD requires that elementary functions should be differentiable and, therefore, have derivatives, we start by listing all the functions in the computational graph shown in Figure 3-1:

$$a = \sin(x_1)$$
$$b = \log_2(x_2)$$
$$c = a + b$$

Now we list their derivatives as follows:

$$\frac{da}{dx_1} = \cos(x_1) \times \frac{dx_1}{dx_1} = \cos(x_1)$$

$$\frac{db}{dx_2} = \frac{1}{x_2} \times \frac{dx_2}{dx_2} = \frac{1}{x_2}$$

$$\frac{dc}{da} = \frac{da}{da} + \frac{db}{da} = 1 + 0 = 1$$

$$\frac{dc}{db} = \frac{da}{db} + \frac{db}{db} = 0 + 1 = 1$$

Figure 3-2. *The computational graph of an arbitrary vector composite function* $g \circ f(x)$.

Now we will use these derivatives in the chain rule to find partial derivatives of the composite function $f(x_1, x_2)$ with respect to each input variable in forward- and reverse-mode ADs, described next. We demonstrate forward mode for finding partial derivative $\partial c/\partial x_2$ and reverse mode for both $\partial c/\partial x_1$ and $\partial c/\partial x_2$. For forward mode, we denote the partial derivative of each variable followed by apostrophe, for instance, $a' = \partial a/\partial x_2$ (also called *tangent*). And for reverse mode, we denote the partial derivative of each output variable c with a bar at its head, for instance, $\bar{a} = \partial c/\partial a$ (also called *adjoint*).

3.3.2.1 Forward Mode

In forward mode, we perform forward primal (numeric program) and forward tangent tracing (derivative of the numeric program). We pass the input values (x_1, x_2) to the function $f(x_1, x_2)$ and start tracing the forward primal program and store the intermediate values a, b, and c. With a corresponding step of primal tracing, we also trace the tangent values of corresponding variables. Before we start the tracing, we set the derivative of a specific input variable with respect to itself equal to one and others with respect to this variable equal to zero.

Table 3-1. *Computation traces for forward mode algorithmic differentiation.*

Forward Primal Trace		Forward Tangent Trace	
x_1	$= 3\pi/2$	x_1'	$= 0$
x_2	$= 4$	x_2'	$= 1$
$a = \sin(x_1)$	$= -1$	$a' = \cos(x_1) * x_1' = 0$	
$b = \log_2(x_2)$	$= 2$	$b' = (1/x_2) * x_2' = 1/4$	
$c = a + b$	$= 1$	$c' = a' + b'$	$= 0.25$

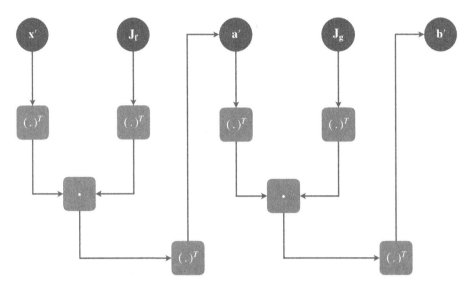

Figure 3-3. *The forward-mode algorithmic differentiation computational graph of an arbitrary vector composite function g ∘ f (x).*

Notice that the already available derivatives of elementary functions are used in the chain rule, starting from input variables, to compute the partial derivative of the output variable with respect to input variables. Here, we get $\partial c / \partial x_2 = c' = 0.25$.

The word "forward" in forward-mode AD comes from the fact that we sequentially compute tangents of input variables, intermediate variables, and then output variables with respect to input variable. Forward-mode AD is also called *push-forward AD* because we are pushing the derivatives from input variable toward output variables using the chain rule.

Now consider two arbitrary vector functions $\mathbf{f}: \mathbb{R}^m \rightarrow \mathbb{R}^n$ and $\mathbf{g}: \mathbb{R}^n \rightarrow \mathbb{R}^o$ and input vector variable $\mathbf{x} \in \mathbb{R}^{1 \times m}$ (we represent it as a matrix for matrix multiplication). Here, we are interested in composite function $\mathbf{g} \circ \mathbf{f}$, shown in Figure 3-2. Because these functions are composed of elementary functions, akin to the previous multivariate function's example, we have their partial derivatives already available stored in their respective

Jacobian matrices, that is, $\mathbf{J_f} \in \mathbb{R}^{m \times n}$ and $\mathbf{J_g} \in \mathbb{R}^{n \times o}$. Now we perform forward primal tracing as follows:

$$\mathbf{a} = \mathbf{f}(\mathbf{x})$$

$$\mathbf{b} = \mathbf{g}(\mathbf{a})$$

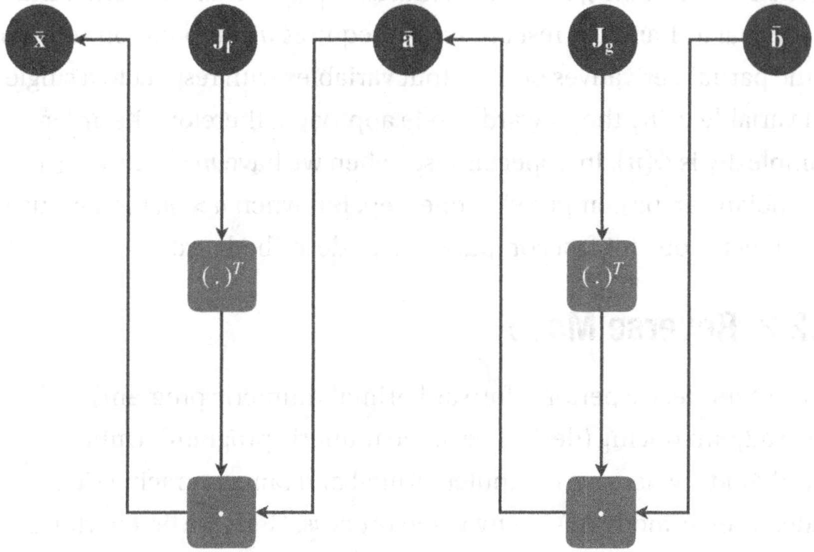

Figure 3-4. *The reverse-mode algorithmic differentiation computational graph of an arbitrary vector composite function $g \circ f(x)$.*

Here, we have intermediate variable $\mathbf{a} \in \mathbb{R}^{1 \times n}$ and output variable $\mathbf{b} \in \mathbb{R}^{1 \times o}$. We will set $d\mathbf{x}/d\mathbf{x}$, which is a $1 \times m$ matrix and denoted as $\mathbf{x}'$, with only one element set equal to one. We can now perform forward tangent tracing (shown in Figure 3-3) as follows:

$$\mathbf{a}' = \left(\mathbf{J_f^T} \cdot \mathbf{x}'^T\right)^T$$

$$\mathbf{b}' = \left(\mathbf{J_g^T} \cdot \mathbf{a}'^T\right)^T$$

Here, we have intermediate variable's derivative $\mathbf{a}' \in \mathbb{R}^{1 \times n}$ and output variable's derivative $\mathbf{b}' \in \mathbb{R}^{1 \times o}$ which are of the same dimension sizes as their forward primal traced variable counterparts. Because we matrix multiplied, denoted by $\cdot$ operator, Jacobian and vector (represented as a matrix), forward-mode AD can be represented as a chained application of *Jacobian-vector products* (JVP).

When we evaluate $\mathbf{J}_f$ at point $\mathbf{a}'$, that is, $\mathbf{J}_f\big|_{x=a'}$ where only one variable of $\mathbf{a}'$ is equal to 1 and the rest are zero, it requires n computation steps to find the partial derivatives of all output variables with respect to a single input variable using the forward-mode approach; therefore, its order of complexity is $\mathcal{O}(n)$. In a special case, when we have $m = 1$ and $n \geq 1$, the Jacobian can be computed in one step. But when $n > m$, then we use another technique for fast computation, as described next.

3.3.2.2 Reverse Mode

In reverse mode, we perform forward primal (numeric program) and reverse adjoint tracing (derivative of the numeric program). Unlike forward mode, where we computed primal and tangent tracing side by side, reverse-mode AD is a two-step process. Here, we first perform forward primal tracing and then reverse adjoint tracing in the second step. In the first step, also called *forward pass*, we pass the input values (x_1, x_2) to the function $f(x_1, x_2)$ and start tracing the forward primal program and store the intermediate values a, b, and c. In the second step, also called *backward pass*, we trace the adjoint values of variables starting from the output variable toward the input variables. Before we start the tracing, we set the derivative of a scalar output variable with respect to itself equal to one.

Table 3-2. *Computation traces for reverse mode algorithmic differentiation*

Forward Primal Trace	Reverse Adjoint Trace
$x_1 = 3\pi / 2$	$\bar{c} = 1$
$x_2 = 4$	$\bar{b} = 1$
$a = \sin(x_1) = -1$	$\bar{a} = 1$
$b = \log_2(x_2) = 2$	$\bar{x}_2 = \bar{b} \cdot dx_2 / dx_2 = 1.1 / 4 = 0.25$
$c = a + b = 1$	$\bar{x}_1 = \bar{a} \cdot dx_1 / dx_1 = 1$

Here, we get $\partial c / \partial x_1 = \bar{x}_1 = 1$ and $\partial c / \partial x_2 = \bar{x}_2 = 0.25$.

The word "reverse" in reverse-mode AD comes from the fact that we sequentially compute partial derivatives of output variables with respect to output variables, intermediate variables, and then input variables. Reverse-mode AD is also called *pullback AD* because we are pulling the derivatives from the output variable toward the input variables using the chain rule.

From the previous forward-mode AD discussion, we consider the same assumptions about vector functions **f** and **g** and their Jacobians $\mathbf{J}_f$ and $\mathbf{J}_g$. We then perform forward primal tracing (shown in Figure 3-4) as follows:

$$\mathbf{a} = \mathbf{f}(\mathbf{x})$$

$$\mathbf{b} = \mathbf{g}(\mathbf{a})$$

Here, again, we have intermediate variable $\mathbf{a} \in \mathrm{R}^{1 \times n}$ and output variable $\mathbf{b} \in \mathbb{R}^{1 \times o}$. We will set $d\mathbf{b}/d\mathbf{b}$, which is a $1 \times o$ matrix and denoted as $\bar{\mathbf{b}}$, with only one element set equal to one. We can now perform reverse adjoint tracing as follows:

$$\bar{\mathbf{a}} = \bar{\mathbf{b}} \cdot \mathbf{J}_g^T$$
$$\bar{\mathbf{x}} = \bar{\mathbf{a}} \cdot \mathbf{J}_f^T$$

Here, we have the output's derivative with respect to intermediate variable $\bar{\mathbf{a}} \in \mathbb{R}^{1 \times n}$ and input variable $\bar{\mathbf{x}} \in \mathbb{R}^{1 \times m}$ which are of the same dimension sizes as their forward primal traced variable counterparts. Because we matrix multiplied vector and Jacobian, reverse mode AD can be represented as a chained application of *vector-Jacobian products* (VJP).

When we evaluate $\mathbf{J_g}$ at point $\bar{\mathbf{b}}$, that is, $\mathbf{J_g}\big|_{\mathbf{b}=\bar{\mathbf{b}}}$ where only one variable of $\bar{\mathbf{b}}$ is equal to 1 and the rest are zero, it requires m computation steps to find partial derivatives of all output variables with respect to all intermediate and input variables using the reverse-mode approach; therefore, its order of complexity is $\mathcal{O}(m)$. In a special case when we have $m = 1$ and $n \geq 1$, the Jacobian can be computed in one step.

When we study neural networks in the next chapter, we'll see that neural networks' gradient computation is always this special case because a loss function emits a scalar value. This is the primary reason why today's deep learning libraries only implement reverse-mode AD (although Swift implements both forward and reverse modes which makes it a more general language and open to be applied in various other domains than just deep learning) because the gradient of an output scalar with respect to all intermediate and input variables can be computed in just a single backward pass. In this book, we are also concerned with using reverse-mode AD functions (Subsection 3.4.9) of Swift.

3.3.3 Implementation Approaches

Here we discuss two ways to implement AD, namely, operator overloading (OO) and source code transformation (SCT).

3.3.3.1 Operator Overloading

Algorithmic differentiation can be easily implemented by defining advanced operators (see Subsection 3.4.8), also called operator overloading (OO), for numerical custom type. Some Python libraries such as autograd (Maclaurin et al., 2015; Maclaurin, 2016),[5] PyTorch (Paszke et al., 2017, 2019),[6] Pythonic TensorFlow (Abadi et al., 2016),[7] Keras (Chollet et al., 2015),[8] Theano (Al-Rfou et al., 2016),[9] and others implement reverse-mode AD using the OO approach. These are known as embedded (their host language is Python) *domain-specific languages* (DSLs) because they solve a specific domain's problem (deep learning here) and are distributed as libraries.

The code in Listing 3-1 presents a simple example (adapted from (Wei et al., 2018)) of operator overloading using dual numbers to implement forward-mode algorithmic differentiation in Swift for computing a given expression's derivative.

Listing 3-1. Demonstrate operator-overloaded forward-mode algorithmic differentiation using dual numbers

```
struct DualNumber<T: FloatingPoint> {
  var value: T
  var derivative: T
}

extension DualNumber {
  /// Applies sum rule
  static func + (left: Self, right: Self) -> Self {
    DualNumber(
      value: left.value + right.value,
      derivative: left.derivative + right.derivative)
  }
```

---

[5]https://github.com/HIPS/autograd
[6]https://pytorch.org/
[7]https://tensorflow.org/
[8]https://keras.io
[9]www.deeplearning.net/software/theano/

```swift
    /// Applies sum rule
    static func - (left: Self, right: Self) -> Self {
      DualNumber(
        value: left.value - right.value,
        derivative: left.derivative - right.derivative)
    }
    /// Applies product rule
    static func * (left: Self, right: Self) -> Self {
      DualNumber(
        value: left.value * right.value,
        derivative: left.derivative * right.value +
                    left.value * right.derivative)
    }
    /// Applies quotient rule
    static func / (left: Self, right: Self) -> Self {
      DualNumber(
        value: left.value / right.value,
        derivative: (left.derivative * right.value -
                     left.value * right.derivative) /
                     (right.value * right.value))
    }
}
let x = DualNumber(value: 3, derivative: 1)
let expression = x*x*x + x
print("expression value: \(expression.value)")
print("expression derivative: \(expression.derivative)")
```

Output

```
expression value: 30.0
expression derivative: 28.0
```

We have declared a `DualNumber` structure containing two stored properties, `value` and `derivative,` of type `T` conforming to the `FloatingPoint` protocol. Then `DualNumber` is extended to include various advanced operators such as addition, subtraction, multiplication, and division. Each of these returns a `DualNumber` instance containing `value` and `derivative`. Here, addition and subtraction, multiplication, and division use sum, product, and quotient rules of differentiation, respectively, to initialize the `derivative` property of a `DualNumber` instance to return.

Then we initialized the `DualNumber` literal x with `value` of 3 and `derivative` of 1. Setting `derivative` equal to 1 here means the derivative of x with respect to itself is equal to 1. We declare the `expression` literal which computes $x^3 + x$ and whose derivative with respect to x is $3x^2 + 1$. When we access the `derivative` property, we get the `value` $3 * 3^2 + 1 = 28$ as expected.

Note that the limitation of any DSL is that it is restricted by being capable of implementing only one mode of AD, that is, either forward or reverse mode. But compiler-level code transformation, as in the Swift language, lets us implement both.

3.3.3.2 Source Code Transformation

A better way to implement AD is to perform compiler-level source code transformation (SCT) of the program which allows implementing *both* forward and reverse modes in the language itself! The programmer can simply call APIs to differentiate the function using either forward or reverse mode easily. SCT gives more control to perform optimizations at the compiler level during the compilation process for fast differentiation.

One SCT optimization example is as follows. Consider a conditional statement (containing different numeric computations in each condition pass) during numeric execution tracing. During forward tangent or reverse adjoint tracing, a DSL would require to trace each of those conditions to form a computational graph to optimize the program execution performance. If there are c number of conditional statements, then it would need to run the tracing c times; and now if you also consider control transfer statements, then even more tracing will be required. In contrast, compiler-level SCT can consider every feature of Swift and optimize all the possible cases during the compilation process. This would require just tracing once to accumulate variable values, and partial derivatives will be computed fast.

SCT is exactly how Swift approaches to tackle the shortcomings of previously described techniques. Although discussing SCT lies beyond the scope of this book, we do discuss various differentiation APIs (Subsection 3.4.9) available in Swift. But before that, let us familiarize ourselves with the Swift language itself in the following section.

3.4 Swift Language

In this section, we will go through enough features of the Swift language to understand the machine learning programs in the book. Experienced programmers familiar with Python or C++ will find Swift syntax easy to grasp. To beginner-level programmers, Swift code feels like reading English sentences, so the intention behind the code statement becomes intuitively understandable. In addition to simple syntax, Swift is a fast, cross-platform, compiled, and type-safe language with modern features like generics, retroactive modeling, protocols, optionals, and much more. Covering all the features of Swift lies beyond the scope of this book. Apple's fantastic Swift book available online[10] will be very helpful for readers interested in other features of Swift.

We start with simple values (Subsection 3.4.1) and then see how to use various collection types (Subsection 3.4.2) in Swift. Subsection

---

[10]https://docs.swift.org/swift-book/

3.4.3 introduces control flow statements. The three forms of functions in Swift are discussed in Section 3.4.4. We then introduce custom types (Subsection 3.4.5). Subsection 3.4.6 discusses some powerful and modern features of Swift. Subsection 3.4.7 shows how to handle errors in Swift with a breeze. Custom operators for types are introduced in Subsection 3.4.8. Finally, we close this section with an introduction to the algorithmic differentiation feature of Swift in Subsection 3.4.9.

3.4.1 Values

In Swift, you declare an instance as either a variable or a constant with the **var** or **let** keyword, respectively. You can change the value of a variable instance during program execution, whereas the value of a constant instance cannot be changed.

Following the Swift conventions, you should declare an instance with lower camel case letters.

Listing 3-2. Declare instances containing simple values

```
var firstNumber = 10
let pi = 3.14159
var secondNumber: Float = 123.456
```

Here, `firstNumber` is inferred to be of type `Int`. A constant `pi` declared in the preceding code is inferred to be of type `Double` because it contains decimal values. In some cases, you might need to declare a floating-point number. In this case, simply provide `Float` as type information about the variable. You can also verify the type of each instance using the `type(of:)` function.

Listing 3-3. Check the type of instance

```
print("firstNumber: \(type(of: firstNumber))")
print("pi: \(type(of: pi))")
print("secondNumber: \(type(of: secondNumber))")
```

Output

```
firstNumber: Int
pi: Double
secondNumber: Float
```

The type information is automatically inferred from the value assigned to the instance. In other cases, you can provide the type information by writing the type name followed by the instance separated by a colon.

This is a good example demonstrating that reading a code statement in Swift feels like reading an English sentence. Swift's simple syntax makes it easy for newcomers to learn programming.

In some situations, an instance might not contain a value. To represent this state of an instance, Swift provides optional values which either contain a value or nothing represented by **nil**. To define an optional, provide the type information during declaration followed by a question mark (?) without any white space.

Listing 3-4. Declare an optional-type instance

```
var optionalInt: Int? = 5
if let value = optionalInt {
  print("optionalInt has value: \(value)")
}
```

Output

```
optionalInt has value: 5
```

Here, optionalInt is of type Int? having a value of 5. It could have contained **nil** because it is an optional. Then an **if let** statement extracts and binds the value in the value constant for use in the code block of the **if** statement. This is called *optional binding*.

You can also define the computed property which computes the value instead of storing it. The computed property must always be declared as a variable instance. See Listing 3-24 for an example.

3.4.2 Collections

You can declare three kinds of collections in Swift, namely, array, set, and dictionary. Collections are generic structures for which you have to provide type information in case it cannot be inferred. Every collection type conforms to the Sequence protocol which allows you to iterate over its elements.

3.4.2.1 Array

An array is an ordered collection of elements. You access an element with its index as subscript representing its position in the array. Arrays are zero-indexed in Swift, that is, the first element of an array has position zero, the second element has position one, and so on.

Listing 3-5. Iterate over an array instance

```
let deepLearningPioneers = ["Geoffrey Hinton", "Yoshua Bengio",
"Yann LeCun", "Jürgen Schmidhuber"]
for name in deepLearningPioneers {
  print(name)
}
```

Output

```
Geoffrey Hinton
Yoshua Bengio
Yann LeCun
Jürgen Schmidhuber
```

You can also access each element's index position with the enumerated() instance method. Code in Listing 3-6 sorts and then enumerates over the array.

Listing 3-6. Access each element with its index in a sorted array

```
for (index, name) in deepLearningPioneers.sorted().enumerated()
{
  print("\(index). \(name)")
}
```

Output

```
0. Geoffrey Hinton
1. Jürgen Schmidhuber
2. Yann LeCun
3. Yoshua Bengio
```

3.4.2.2 Set

A set is an unordered collection of unique elements. In the declaration, specify that the instance is of Set type. You can perform mathematical set operations. A set also has some methods akin to those of an array in standard library.

Listing 3-7. Set operations on even, odd, and whole numbers

```
let oddNumbers: Set<Int> = [1, 3, 5, 7, 9]
let evenNumbers: Set = [0, 2, 4, 6, 8]
let wholeNumbers = oddNumbers.union(evenNumbers).sorted()
print("wholeNumbers: \(wholeNumbers)")
print("Even and odd numbers are subset of whole numbers:
\(evenNumbers.union(oddNumbers).isSubset(of: wholeNumbers) ?
"✓" : "×")")
```

Output

Even and odd numbers are a subset of whole numbers: ✓

You can define a set with Set type followed by the type information in an angle bracket, for instance, Set<Int>, because Set is a generic structure type. But in case information is available, you may omit the type information. Although sets are unordered, you can sort them using the sorted() instance method. Note the usage of the ternary operator here written as condition ? result1 : result2. If the condition is true, then result1 is returned – otherwise, result2. Here, union of even and odd numbers is a subset of whole numbers is a true statement so "✓" is returned.

3.4.2.3 Dictionary

A dictionary is a collection of unordered elements where each element is a key and value pair. You access a value by using a key as subscript on an instance.

Listing 3-8. Define a dictionary and access its value

```
let wheelsCount = ["unicycle": 1, "bicycle": 2, "rickshaw": 3,
"car": 4]
print("A rickshaw has \(wheelsCount["rickshaw"]!) wheel(s).")
```

Output

```
A rickshaw has 3 wheel(s).
```

Note that we use the exclamation mark when accessing the wheel count for rickshaw. An optional value is returned because a key may not exist in the dictionary. Using an exclamation mark to access the value of an optional is called *forced unwrapping*. Note that this can fail, so try using optional binding in situations where you are not sure about the presence of a key in a dictionary as follows.

Listing 3-9. Safely access a dictionary value with optional binding

```
if let unicycle = wheelsCount["unicycle"] {
  print("A unicycle has \(unicycle) wheel(s).")
}
```

Output

```
A unicycle has 1 wheel(s).
```

The **if** conditional statement used in the preceding code is a part of many other control flows discussed in the following.

3.4.3 Control Flow

Swift provides various control flow statements. You can loop through a sequence of statements with three kinds of loops. Conditional statements allow you to execute a particular statement based on truthfulness of a condition. You can also transfer the control of execution to certain statements with control transfer statements.

3.4.3.1 Loops

Swift has three kinds of loops, namely, **for-in** loop, **while** loop, and **repeat-while** loop. Each has its own importance as described in the following.

The **for-in** loop lets you iteratively access each element in a collection instance. You can also access the index of each element during iteration by calling the enumerated() instance method on that collection.

Listing 3-10. Declare a for-in loop to iterate over a range of values

```
for value in 1...5 {
  print("5 x \(value) = \(5 * value)")
}
```

Output

```
5 x 1 = 5
5 x 2 = 10
5 x 3 = 15
5 x 4 = 20
5 x 5 = 25
```

This example simply iterates over a range from 1 to 5. You can exclude the last number (5) in the range with 1..<5 syntax.

Listing 3-11. Access corresponding elements of two arrays simultaneously

```
let fruits = ["Apple", "Banana", "Orange", "Watermelon"]
let colors = ["red", "yellow", "orange", "green"]
for (fruit, color) in zip(fruits, colors) {
  print("\(fruit) has \(color) color.")
}
```

Output

```
Apple has red color.
Banana has yellow color.
Orange has orange color.
Watermelon has green color.
```

Using the zip(_:_:) function with two instances conforming to Sequence lets you access elements from each instance at corresponding index positions. Here, "Apple" and "red" are at zero index in fruits and colors, respectively. Running the **for-in** loop accesses both of these in the first iteration and prints "Apple has red color." Similarly, other sentences are printed for each corresponding element pair.

The **for-in** loop is good for situations when iterating over a range or Sequence of conforming instances. But when the number of iterations is not known, then while loops can be helpful. While loops simply run a block of code if the condition is true and terminate otherwise. There are two kinds of while loops, namely, **while** loop and **repeat-while** loop.

The **while** loop checks the condition at the start and repeats a set of statements until the condition becomes false. In contrast, a **repeat-while** loop executes a set of statements when a condition is true for all passes except the first pass which requires no condition check.

Listing 3-12. Demonstrate the while loop

```swift
var a = 5
while a > 0 {
  print(a, terminator: " ")
  a -= 1
}
```

Output

```
5 4 3 2 1
```

Here, the **while** loop checks, at the beginning, if the value of a is greater than zero. If this condition is true, then the statements in curly braces are executed. But when the value of a becomes equal to or less than zero, the loop terminates returning the control to the code after the closing curly brace, if any.

Listing 3-13. Demonstrate the repeat-while loop

```
var b = 0
repeat {
  print(b, terminator: " ")
  b += 1
  if b > 6 { break }
} while b > 0
```

Output

```
1 2 3 4 5
```

In preceding **repeat-while** loop, a set of statements between curly braces are executed in the first pass. It first prints the value of b with the terminating character " " instead of "\n" (carriage return character, which moves the cursor to newline) and then updates the value of b by adding one to it. Finally, it breaks the loop if the value of b exceeds 6. This is the loop termination condition. After running these statements once, the condition is checked if b is greater than zero to execute the loop again. Notice that **while** loops might infinitely execute a sequence of statements, and you must provide a terminating condition as we have provided in the preceding code (inside loop).

3.4.3.2 Conditional Statements

Swift has support for two kinds of conditional statements, namely, **if** and **switch**.

In an **if** statement, a block of code is executed if a condition is true. In addition, you can define an **else** code block to execute if your **if** condition is false. You can also provide an **else if** statement between **if** and **else** code blocks if you want to check for more than one condition for success, given that it cannot be provided within an **if** statement altogether separated by commas.

Listing 3-14. Demonstrate an if-else statement

```swift
let marks = 75
if marks < 60 {
  print("Poor")
} else if marks >= 60 && marks <= 80 {
  print("Average")
} else {
  print("Excellent")
}
```

Output

```
Average
```

This example shows how an **if** conditional statement can be combined with **else** and **else if** statements for fine-grained control over the code execution. Since marks are within the range of 60 and 80, this code prints "Average."

Another useful conditional statement is **switch**. The **switch** statement is used to compare a single instance with multiple possible values.

Listing 3-15. Demonstrate the `switch` statement

```
switch marks {
case let x where x < 60:
  print("Poor")
case 60...80:
  print("Average")
  fallthrough
default:
  print("Excellent")
}
```

Output

```
Average
Excellent
```

Here, the **switch** statement compares a single variable with many possible cases. Notice how you can define a local variable or constant in a case using the **let** or **var** keyword and compare its value right there. You can also check the value for lying in a particular interval. In **switch** statements, **default** acts as an **else** block in **if** statements. It must be included if your **switch** statement is not exhaustive. The control of the program is transferred to the line of code after the closing curly brace of the **switch** statement when any first encountered case is matched and its code is executed. But in case you want to execute a succeeding case code irrespective of it matching the value, you can use the **fallthrough** control transfer statement. If **fallthrough** was not included in this example, then it would have only printed "Average." The **fallthrough** statement imitates the behavior of the **switch** conditional statement in C and C++ languages.

3.4.3.3 Control Transfer Statements

Swift provides five control transfer statements, namely, **continue**, **break**, **return**, **fallthrough**, and **throw**. The **throw** statement is discussed in error handling in the following. And **fallthrough** has been discussed in the preceding text. The **return** statement is used in functions, as well as the **guard** statement. You have also already seen an example of the **break** statement in Listing 3-13.

Here, we focus on **continue** control transfer statements used in loops.

Listing 3-16. Use a continue control transfer statement in a for-in loop

```swift
let totalSteps = 50
let range = stride(from: 0, to: totalSteps, by: 10)
print("range: \(Array(range))")
for step in range {
  if step == 30 { continue }
  print("step: \(step)")
}
```

Output

```
range: [0, 10, 20, 30, 40]
step: 0
step: 10
step: 20
step: 40
```

In this code, the stride(from:to:by:) function produces a range of values starting from 0 to 40 distanced by 10, excluding the last value, that is, 50. Printing the range by converting into an array shows the values described by it. To include the last value, substitute the to argument with through in this function. Then **for-in** loop iterates over all the values printing each value but not 30. This is done by using a **continue** statement which transfers the control of execution to the first statement of the **for-in** loop for the next iteration, skipping all the following statements.

3.4.3.4 Early Exit

In a **guard** statement, the code following the **guard** keyword must be true if it is a condition, or contain a value if it is an optional, for the code after the **guard** statement to execute. In the case of optional binding, the instance is made available in the code in which the **guard** statement appears for further use. But if it fails, then the code inside the **else** code block is executed. This **else** block must also contain some control transfer statement that transfers the control to outside the code block in which the **guard** statement is written.

Listing 3-17. Demonstrate the usage of the guard statement

```
func welcome(language: [String: String]) {
  guard let name = language["name"] else {
    print("Welcome!")
    return
  }
  print("Welcome \(name)!")
}
welcome(language: [:])
welcome(language: ["name": "Swift"])
```

Output

```
Welcome!
Welcome Swift!
```

Here, the `welcome(language:)` function takes a dictionary as an argument. Then the **guard** statement tries to extract the value for the "name" key from the dictionary. Optional binding might fail in case the "name" key is not present in the dictionary. In this case, the **else** code block is executed which simply prints a "Welcome!" message to the console. But when the value exists, then it is stored in a name constant which is used to print a much finer message. This example uses a function feature which is discussed in more detail next.

3.4.4 Closures and Functions

In Swift, closures are code blocks of functionality which can be reused in different parts of your program. Putting it more clearly, Swift provides three kinds of closures, and function is one of them:

1. *Global functions* are named closures that can be called by explicitly referring to them with their names.

2. *Nested functions* are named closures declared in another function.

3. *Closure expressions* are an unnamed block of functionality that is implicitly executed wherever it is declared.

Calling a function means to execute the code statements written inside that function by referring to that function's name.

3.4.4.1 Global Functions

You define a global function with the **func** keyword followed by the name, the parameter list in round brackets, and the body of the function containing functionality within curly braces.

Listing 3-18. Declare a global function

```
enum Vehicle {
  case car, train
}
func drive(vehicle: Vehicle) -> String {
  switch vehicle {
    case .car:
      return "Vroom vroom!"
    case .train:
      return "Choo choo!"
  }
}
let sound = drive(vehicle: .car)
print(sound)
print(type(of: drive))
```

Output

```
Vroom vroom!
(Vehicle) -> String
```

The preceding function drive(vehicle:) takes a vehicle argument
of Vehicle enumeration type (discussed later) representing two vehicles.
Based on the vehicle value, it returns a string representing the sound it
makes while driving. Finally, we print the sound.

In Swift, every function is a reference type. And only classes and
functions are reference types in Swift. Here, drive(vehicle:) is a function
of type (Vehicle) -> String. You can read it as "function named drive
takes one argument value of Vehicle type and returns a String value."
Printing the type of this function using the type(of:) function confirms
this function's type.

3.4.4.2 Nested Functions

A nested function is a function declared inside another function.

Listing 3-19. Declare a nested function

```
func outerFunction() -> () -> Int {
  func innerFunction() -> Int {
    print("Running inner function.")
    return 0
  }
  print("Running outer function.")
  return innerFunction
}
let someInnerFunction = outerFunction()
print("someInnerFunction type: \(type(of: someInnerFunction))")
let someInt = someInnerFunction()
print("someInt: \(someInt)")
```

Output

```
Running outer function.
someInnerFunction type: () -> Int
Running inner function.
someInt: 0
```

The type of outerFunction() is () -> () -> Int that takes nothing as a parameter and returns a function of type () -> Int. The nested function innerFunction() has type () -> Int and returns 0. Calling outerFunction() only prints a statement in an outer function, before returning the preceding innerFunction(). The variable inside someInnerFunction() is innerFunction() that when called prints a statement inside it and returns 0 which is then stored in someInt.

3.4.4.3 Closure Expressions

Closure expressions are simple but powerful nameless functional code blocks. Closure is written inside a set of opening and closing curly braces. Closure takes parameters in round brackets just like a named function and represents the return type following a right arrow. The body of closure is written after the **in** keyword. We will use closure expressions very often to compute gradients of the loss function with respect to neural networks later.

Listing 3-20. Declare a closure to return Bool representing an integer's positivity

```
let isPositive = { (_ x: Float) -> Bool in
  return x > 0
}
print(isPositive(-5))
```

Output

```
false
```

Here, closure has type (Float) -> Bool, that is, it takes an Int and returns a Bool. The body following the in keyword computes the operation and returns the result. This closure returns a function to the isPositive(_:) instance which is later called to check if -5 is positive and correctly prints that it is not.

Listing 3-21. Demonstrate trailing closures

```
func isEven(_ x: Int, also hasProperty: (Int) -> Bool) -> Bool
{
  x % 2 == 0 && hasProperty(x)
}
```

```
let number = 2
let isEvenAndPositive = isEven(number, also: isPositive)
print(isEvenAndPositive)
let isEvenAndFibonacciNumber = isEven(number) { number in
  fibonacciNumbers.contains(number)
}
print(isEvenAndFibonacciNumber)
```

Output

```
true
true
```

The function isEven(_:also:) takes a number and a closure also representing the second property of the number. Passing number as 2 and the isPositive function to isEven(_:also:) returns true signifying that 2 is a positive and even integer. The array fibonacciNumbers is declared in Listing 3-31.

When a closure is a last argument to the function, you can drop its argument label and round brackets of the function call and simply write closure in the opening and closing curly braces, for simplicity. This is called *trailing closure*. To provide a custom closure to isEven(_:also:), we simply write a closure that returns a Boolean value signaling the presence of a number in the Fibonacci series. In our case, 2 is even and also contained in the Fibonacci series, so it returns true.

Closures are much more powerful, and explaining all their features lies beyond the scope of this book. For instance, Swift also has *multiple trailing closures* allowing you to write more than one closure as trailing closures to a function's arguments. We advice you to refer to the official Swift book available online for deeper understanding on closures and many other features.

3.4.5 Custom Types

You can also declare new types in Swift known as *custom types*. It can be any of the enumeration, structure, and class types. Enumeration and structure are value types (instances are copied), and class is a reference type (instances are only referenced, not copied). Each of these types is useful in different situations.

Following the naming conventions, you should declare types with upper camel case letters to align with other types already defined in Swift's standard library.

3.4.5.1 Enumerations

Enumeration allows you to define a group of types having similar relation to each other. For example, you can define a `Rainbow` enumeration containing a group of color cases. Note that these colors are types in their right. Use the **enum** keyword to define your enumeration.

Listing 3-22. Declare an enumeration and print a statement according to an instance

```
enum Rainbow {
  case violet, indigo, blue, green, yellow, orange, red
}
// `Rainbow.violet` is similar to the following approach.
let favoriteColor: Rainbow = .indigo
switch favoriteColor {
case .violet:
  print("\(favoriteColor) has low wavelength and high
  frequency.")
case .red:
  print("\(favoriteColor) has high wavelength and low
  frequency.")
```

default:
```
  print("\(favoriteColor) has wavelength and frequency within
  the range of visible spectrum.")
}
```

  Output

```
indigo has wavelength and frequency within the range of
visible spectrum.
```

We have declared an enumeration named Rainbow which contains all the dominant colors naturally occurring in the rainbow. The values of Rainbow are declared with the **case** keyword and are self-contained values in their own right.

The favoriteColor instance has been declared by setting its value to indigo of type Rainbow. Then a suitable statement is printed by checking the value of favoriteColor against different colors. Note how dot syntax is used here. The compiler automatically understands that the value being compared in each **switch** case is of Rainbow type, so using dot syntax is sufficient.

3.4.5.2 Structures

Structures are the basic building blocks of your program which can contain properties, methods, and subscripts to add capabilities to your type. Structures can also conform to protocols and be extended with more features. We will be using structures extensively throughout the book.

The structure code snippet in Listing 3-23 declares a Mammal structure and a nested enumeration type named LivingZone. Mammal has two properties, namely, livingZone, and legsCount. Here, legsCount is an optional integer instance because some mammals might not have legs and others might have lost them during their lifetime. The livingZone is an instance of LivingZone describing the survival surroundings of a mammal.

Listing 3-23. Declare a nested structure and initialize its instances

```
struct Mammal {
  enum LivingZone {
    case land, water
  }
  var livingZone: LivingZone
  var legsCount: Int?
}
let human = Mammal(livingZone: .land, legsCount: 2)
let injuredHuman = Mammal(livingZone: .land, legsCount: 0)
let fish = Mammal(livingZone: .water, legsCount: nil)
```

We have declared three instances of Mammal named human, injuredHuman, and fish, each initialized with varying instance property values. You can read the human instance as "human lives on land and has 2 legs." Similarly, injuredHuman can be described as "injured human also lives on land but has lost both of its legs." Finally, you can read the fish instance as "fish lives under water and requires no legs for survival."

Listing 3-24. Extend Mammal to include a curated description

```
extension Mammal {
  var description: String {
    var text = "Lives \(livingZone == .land ? "on" ? "in") \
    (livingZone)"
    if let legsCount = legsCount {
      if legsCount == 0 {
        text += " and cannot walk because it has \(legsCount)
        legs."
      } else if legsCount > 0 {
          text += " and can walk with its \(legsCount) legs."
      }
```

```
    } else {
      text += " and swims."
    }
    return text
  }
}
print(human.description)
print(injuredHuman.description)
print(fish.description)
```

Output

```
Lives on land and can walk with its 2 legs.
Lives on land and cannot walk because it has 0 legs.
Lives in water and swims.
```

The preceding code extends the Mammal structure to include a curated description of a mammal instance. See how a text instance property is modified inside the description computed instance property to include refined information based on the properties of a Mammal instance. The final printed sentences make meaningful descriptions of each instance. Notice how extending the Mammal structure even after the declaration of instances still allows those instances to use the extended functionality; this is applicable for all custom types in Swift.

You can also call your type instances as functions. This *functional programming* approach makes it convenient to perform forward pass in neural networks in our case. You make it happen by declaring a callAsFunction() in your custom type with any number of arguments. We will declare this function in our structures describing neural network models in later chapters.

But sometimes you might require to do more than just creating instances with properties, subscripts, and methods. You might need to inherit functionalities from other types, override some features, and so on. Classes provide such capabilities in your types as described in the following.

3.4.5.3 Classes

Just like structures, classes are also the basic building blocks of your program which can contain properties, methods, and subscripts to add capabilities to your type. Similar to structures, classes can also conform to protocols and be extended with more features.

In addition to sharing capabilities with structures, classes also let you inherit properties, methods, and subscripts from other classes, override them, typecast to check the instance's class, deinitialize an instance, and allow more than one reference to a class instance. But all the features are not discussed in this book. We only go through the features that are important to understand deep learning programs in the book.

Listing 3-25. Declare the Rocket class with stored and computed properties and an initializer

```
class Rocket {
  var name: String? = nil
  var vacuumThrust: Int = 0
  var description: String {
    return "\(name ?? "Rocket") has \(vacuumThrust) kN
thrust in vacuum."
  }
  init(name: String? = nil, vacuumThrust: Int = 0) {
    self.name = name
    self.vacuumThrust = vacuumThrust
  }
}
```

```
var rocketA = Rocket()
var rocketB = Rocket(name: "ABCRocket")
print(rocketA.description)
print(rocketB.description)
```

Output

```
Rocket has 0 kN thrust in vacuum.
ABCRocket has 0 kN thrust in vacuum.
```

The preceding code declares a base class Rocket containing two stored properties and a computed property. Based on name and thrust applied by a rocket in space, a description is generated. We declare two Rocket instances and print their descriptions.

Note that a class does not automatically get an implementation of an initializer (code block starting with the **init** keyword) which must be provided by you if stored properties don't contain initial values.

Listing 3-26. Inherit features of Rocket and refine to carry payload

```
final class CargoRocket: Rocket {
  var payload: Int
  override var description: String {
    return "\(name!) carries \(payload) kg and has \
(vacuumThrust) kN thrust in vacuum."
  }
  init(name: String?, vacuumThrust: Int, payload: Int) {
    self.payload = payload
    super.init(name: name, vacuumThrust: vacuumThrust)
  }
}
var falcon9 = CargoRocket(name: "Falcon 9",
vacuumThrust: 8_227, payload: 22_800)
```

```
var falconHeavy = CargoRocket(name:
"Falcon Heavy", vacuumThrust: 24_681, payload: 63_800)
print(falcon9.description)
print(falconHeavy.description)
```

Output

```
Falcon 9 carries 22800 kg and has 8227 kN thrust in vacuum.
Falcon Heavy carries 63800 kg and has 24681 kN thrust in
vacuum.
```

Some rockets are more powerful than the others and can carry larger payloads. These rockets have a payload feature in addition to features of normal rockets. Using this idea, the preceding code inherits the features from Rocket and provides an additional stored property payload. We also modify the description to describe the CargoRocket with finer details. You have to mark the description with the **override** keyword here. Notice that **final** keyword? It means this CargoRocket class is not allowed to be inherited further by any other class.

We create two instances of CargoRocket, namely, falcon9 and falconHeavy. Each of these has different capabilities which we provide the details of in the initializer. The details are then correctly printed out to the console by accessing the description computed property.

3.4.6 Modern Features

Swift also has modern programming capabilities, namely, extensions, protocols, generics, and differentiation. With extensions, you can provide implementation of types that you don't even have access to the source code of. Protocol lets you define a set of standards (requirements) for a type. The type implementing all requirements of a protocol is said to conform to that protocol. Swift provides generics which make your code usable in a wide number of possible scenarios. The first-class support for differentiation, built right in the compiler, lets you build differentiable programs ranging from computational fluid dynamics (Kutz, 2017) to robotic hand movement (Akkaya et al., 2019) with deep reinforcement learning. The differentiation feature is discussed in Subsection 3.4.9.

3.4.6.1 Extensions

Extensions let you extend the capabilities of a type by providing implementation of new features. You can also do *retroactive modeling* in Swift. In other words, you can extend any type you don't even have access to the source code of, for instance, Swift's standard library types like Array and Tensor (available in TensorFlow library) or even types declared in other libraries like Foundation, Vision, and others can be extended.

Listing 3-27. Extend Int to mutate its value when raised to some power

```
extension Int {
  mutating func raised(to power: Self) {
    assert(power > 0, "`power` must be a non-negative integer.")
    if power == 0 {
      self = 1
      return
    }
    var result = 1
    for _ in 1...power {
      result = result * self
    }
    self = result
  }
}
```

```
var number = 5
number.raised(to: 3)
print("Now `number` is \(number).")
```

Output

```
Now `number` is 125.
```

The preceding example extends Int to include an instance method raised(to:) that changes the instance's value by raising itself to some power value given during the method call. The method has been marked **mutating** because Int is declared as a structure in standard library and structures are value types which, unlike classes that are reference types, cannot modify themselves. We first write an assertion which ensures that power is not a negative number. Then an **if** condition sets the value of the instance equal to one if power is zero. Later, a **for-in** loop computes the value of the instance raised to power, iteratively. Finally, the instance is set equal to result once calculation finishes.

Extensions are capable of providing implementation of computed properties, methods, subscripts, initializers, nested types, even conform types to protocols, and much more.

In Chapter 6, we will see how to extend TensorFlow's Layer protocol to define custom checkpoint writing and reading instance methods via interoperation with the Python language. This will demonstrate how much we can hack into Swift with these modern and powerful features.

3.4.6.2 Protocols

Most programmers are usually familiar with object-oriented programming. In contrast, Swift was designed to be a *protocol-oriented language* since its incarnation. Because Swift is also object-oriented, we first begin with protocol declarations and then make other types like enumerations, structures, and classes conform to them under suitable scenarios.

Listing 3-28. Declare and use `ProfileProtocol`

```
protocol ProfileProtocol {
  let name: String { get }
  var age: Int { get set }
  var email: Int { get set }
}
struct Person: ProfileProtocol {
  let name: String
  var age: Int
  var email: String
}
var rahulbhalley = Person(name: "Rahul Bhalley", age: 24,
email: "rahulbhalley@icloud.com")
```

Here, `ProfileProtocol` has three requirements, namely, gettable name of type `String`, gettable and settable age of type `Int`, and gettable and settable email of type `String`. It requires the conforming type to provide their implementations. The `Person` structure adopts `ProfileProtocol` by providing an implementation of its requirements.

You can also extend a protocol to provide implementations instead of only requirements information. This way, the types conforming to that protocol automatically get those implementations.

Listing 3-29. Extend `ProfileProtocol` to provide common implementation

```
extension ProfileProtocol {
  var details: String { "Name: \(name), age: \(age), email: \
  (email)" }
}
print(rahulbhalley.details)
```

Output

```
Name: Rahul Bhalley, age: 24, email: rahulbhalley@icloud.com
```

Now any type, including previous implementations, conforming to
ProfileProtocol can access the details property. Note that we can
eliminate the **return** keyword if there's only one statement in the body of
function, closure, computed property, or subscript which returns some value.

3.4.6.3 Generics

Generics allows you to program a single code block and execute it with
many different possible data types. This is one of the basic principles of
object-oriented programming known as *polymorphism*. And Swift syntax
makes it very easy to implement and use a generic code block. In Swift, you
can define generics of properties, subscripts, functions, methods, and even
enumerations, structures, and classes.

Listing 3-30. Swap values of two variables of the same type

```swift
func swapValues<T>(_ x: inout T, _ y: inout T) {
  let temporaryX = x
  x = y
  y = temporaryX
}
// Swapping String values
var x = "x"
var y = "y"
swapValues(&x, &y)
print("x: \(x) y: \(y)")
// Swapping custom type instance values
swapValues(&falcon9, &falconHeavy)
print(falcon9.description)
print(falconHeavy.description)
```

Output

```
x: y, y: x
Falcon Heavy carries 63800 kg and has 24681 kN thrust in
vacuum.
Falcon 9 carries 22800 kg and has 8227 kN thrust in vacuum.
```

Swift already provides the swap(_:_:) function to swap values of any two same-typed instances. But we have implemented our own version of it named swapValues(_:_:) in the preceding code to get familiar with generic programming.

Here, T is a *type placeholder* whose type is not known until you use the function. The type is inferred by the compiler when you provide the variables in the function call. The **inout** keyword allows you to modify the values of parameters in the function body and writes these modifications back to the external variables. The ampersand (**&**) sign before variables in the function call makes it clear to you that their values are mutable inside the function body. Note that you should always declare these instances with the **var** keyword or they will not be mutated. You can read the function declaration as "declare a generic function named swapValues with type placeholder T and which takes two **inout** variables x and y."

We have successfully swapped the values of two strings and even our own structure instances! You can swap the values of any two variable instances as long as they are of the same type. Next, we use two generic types to describe more complex usage of generics.

Listing 3-31. Find common and unique elements from two Array<Int> instances

```
func allCommonAndUniqueElements<T: Sequence, U: Sequence>
(_ left: T, _ right: U) -> [T.Element]
where T.Element: Equatable, T.Element == U.Element {
  var result = [T.Element]()
```

```
  for leftItem in left {
    for rightItem in right {
      if leftItem == rightItem && !result.contains(leftItem) {
        result.append(leftItem)
      }
    }
  }
  return result
}
let fibonacciNumbers = [0, 1, 1, 2, 3, 5, 8, 13, 21]
let oddNumbers = [1, 3, 5, 7, 9, 11, 13, 15, 17, 19, 21]
let commonNumbers =
allCommonAndUniqueElements(fibonacciNumbers, oddNumbers)
print(commonNumbers)
```

Output

```
[1, 3, 5, 13, 21]
```

The preceding allCommonAndUniqueElements(_:_:) has two
generic types T and U which both conform to the Sequence protocol. The
statements after the **where** clause state that each element of T sequence
must conform to Equatable (must be equatable) and both T and U should
have the same type of elements. The function takes left and right
conforming to T and U, respectively, as parameters and returns an array of
elements of type T. Finally, calling the function simply finds and returns an
array of unique and common elements.

Listing 3-32. Find common and unique elements from two
Array<Character> or String instances

```
let machineLearning = "machine learning"
let deepLearning = "deep learning"
let commonCharacters =
allCommonAndUniqueElements(machineLearning, deepLearning)
print(commonCharacters)
```

Output

```
["a", "i", "n", "e", " ", "l", "r", "g"]
```

This generic function works with any instance that is a sequence and
whose elements can be equated. This is true for the String instance also
because it is an array of Characters.

Listing 3-33. Demonstrate the generic type

```
struct Pair<T, U> {
  var x: T
  var y: U
  var description: String { "x: \(x) and y: \(y)" }
}
let pair = Pair(x: "x", y: 5)
print(pair.description)
let anotherPair = Pair<Vehicle,
CargoRocket>(x: .car, y: falconHeavy)
print(type(of: pair))
print(type(of: anotherPair))
```

Output

```
x: x and y: 5
Pair<String, Int>
Pair<Vehicle, CargoRocket>
```

Just like generic functions, we can also declare generic types in Swift making the type reusable in remarkably various scenarios. Here, the `Pair` structure is declared as a generic type with two generic types T and U. The two stored properties are of different generic types. Two instances `pair` and `anotherPair` are declared with generic types `Pair<String, Int>` and `Pair<Vehicle, CargoRocket>`, respectively. This is confirmed by printing their type information.

The generics are not limited to only structures but also work for enumerations and classes. They can be considered as a very powerful way of implementing polymorphism in Swift.

Swift's another modern and powerful feature is differentiation, discussed at length in Subsection 3.4.9.

3.4.7 Error Handling

Error handling is a way of making your program more robust in error-prone situations. With error handling, you can save your program from crashing and get the clearer picture about the error by printing its information to the console. Swift's simple syntax helps in making error handling code easier to read and understand.

A convenient approach to handling errors in Swift is through the usage of **do-catch** code blocks for it.

Listing 3-34. Respond to possible errors when requesting a web page

```
enum RequestError: Error {
  case noInternet
  case notFound
  case timeOut
}
```

```swift
func ping(website link: String) throws -> String {
  if link == "Wrong address" {
    throw RequestError.notFound
  } else if link == "No connection" {
    throw RequestError.noInternet
  } else if link == "Request timeout" {
    throw RequestError.timeOut
  }
  return #"Website: "\#(link)" is live."#
}
do {
  let pingResponse = try ping(website: "Wrong address")
  print(pingResponse)
} catch RequestError.noInternet {
  print("Could not connect to the Internet.")
} catch let pingError as RequestError {
  print("Error: \(pingError)")
}
```

Output

```
Error: notFound
```

To represent an error, simply conform your custom type (here, RequestError) to the Error protocol. It is an empty protocol only used for representing errors. The enumeration type is well suited for error representation in Swift.

Only functions can throw errors. Write the **throws** keyword after the parameter list to tell the compiler that this function can throw an error. And write the **try** keyword before the function call that can throw an error. Finally, when an error has occurred, then throw an error using the **throw** keyword followed by the error, for example, **throw** RequestError. noInternet.

The preceding code shows how to throw an error when a ping to some website fails. Possible errors are written as cases in RequestError enumeration. Call to the ping(website:) function in the do block takes a link for pinging. If the error occurs while pinging, then an appropriate error is thrown in **catch** blocks. You should consider manipulating the website argument label values to see what error messages are printed for each value.

One interesting thing to notice here is the usage of the hash symbol (#) for using double quotes inside a string. Using hash before and after a string double quotes lets you write the double quotes inside the string itself. One additive change for interpolation is the usage of the hash symbol between the backslash (\) and left round bracket.

3.4.8 Advanced Operators

Swift has support for implementing custom operators on types using functions easily in a meaningful syntax. Listing 3-35 is a simple example of adding two instances of structure.

Listing 3-35. Declare a structure and implement an advanced operator

```
struct Point3D {
  var (x, y, z) = (0.0, 0.0, 0.0)
  var description: String {
    "Coordinates: (\(x), \(y), \(z))"
  }
}
extension Point3D {
  static func + (left: Self, right: Self) -> Self {
    Point3D(x: left.x + right.x, y: left.y + right.y, z: left.z
    + right.z)
  }
}
```

```
var pointA = Point3D(x: 1, y: 2, z: 3)
var pointB = Point3D(x: 4, y: 5, z: 6)
print((pointA + pointB).description)
```

Output

```
Coordinates: (5.0, 7.0, 9.0)
```

When you define your own structure, the compiler doesn't know what any mathematical operation means for it. Here, you can define your own operation for a specific operator, for instance, addition for the plus operator as in the preceding code. This plus sign (+) instance method returns the Point3D instance after adding each element of two parameters. The operation simply adds two Point3D instances as can be verified with the preceding description.

Usually, domain-specific languages (DSLs) in deep learning like Pythonic TensorFlow (Abadi et al., 2016), PyTorch (Paszke et al., 2017, 2019), autograd (Maclaurin et al., 2015; Maclaurin, 2016), and many others use this feature in the C++ codebase for implementing tensor operations and automatic differentiation (usually, reverse mode). In contrast, Swift takes a radical approach to tackle this problem by implementing automatic differentiation, introduced next, right in the compiler for optimal performance and allowing statically compiled language features and benefits of Swift.

3.4.9 Differentiation

Swift has first-class support for the algorithmic differentiation feature. Differentiation has been baked inside the compiler making Swift's type system differentiable. The amazing part is that you don't have to restrict your program's expressivity and you can freely write control flow statements, loops, and recursions and the program will still be differentiable! You import the _Differentiation library with the statement in Listing 3-36.

Listing 3-36. Import the _Differentiation library

```
import _Differentiation
```

Notice the underscore before the library name? This means the library is not yet ready for production (but soon it will be) and, therefore, cannot be used to build apps in Xcode for distribution. But you can use this feature for learning, practicing, and researching with differentiable programming (and even deep learning, as we shall see later) in Swift! And if you're an app developer, then, in the future, you'll be able to develop and distribute differentially programmed apps to your users.

Once the _Differentiation library is imported, you get access to all the available differentiation APIs. The following code listings expect this import statement at the top. It's not possible to cover every detail of programming in a single book. We suggest you to refer to the (Wei et al., 2018).

3.4.9.1 Differentiable Types

Strictly speaking, only functions can be differentiated and can therefore have derivatives or partial derivatives. More specifically, a function is differentiable if its parameter(s) and result values are both differentiable. Programmatically, this means the parameter and result types must be differentiable for a function to be differentiable given that computation inside its body is also differentiable. And these types are not to be limited to only scalar real numbers represented by Float or Double types in Swift's type system. But they also extend to vector, matrix, or tensor data structures of any dimensions. Swift makes differentiation of such custom types and functions possible.

At the time of writing, Swift provides the syntactically most meaningful and mathematically most plausible way of declaring differentiable custom types with the Differentiable protocol.

A fun fact about Swift's type system is that types such as `Float`, `Int`, `Double`, `String`, `Dictionary`, `Array`, and others are defined in Swift's standard library instead of in Swift's compiler. This allows the addition of types for numerical computation and treatment of them as first-class citizens to the language.

There are different branches of mathematics that allow differentiation of functions over various types of parameter and result:

1. **Elementary calculus**: A branch of mathematics where we simply compute the derivative of a function scalar result with respect to an input scalar.

2. **Vector calculus**: A branch of mathematics concerned with differentiation involving vector fields as parameter/result. This branch further extends to matrix and tensor fields.

3. **Differential geometry**: A branch of mathematics where functions are differentiated over manifolds. A *manifold* is a connected region in high-dimensional space where points near to one another seem to be in a Euclidean space.

We next introduce the general protocol that allows custom types to perform differentiation. This protocol also collectively suffices the requirements of above-mentioned mathematics subfields.

3.4.9.2 Differentiable Protocol

Following Swift's protocol-oriented programming paradigm, to conform with the mathematical theory of differentiation in different branches, Swift introduces the notion of differentiable types with the `Differentiable` protocol. Mathematically speaking, types which can represent real numbers (such as `Float` or `Double`) are differentiable, whereas others are not (such as `String` or `Int`). The Swift compiler emits an error with a human-readable message when you try to differentiate a non-differentiable type. For instance, code in Listing 3-37 cannot be differentiated.

Listing 3-37. Show that differentiation of an `Int` instance is not possible

```
@differentiable
func failedDifferentiation(_ input: Float) -> Float {
  Float(Int(x))
}
```

This code does not compile and reports an error: "Function is not differentiable." Although the input and return types are both differentiable, the computation inside the function is not. This is because the value is converted to `Int` and then back to `Float` which makes the computation non-differentiable and `Int` cannot represent real numbers. Whenever such mistakes occur in your code, Swift will guide you through warning or error messages (in this case) to make modifications to your code, especially in Xcode. This way Swift can be very helpful for beginners in machine learning to understand differentiation and machine learning itself.

Any type that conforms to the `Differentiable` protocol can be passed as a parameter to and returned from a differentiable function. This means we can compute the derivative or partial derivative of a function's result with respect to its parameter(s) in pure Swift (i.e., no C or C++ code under the hood like many Python libraries). Note that for a function to be differentiable, the computation inside its body must also be differentiable (see Listing 3-37).

Swift already provides conformance for its fundamental types (such as `Float`, `Double`, `Array`, `Dictionary`, etc.) to the `Differentiable` protocol in its standard library. But this conformance is not limited to only fundamental types but also extends to user-defined custom types (for instance, Tensor custom type from the TensorFlow library) that can contain instance and type properties (stored and computed), subscripts, and methods. (Avoid declaring enumeration types because they cannot have stored properties.) If there is some type that currently doesn't conform to the Differentiable protocol, you can simply extend it, and the compiler will automatically synthesize all the differentiation-specific requirements, discussed in the following, via code generation for you.

Let us code a three-dimensional vector with the name Point3D (adapted from Listing 3-35) and make it differentiable.

Listing 3-38. Make the Point3D structure differentiable

```
struct Point3D: Differentiable, AdditiveArithmetic {
  var (x, y, z) = (0.0, 0.0, 0.0)
  @noDerivative
  var description: String {
    "Coordinates: (\(x), \(y), \(z))"
  }
}
var pointA = Point3D(x: 5, y: 2, z: 3)
var pointB = Point3D(x: 5, y: 2, z: 3)
let result = valueWithGradient(at: pointA) { pointA in
  (pointA + pointB).y
}
print("sum: \(result.value)")
print("∇sum:  \(result.gradient.description)")
```

Output

```
sum: 4.0
∇sum: Point3D(x: 0.0, y: 1.0, z: 0.0)
```

Here, `Point3D` conforms to `Differentiable` and `AdditiveArithmetic` protocols. The implementation for addition advanced operators is adopted from `AdditiveArithmetic`. The adoption of the `Differentiable` protocol makes `Point3D` differentiable. Since the `Differentiable` protocol requires the properties to conform to `Differentiable` themselves, we marked the description **@noDerivative** because `String` is not differentiable. `Point3D` successfully conforms to `Differentiable` because all properties are now differentiable including `x`, `y`, and `z` which are inferred as `Double`.

The `valueWithGradient(at:in:)` function returns the result of the `(pointA + pointB).y` function and its derivative with respect to `pointA` as named tuples. This allows you to access each value with that name following dot syntax (.), making it easy to understand what values are being returned. Note that the output must always be a differentiable scalar (here, `Double`) only for computing its gradient with respect to varying parameters (here, `pointA`). This is because `gradient(at:in:)` and its variants implement reverse-mode AD. Here, we get the partial derivative of the `(pointA + pointB).y` output at (or with respect to) `pointA`. This is why the values of `x` and `z` in the ∇result are zero each.

When you conform any custom type (for instance, the preceding `Point3D`) to the `Differentiable` protocol, then Swift's compiler automatically synthesizes the implementation for various requirements as follows. Please refer to (Wei et al., 2018) for more details:

1. **Structure types**: The compiler provides implementation of the `TangentVector` structure automatically. The `TangentVector` structure contains the derivative for every differentiable stored property. Those properties marked with the **@noDerivative** attribute are not introduced in synthesized `TangentVector`.

2. **Properties**: Accessing the `zeroTangentVector` property returns an instance with all differentiable stored properties initialized with zero values (`Point3D(x: 0.0, y: 0.0, z: 0.0)` in our case).

3. **Instance methods**: The `move(along:)` mutating method is described in the documentation as "Moves **self** along the given direction. In Riemannian geometry, this is equivalent to exponential map, which moves **self** on the geodesic surface along the given tangent vector." Internally, `move(along:)` mutates **self**'s all differentiable properties by adding the corresponding properties of the `along` argument. Here, `along` expects an instance of the same type on which this method is called.

In Listing 3-38, we simply conformed `Point3D` to `AdditiveArithmetic`, and advanced operator + was automatically provided for differentiable addition operation. Now we will look at how to construct our own differentiable functions.

3.4.9.3 @differentiable Attribute

Swift allows two kinds of attributes, namely, declaration attribute and type attribute. Attributes provide more information to declarations for modified behavior. The *declaration attribute* is applied on the function-like declarations (including methods, properties, and initializers), whereas the *type attribute* is applied on the type of declaration. As a simple example, the **@discardableResult** declaration attribute when applied on a function does not emit the warning if the result returned by the function is not used or stored in another variable.

Swift provides the **@differentiable** attribute that can be used to annotate both the declaration and type of declaration. Let us see how to declare a differentiable function using the **@differentiable** declaration attribute in action.

Listing 3-39. Declare and demonstrate the usage of the @differentiable declaration attribute on a computed property

```
extension Double {
  @differentiable
  var cubed: Self { self * self * self }
}
let x: Double = 5
print("\(x)^3 = \(x.cubed)")
let grad = gradient(at: x) { x in x.cubed }
print("Gradient of x^3 at \(x) is \(grad)")
```

Output

```
5.0^3 = 125.0
Gradient of x^3 at 5.0 is 75.0
```

Using retroactive modeling, we first declare the differentiable computed property named cubed. This simple use of the **@differentiable** declaration attribute makes the computed property differentiable. Then we simply take the gradient of cubed at 5 and store its result in the grad constant. Mathematically, $dx^3/dx = 3x^2$ which when evaluated at $x = 5$ gives 75, so our code also gives this result as expected.

This concludes the basic features of Swift. Next, we move on to S4TF-specific features which make it a powerful language for machine learning. Chapter 4 is dedicated to introducing the machine learning–specific features in TensorFlow and related libraries. The next section shows how S4TF can interoperate with the Python language and access its built-in and custom functions with a breeze.

3.4.9.4 Differentiation APIs

The differentiation APIs follow a naming pattern. Let us explain how to read these closures by considering some examples. First of all, argument labels at, in, and of take variable, closure, and closure as input, respectively. Here, `gradient(at:in:)` can be read as "calculate the gradient of closure at a point and return the gradient value." The function `gradient(of:)` is also simple to read, "calculate the gradient of closure and return it," which can be evaluated at a desired value. The prefix `valueWith` returns a named tuple containing `value` and `gradient`, `pullback`, or other closures.

There are various forward-mode differentiation closures in Swift listed in the following. But we don't discuss these because they're still under development and experimental:

1. `differential(at:in:)` and `valueWithDifferential(at:in:)`

2. `derivative(of:)`, `derivative(at:in:)`, `valueWithDerivative(of:)`, and `valueWithDerivative(at:in:)`

We mainly focus on reverse-mode algorithmic differentiation functions in the book which are discussed as follows:

1. `pullback(at:in:)` and `valueWithPullback(at:in:)`: These compute the partial derivatives of closure's scalar output with respect to the input scalar variable(s) (i.e., either univariate or multivariate variable) and return a `pullback` closure. This closure takes the derivative of the output with respect to itself as argument, that is, dy/dy where y is the output variable. We usually set $dy/dy = 1$. During evaluation of pullback, this value is multiplied in the chain rule as $dy/dx = dy/dy \cdot dy/dx$ where x is an input variable to the returned `pullback` closure.

2. gradient(at:in:) and valueWithGradient(at:in:):
    These are based on pullback(at:in:) and
    valueWithPullback(at:in:); therefore, they work
    the same as them but instead always set dy/dy = 1
    and simply return the evaluated gradient instead of a
    pullback closure.

3. gradient(of:) and valueWithGradient(of:):
    These are also based on pullback(at:in:) and
    valueWithPullback(at:in:); therefore, they work
    the same as them but return a gradient closure
    which when evaluated at some point returns a tuple
    of closure-evaluated value and gradient value.

We have already demonstrated some of these differentiation closures of our later interest in Listings 3-37, 3-38, and 3-39. Now we demonstrate how to define custom derivatives for functions.

3.4.9.5 Custom Derivatives

We know that the derivative of cube function $f(x) = x^3$ is $f'(x) = 3x^2$. But what if we want to customize the derivative of this function? Swift lets us define custom derivatives of functions in reverse-mode differentiation using the **@derivative(of:)** function declaration attribute, whereas **@transpose(of:)** is used for forward-mode differentiation, but it is under development. Let us define the desired custom derivative.

Listing 3-40. Demonstrate the declaration of custom derivatives in reverse-mode differentiation

```
func cube(_ x: Float) -> Float {
  x * x * x
}
```

```
let anotherX: Float = 4
print("Before customization, df/dx =", gradient(at: anotherX,
in: { x in
  cube(x)
}))
```

@derivative(of: cube)
```
func vjpCube(_ x: Float) -> (value: Float, pullback: (Float) ->
Float) {
  (value: cube(x), pullback: { chain in chain * 2 * x })
}
print("After customization, df/dx =", gradient(at: anotherX,
in: { x in cube(x) }))
```

Output

```
Before customization, df/dx = 48.0
After customization, df/dx = 8.0
```

We declared a cube(_:) function that returns the cube of argument
x and initialized a Float constant anotherX equal to 4. Then using the
gradient(at:in:) function, we compute the derivative of the cube(_:)
closure at point anotherX.

Next, we declared a vjpCube(_:) function and applied the
@derivative(of: cube) attribute to it which tells the compiler to compute
the derivative of the cube(_:) closure according to the pullback closure
declaration returned by this function. This function returns a named tuple
containing value and pullback of types Float and (Float) -> Float,
respectively. Inside the function body of vjpCube(_:), we return cube(x)
as value and chain * 2 * x as pullback closure. Here, chain represents
dy/dy whose value is 1 if you pass it to gradient(at:in:) variants, but its
value actually depends on you if it's passed to pullback(at:in:) variants.
Now when we compute the gradient of the cube(_:) closure at anotherX,
we get 8 as output, successfully.

We can also define custom derivatives for forward-mode differentiation with the **@transpose(of:)** function declaration attribute; but, unfortunately, it is experimental and under development at the time of writing.

3.4.9.6 Stop Derivative Propagation

You can also stop the derivatives from propagating through a subgraph of the whole computational graph. Swift provides two closures, namely, withoutDerivative(at:) and withoutDerivative(at:in:), to stop derivatives from being computed. Here, the at argument takes a mathematical expression evaluated at some point which will not participate in derivative computation of the whole expression and simply returns the value of itself. The **in** argument takes a closure whose derivative is not desired to be computed, and it returns a value by evaluating the mathematical expression inside it at a given point.

Listing 3-41. Demonstrate the stopping of gradient computation through a graph

```
let yetAnotherX: Float = 5
let result1 = valueWithGradient(at: yetAnotherX) { x in
    x * x * withoutDerivative(at: x)
}
print("result1: \(result1)")
let result2 = valueWithGradient(at: yetAnotherX) { x in
    x * x * withoutDerivative(at: x) { y in
        y + 10
    }
}
print("result2: \(result2)")
```

Output

```
result1: (value: 125.0, gradient: 50.0)
result2: (value: 375.0, gradient: 150.0)
```

All the expressions in this example are evaluated at 5. Here, the closure expression for `result1` computes x^3 which when evaluated returns 125. But its derivative is $3x^2$ that should return 75, but because `withoutDerivative(at: x)` doesn't involve derivative, we get $(x^2)' \cdot (x + 10) = 2x \cdot (x + 10)$ which when evaluated gives 50.

The closure expression for `result2` demonstrates a more complex computation $x^2 \cdot (x + 10)$ which when evaluated returns 375. When its derivative $3x^2 + 20x$ is evaluated at 5, we should get 175, but we don't. This is because the subexpression $x + 10$ never participates in derivative computation and the actual derivative, here, is $2x \cdot (x + 10)$ which when evaluated at 5 returns 150.

Stopping the gradient computation plays an important role in training various neural networks. For instance, generative adversarial networks contain two different neural networks which are connected, that is, they act as a single neural network, but they should be trained individually although they together act as a whole single computational graph. To stop the derivatives of parameters of a network from being computed, we can pass the closure that performs its computation to the `in` argument of the `withoutDerivative(at:in:)` function. Some famously important deep learning tasks such as image stylization, adversarial example generation, and others also require stopping the gradient propagation through the sub-computational graph.

This concludes the basic features of Swift. Next section shows how easily Swift can interoperate with Python language and access its builtin and custom functions and also any of its installed libraries with a breeze.

3.5 Python Interoperability

We know that Python is currently a very important language for machine learning. If you are already a Python programmer, you might know there are many important and useful libraries written in Python. We might still want to use these libraries to keep ourselves productive. So, instead of rewriting all these libraries in Swift, you can easily interoperate with Python's built-in functions and all the Python libraries installed on your system directly in Swift.

Internally, when S4TF accesses the Python entities, then Python interpreter is invoked which executes the process and returns the data to S4TF. So the execution time of Python operations depends on Python's interpreter and not S4TF's compiler. To make the interaction with the dynamic nature of Python possible, S4TF introduces the `PythonObject` structure which can store any data returned by Python's interpreter. Any imported Python library, class, instance, or any other entity from Python in S4TF is represented with `PythonObject`. This way you can also perform operations on `PythonObject` in S4TF itself as we shall see in the following. Note that the Python library available in S4TF can be made available in Swift by including a package with the code: .package(url: "`https://github.com/pvieito/PythonKit.git`", .branch("master")) in Package.swift file in Xcode.

This section assumes the import statement in Listing 3-42 to be written on top of every code listing in this section.

Listing 3-42. Import the `PythonKit` library

```
import PythonKit
```

The code in Listing 3-43 shows a simple example to demonstrate working with Python's NumPy library in S4TF.

Listing 3-43. Add two NumPy arrays

```
let np: PythonObject = Python.import("numpy")
let x = np.array([1, 4, 2, 5], dtype: np.float32)
let y = np.array([5, 2, 4, 1], dtype: np.float32)
print(x * y)
```

Output

```
[5. 8. 8. 5.]
```

We first import Python's NumPy library. Then we declare and initialize two NumPy arrays x and y. Finally, we print their product. Notice how easy it is to multiply Python objects directly in S4TF using the simple multiplication operator (an asterisk sign). This is because `PythonObject` implements such advanced operators.

Note that some global functions and keywords like `type`, `import`, and others exist in both Swift and Python. Since the programs we will write are in S4TF, this makes it ambiguous for the compiler to understand which global function we intend the compiler to call. So, to prevent such unwanted cases from appearing in practice, S4TF adds a namespace to Python entities, adding a separation layer between global functions of Python and S4TF, thereby making it totally unambiguous for the S4TF compiler about which language's global function it should call. See Listing 3-44 for an example of how a Python namespace effectively separates the global functions of these both languages.

Listing 3-44. Demonstrate the Python namespace

```
import Python
let myNamePy: PythonObject = "Rahul Bhalley"
print("myNamePy Swift type: \(type(of: myNamePy))")
print("myNamePy Python type: \(Python.type(myNamePy))")
```

Output

```
myNamePy Swift type: PythonObject
myNamePy Python type: str
```

In the preceding code, we initialize the myNamePy literal as a PythonObject. Then we can use Swift's type(of:) function and Python's type() method with the Python namespace. It's important to note that although Swift doesn't have any notion of namespaces, such behavior can be achieved by using type methods and enumerations.

As discussed in the preceding text, Python is a dynamically typed language in which every type is inherited from the base class known as object. At one time, your declared variable may contain an str value, and at another instant, it can store an int value or even any other user-defined class. Also there are no type-safe checks in Python. But S4TF is a strongly typed language which can be statically and dynamically executed. The ability of S4TF to operate dynamically lets us to interoperate with Python in a dynamic manner without compromising the dynamic nature of Python. This is the most basic Pythonic requirement that users come to expect even in S4TF. Instead of providing primitive types of Python directly, the S4TF gives an access to the PythonObject type which acts as a separation between fundamental types of S4TF and Python. You can simply declare a variable in S4TF of PythonObject type which behaves the same as Python variables, that is, its values can be manipulated between different types (such as Python.str, Python.float, etc.). In addition to calling methods on such instances, we can also perform arithmetic operations on these Python instances directly.

Note that these operations are actually performed by the Python interpreter, but the operators of PythonObject are declared in S4TF. See Listing 3-45 for an example of operations on PythonObjects.

Listing 3-45. Demonstrate operations on `PythonObjects`

```
var firstNumber: PythonObject = 30
var secondNumber: PythonObject = 6
let result = secondNumber / firstNumber
print("The result is \(result).")
print("Swift type is \(type(of: result)).")
print("Python type is \(Python.type(result)).")
```

Output

```
The result is 5.
Swift type is PythonObject.
Python type is int.
```

We declare and initialize two `PythonObject` variables `firstNumber` and `secondNumber` with 30 and 6 values, respectively. Although these are `PythonObjects`, we can perform various operations such as addition, multiplication, subtraction, and division on them. Here, we divide `secondNumber` by `firstNumber`.

Because interoperability lets us interact with Python objects directly from S4TF, we can also perform type conversion between these languages! To convert the S4TF type to Python's counterpart, you only need to typecast a S4TF instance with `PythonObject` type. In the case you need to perform Python to S4TF type conversion, you will typecast `PythonObject` with your desired S4TF type. But this typecasting returns an optional type in S4TF, that is, `PythonObject?`, because this conversion can fail. For instance, when you typecast Python's `str` object to Swift's `Int` type, then this conversion is not possible, and a `nil` is returned.

Undoubtedly, this feature is extremely helpful in situations, especially machine learning, when we have to initialize S4TF's `Tensor` instance with values from a NumPy's `ndarray` object because we might require to pass these values through a neural network instance on some hardware accelerator which is nearly always the case. Listing 3-46 describes a simple type conversion between these languages.

Listing 3-46. Type conversions between Swift types and PythonObject

```
// Conversion from Swift to Python type
let swiftFive: Int = 5 // Swift Int value
let pyFive = PythonObject(swiftFive) // Python int value
print("Python type of pyFive is \(Python.type(pyFive)).")
print("Swift type of pyFive is \(type(of: pyFive)).")
// Conversion from Python to Swift type
let pyDescription: PythonObject = "Python interoperability
feature is beautiful!" // Python str type
if let swiftDescription = "Swift's \(String(pyDescription))" {
  print("swiftDescription (conversion accomplished!): \
(swiftDescription)")
}
```

Output

```
Python type of pyFive is int.
Swift type of pyFive is PythonObject.
swiftDescription (conversion accomplished!): Swift's Python
interoperability feature is beautiful!
```

One of the most important tools in a data scientist's toolkit is visualization which even machine learning researchers and practitioners also require. With the help of Python interoperability, we can do data visualization in S4TF easily. See Listing 3-47 for a simple example. Make sure you have already installed the Matplotlib library via the Pip package manager; otherwise, simply run the following command in the terminal: `pip install --upgrade matplotlib`.

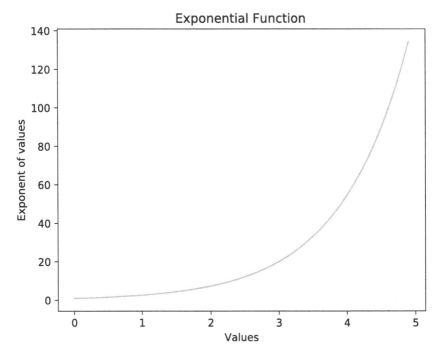

Figure 3-5. *The graph of an exponential function plotted with the Matplotlib library of Python via interoperation with S4TF*

Listing 3-47. Plot an exponential function

```
// Import Python libraries
let np = Python.import("numpy")
let plt = Python.import("matplotlib.pyplot")

// Declare variables
let x = np.linspace(0, 5, 50)
let y = np.exp(x)

// Plot the values
plt.xlabel("Values")
plt.ylabel("Exponent of values")
```

```
plt.title("Exponential Function")
plt.plot(x, y, color: "violet")
plt.show()
```

Running the preceding code displays an image (see Figure 3-5) displaying the plot of an exponential function in range [0,5). Here, the Matplotlib library's plt module performs the plotting of x and y variables.

Python interoperability helps us use Python's well-known powerful libraries in S4TF. This eliminates the hindrance for current Python users of deep learning to easily transit to S4TF.

3.6 Summary

This chapter was focused on programming with the Swift language. Swift introduces differentiable programming with compiler-level implementation, whereas the Swift for TensorFlow language is an extension of Swift implementing deep learning–specific features. The chapter started with motivating the current deep learning community (using Python) to adopt the Swift language. Next, we introduced the nuts and bolts of the algorithmic differentiation feature implemented in Swift. Then a quick tour of the Swift language was provided to make it easy for you to understand various basic and powerful features of Swift. Finally, we introduced the Python interoperability feature which makes it easy for users of Swift for TensorFlow to use their favorite Python libraries directly from Swift for TensorFlow.

Now we are ready to understand the basics of TensorFlow (introduced in the next chapter) which will allow us to program deep learning.

CHAPTER 4

TensorFlow Basics

The most important thing now is no longer debating whether differentiable programming should exist for Swift (because Swift + ML is sooo important!), but figuring out the best form that should land in the language!

—Richard Wei on Twitter

This short practical chapter is designed to introduce some deep learning–specific features of Swift for TensorFlow. Section 4.1 introduces the concept of tensor data structure which is essentially what neural networks make prediction from. After reading this chapter, you will be able to load the datasets (Section 4.2), write your own neural networks (Section 4.3), and train your model and test its accuracy (Section 4.4). In addition to all of this, in Section 4.5, you will also learn how to implement your own new layer, activation function, loss function, and optimizer. This will help in prototyping your research code or implementing the advanced building blocks of deep learning algorithms. This chapter requires some understanding of machine learning. We recommend you to refresh your concepts by reading Chapter 1.

© Rahul Bhalley 2021
R. Bhalley, *Deep Learning with Swift for TensorFlow*,
https://doi.org/10.1007/978-1-4842-6330-3_4

4.1 Tensor

In Chapter 2, we have already gone through the concepts of scalar, vector, and matrix and some important operations on them. Here, we will visualize them to aid our understanding and introduce the concept of tensor to generalize them all. It is important to understand tensors because neural networks, which form the main topic of this book, essentially manipulate the tensor values for prediction.

Tensor is a data structure that can store numerical values in n-dimensional space where $n \geq 0$. There are some common tensors such as scalar, vector, and matrix whose number of dimensions (known as *rank*) is zero, one, and two, respectively. We use the term tensor when we require to store values in higher dimensions whose rank is greater than two. In other words, tensor generalizes all the lower-dimensional data structures mentioned in the preceding text.

TensorFlow provides the Tensor type which is used to initialize a tensor of arbitrary dimensions. It provides two important instance computed properties, namely, rank and shape. The rank property returns an Int value representing the number of dimensions of the Tensor instance. For example, a vector instance has rank of 1. The shape property returns an Array value representing the number of elements in each dimension. For example, a matrix containing three rows and two columns has shape of [4, 3] (programmatically), and mathematically, we write [4 × 3]. Listing 4-1 presents some examples of Tensor which are then visualized in Figure 4-1.

Listing 4-1. Declare Tensor instances of various dimensions

```
import TensorFlow

let scalar = Tensor<Float>(10)
let vector = Tensor<Float>(ones: [5])
let matrix = Tensor<Float>(zeros: [4, 3])
let tensor = Tensor<Float>(repeating: 2, shape: [4, 3, 2])
```

```
// Print `Tensor`s
print("scalar: \(scalar)")
print("vector: \(vector)")
print("matrix:\n\(matrix)")
print("tensor:\n\(tensor)")
print()

// Ranks
print("scalar rank: \(scalar.rank)")
print("vector rank: \(vector.rank)")
print("matrix rank: \(matrix.rank)")
print("tensor rank: \(tensor.rank)")
print()

// Shapes
print("scalar shape: \(scalar.shape)")
print("vector shape: \(vector.shape)")
print("matrix shape: \(matrix.shape)")
print("tensor shape: \(tensor.shape)")
print()
```

Output

```
scalar: 10.0
vector: [1.0, 1.0, 1.0, 1.0, 1.0]
matrix:
[[0.0, 0.0, 0.0],
 [0.0, 0.0, 0.0],
 [0.0, 0.0, 0.0],
 [0.0, 0.0, 0.0]]
```

```
tensor:
[[[2.0, 2.0],
  [2.0, 2.0],
  [2.0, 2.0]],

 [[2.0, 2.0],
  [2.0, 2.0],
  [2.0, 2.0]],

 [[2.0, 2.0],
  [2.0, 2.0],
  [2.0, 2.0]],

 [[2.0, 2.0],
  [2.0, 2.0],
  [2.0, 2.0]]]

scalar rank: 0
vector rank: 1
matrix rank: 2
tensor rank: 3

scalar shape: []
vector shape: [5]
matrix shape: [4, 3]
tensor shape: [4, 3, 2]
```

Notice that Tensor is a generic type and requires us to pass the type for the placeholder type Scalar. The type for the placeholder type Scalar is provided during initialization in angle brackets which allows us to store elements of the specified Scalar type in that Tensor instance. For example, all the tensors declared in Listing 4-1 have a Float type for Scalar. Note that Scalar is a type placeholder for Tensor that conforms to the TensorFlowScalar protocol, and because Float conforms to that protocol, we can set Scalar as Float type.

In Listing 4-1, we declare various tensors of varying ranks and shapes which are then printed for demonstration. Notice that the Tensor type has various initializers available for flexible initialization. We declare scalar, vector, matrix, and tensor instances of Tensor. The scalar instance has rank of 0 and shape of [ ]. The vector instance has rank of 1 and shape of [5]. The matrix instance has rank of 2 and shape of [4, 3], that is, four rows and three columns. The tensor instance has rank of 3 and shape of [4, 3, 2]. All these instances are visualized in Figure 4-1.

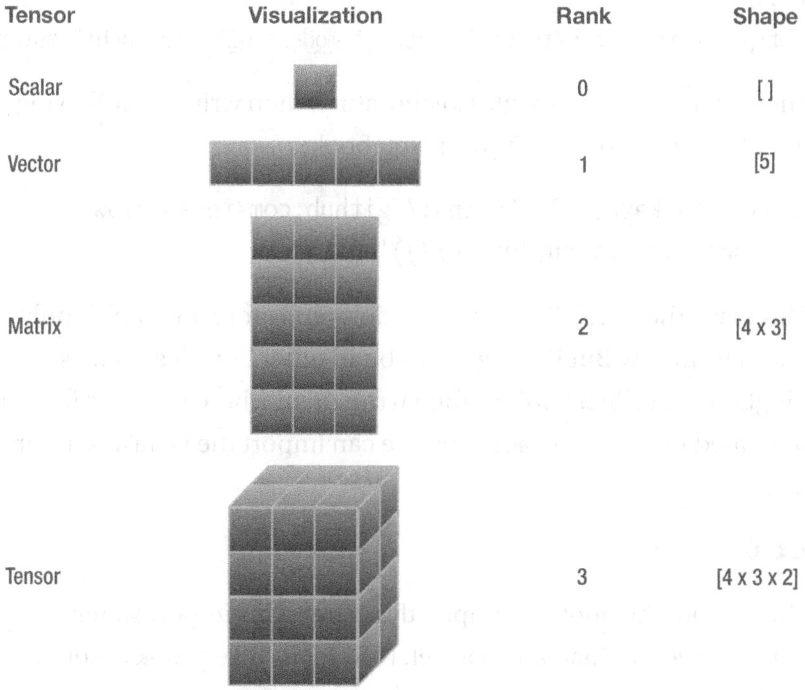

Tensor	Visualization	Rank	Shape
Scalar		0	[]
Vector		1	[5]
Matrix		2	[4 x 3]
Tensor		3	[4 x 3 x 2]

Figure 4-1. *The visualization of various tensors with their corresponding rank and shape properties. Here, each square box contains some numerical value*

Next, we discuss dataset loading in TensorFlow.

4.2 Dataset Loading

At the time of writing, TensorFlow allows loading various datasets in image and text domains. But we will pay attention to image datasets. Before you can load these datasets, you require to add the swift-models package in the Package.swift file of your Xcode Swift package as follows, or you can add the package URL in your Xcode project settings:

```
.package(name: "TensorFlowModels",
    url:
    "https://github.com/tensorflow/swift-models.git", .branch("master"))
```

And if you are using Google Colaboratory, then write the following statement at the top of your Jupyter Notebook:

```
%install '.package(url: "https://github.com/tensorflow/
swift-models", .branch("master"))' Datasets
```

This loads the tensorflow/swift-models repository and builds only the Datasets library. But if you want to build other libraries such as TrainingLoop and Checkpoints, then write them where Datasets is written but separated by a white space. Now we can import the Datasets library as follows:

```
import Datasets
```

Throughout the book, we implicitly assume this import statement written wherever we load any dataset. Now let us take a look at some concepts related to data loading.

4.2.1 Epochs and Batches

There are two main concepts related to dataset sampling, namely, epoch and mini-batch (or simply batch).

The *batch* is a group of individual data samples where batch size defines the number of samples in that batch. For instance, a batch of images (each having a shape of [256 × 128 × 3] where 256 is height (or number of rows), 128 is width (or number of columns), and 3 is the number of color channels) where batch size is 64 has shape [64 × 256 × 128 × 3]. During training, a batch of data samples is passed through the model for making predictions along with the corresponding target labels batch (if we are doing supervised learning).

The *epoch* is the number of times the model gets to experience the whole dataset in batches. A single epoch contains a sequence of different multiple batches (forming the whole dataset) which we iterate through during training to sample batches. For stochastic learning, we usually shuffle the batches during each epoch iteration.

Listing 4-2. Demonstrate epochs and batches

```
let dataset = MNIST(batchSize: 64)
let epochCount = 2

epochLoop: for (epochStep, epoch) in dataset.training.
prefix(epochCount).shuffled().enumerated() {
  batchLoop: for (batchStep, batch) in epoch.enumerated() {
    let data = batch.data
    let label = batch.label
    print("epochStep: \(epochStep) | batchStep: \(batchStep) |
    data shape: \(data.shape) | label shape: \(label.shape)")
    break epochLoop
  }
}
```

Output

```
epochStep: 0 | batchStep: 0 | data shape: [64, 28, 28, 1] |
label shape: [64]
```

Let us break down the so many things that are going on in Listing 4-2. First, we load the MNIST dataset with batch size of 64 samples in the dataset constant. Then we declare the number of epochs in epochCount as 2.

First, we have a loop for the epoch labeled as epochLoop. We iterate through the training instance computed property of the dataset with the prefix(_:) instance method that accepts the number of epochs (epochCount, here) and returns a batch of datapoints in sequence during each iteration step. At each step, we also shuffle the batch sequence with the shuffled() instance method for stochastic sampling.

Then we have a batch loop labeled as batchLoop. We iterate through each batch in an epoch instance. Inside batchLoop's body, we extract the data and label instance stored properties from the batch instance. Then we print the shape of both of these along with the iteration step for both epochLoop and batchLoop.

We use the enumerated() method on both loops to also get the index of the iterated element in sequence. We define the epochLoop and batchLoop labels for the **for-in** loops as reference for control flow statements. You can think of epochLoop and batchLoop as names of the loops. If we had simply written the **break** statement without any following labeled loop statement, then the epoch loop would have executed for two times and the batch loop for one time, that is, this would have stopped only the batch loop from executing multiple times. By writing **break** epochLoop, we tell the compiler to simply stop the iteration for the epoch loop itself and execute the code after its closing curly brace.

Here, we load the MNIST dataset (LeCun, 1998) which is a collection of grayscale images of handwritten digits (one per image) from zero to nine and their corresponding labels. They were written by different people. As we can see from shape in the preceding listing, each image has both height and width of 28 pixels and only one color channel which make it grayscale. Each sample from this dataset is a tuple of a `data` representing image pixel values (as `Tensor<Float>`) and its corresponding `label` value (as `Tensor<Int32>`).

Another important part of the machine learning algorithm is the model definition discussed next.

4.3 Defining Model

We can easily define model architectures whose properties can be differentiated during training. There are mainly two ways to define a model in TensorFlow, namely, conforming the structure to special protocols and using the `Sequential` structure inspired from Keras.

4.3.1 Neural Network Protocols

TensorFlow provides two protocols, namely, `Layer` and `Module`, for defining neural networks. The differentiable model-defining structure must conform to either of these protocols. These protocols require us to provide implementation of `Input` and `Output` type of the model as **typealias**, define the `callAsFunction(_:)` method, and declare at least one `Layer`- or `Module`-conforming or `Sequential` instance property whose parameters will be updated during training.

As an example, let us define a convolutional neural network called LeNet (LeCun et al., 1998).

Listing 4-3. Define the LeNet model by conforming to the Layer protocol

```
struct LeNet: Layer {
  typealias Input = Tensor<Float>
  typealias Output = Tensor<Float>
```

```
var convBlock = Sequential {
  Conv2D<Float>(filterShape: (5, 5, 3, 6), activation: relu)
  MaxPool2D<Float>(poolSize: (2, 2), strides: (2, 2))
  Conv2D<Float>(filterShape: (5, 5, 6, 16), activation: relu)
  MaxPool2D<Float>(poolSize: (2, 2), strides: (2, 2))
}
var flatten = Flatten<Float>()
var denseBlock = Sequential {
  Dense<Float>(inputSize: 16 * 5 * 5, outputSize: 120,
  activation: relu)
  Dense<Float>(inputSize: 120, outputSize: 84, activation: relu)
  Dense<Float>(inputSize: 84, outputSize: 10, activation:
  identity)
}

@differentiable
func callAsFunction(_ input: Input) -> Output {
  input.sequenced(through: convBlock, flatten, denseBlock)
}
}
```

We define two type aliases using the **typealias** keyword of Swift.
This lets us use a new name for an existing type wherever we can
use the existing type. We define Input and Output type names for
Tensor<Float> type. Then we define multiple neural layers conforming
to the Layer protocol, for instance, Flatten, Dense, and Conv2D. Here,
Dense is a densely connected layer (explained in Subsection 5.3.1),
Conv2D is a convolution layer (explained in Section 6.1), and the Flatten
layer simply reshapes the output tensor of the Conv2D layer (here) and
makes it a batched vector of rank 2. Then we define the differentiable
callAsFunction(_:) method which takes input of type Input and returns
an Output-type value. Inside the body, we use the sequenced(through:)

instance method on the instance `input`. `sequenced(through:)` is a protocol method defined on the `Differentiable` protocol and, therefore, can be accessed by any type conforming to it. It accepts comma-separated `Differentiable`-conforming instances and sequentially processes the `input` through them. That is, here, `input` is first processed by the `convBlock` instance whose output is then processed by `flatten`, and then its output is finally processed by `denseBlock` which again returns a new output of type `Tensor<Float>`. This output is then returned by this function. Note that we can eliminate the **return** keyword if there's only one statement in the body of function, closure, computed property, or subscript which returns some value.

Next, we explain the `Sequential` structure used here.

4.3.2 Sequence of Layers

We can define a multiple-layer neural network easily with `Sequential` which is defined as a structure in TensorFlow. You might find it familiar from the Keras design.

We have already defined `convBlock` and `denseBlock` in Listing 4-3 using `Sequential`. In this way, we can simply pass multiple neural layers, each in a different line, to Sequential followed by left curly braces. We don't even need to define the `callAsFunction(_:)` instance method as in protocol conformance. The input to the `Sequential` instance is processed sequentially starting from the first layer (closest to the opening curly brace) to the final layer (closest to the closing curly brace). As discussed in Subsection 5.3.1, the small sequence layers in a neural network are known as *neural blocks*, for instance, `convBlock` and `denseBlock` are great examples of what we mean by neural blocks.

Having loaded the dataset and defined the model, let us now see how to train the model on the dataset.

4.4 Training and Testing

In this section, we first introduce checkpointing of the model's differentiable parameters in TensorFlow. We also train our LeNet model on the CIFAR-10 dataset with a custom training loop. Then we again train our model with a Keras-style training approach.

4.4.1 Checkpointing

Training a neural network is an energy- and time-consuming task. Based on the dataset and neural network sizes, model training can range from minutes to even months! The training finds a set of new parameter values of the model for which the dataset has a very low loss value and high accuracy (in the case of classification). We don't want our time spent on training the model to be wasted. So we can write the optimal parameter values on the disk to save the training progress. This is called *checkpointing*. When we require to use the trained model for inference (for instance, image classification), then we can simply read the parameters into the model from the disk and pass an image to be classified through the trained model.

TensorFlow allows us to make checkpoints of our model. We simply require to conform our model structure to the Checkpointable protocol. We don't need to write anything else other than just Checkpointable followed by opening and closing curly braces (see Listing 4-4), and all the methods callable on the model instance become available for checkpointing purposes. This becomes possible because checkpointing methods are implemented in the Checkpointable protocol.

Listing 4-4. Conform LeNet to the Checkpointable protocol

```
extension LeNet: Checkpointable {}
```

We just conformed LeNet to Checkpointable with extensions! Let us declare a path to a directory where we would like to write and read the checkpoints to and from. This is done by defining the URL instance from the Foundation module as shown in Listing 4-5.

Listing 4-5. Declare directory location for checkpointing the model

```
import Foundation
let checkpointDirectory = URL(
  fileURLWithPath: "/Users/rahulbhalley/Desktop/Checkpoints",
  isDirectory: true)
```

We set isDirectory to **true** to make sure that this location points to the directory and not any file. Both writeCheckpoint(to:name:) and readCheckpoint(from:name:) can throw an error, so we will use a **do-catch** block for error handling and call these methods with the **try** keyword. Instead of demonstrating this here, we will directly demonstrate this when we will train the model in the following.

4.4.2 Model Optimization

Let us train our LeNet with stochastic gradient descent and save checkpoints. Listing 4-6 demonstrates the training.

Listing 4-6. Train the LeNet model and save checkpoints

```
// Define the default device
let device = Device.defaultXLA

// Load CIFAR 10 dataset
let dataset = CIFAR10(batchSize: 128, on: device)

// Initialize the LeNet model
var model = LeNet()
model = .init(copying: model, to: device)
```

```
// Initialize the optimizer
var optimizer = SGD(for: model, learningRate: 0.01, momentum: 0.9)
optimizer = .init(copying: optimizer, to: device)
```

First, we declare a default XLA device on which all the processing will happen. We load the CIFAR-10 dataset into the dataset constant and put it on the device. Then we initialize our LeNet in the model variable and copy it to the device. Finally, we initialize the SGD optimizer (which is also copied to the device) for the model to have learningRate of 0.01 and momentum (explained in Subsection 5.6.2) of 0.9.

Listing 4-7. Define one training step for the model

```
func trainingStep(samples: Tensor<Float>, labels:
Tensor<Int32>) {
    // Compute gradients
    let ∇θmodel = gradient(at: model) { model -> Tensor<Float> in
    let logits = model(samples)
    let loss = softmaxCrossEntropy(logits: logits, labels: labels)
    return loss
  }
  optimizer.update(&model, along: ∇θmodel)
}
```

In Listing 4-7, we define a function trainingStep(samples:labels:) that accepts samples and their labels as arguments. It computes logits for samples passed to the model which are then used along with labels to compute softmax cross-entropy loss. The gradient(at:in:) function takes model as a parameter to the at argument label and takes a closure that computes and returns the loss between logits and labels, the process described by the previous line. It then calculates the gradient of the scalar loss with respect to all the parameters of the model. Finally, the optimizer updates the differentiable parameters of the model along the direction of its gradient ∇θmodel. This concludes the one training step.

Listing 4-8. Define a training loop executable for multiple epochs

```swift
func trainingLoop(epochCount: Int = 5) {
  epochLoop: for (epochStep, epoch) in dataset.training.
  prefix(epochCount).enumerated() {
    batchLoop: for (batchStep, batch) in epoch.enumerated() {
      // Get data
      let samples = Tensor<Float>(copying: batch.data, to: device)
      let labels = Tensor<Int32>(copying: batch.label, to: device)

      // Training step
      trainingStep(samples: samples, labels: labels)
    }

    // Print statistics
    print("epoch: \(epochStep + 1)/\(epochCount)\ttest
    accuracy: \(testAccuracy)")

    // Write checkpoint
    do {
      try model.writeCheckpoint(to: checkpointDirectory,
                                name: "\(type(of: model))")
    } catch {
      print(error)
    }
  }
}
// Train the model
trainingLoop()
```

Output

```
epoch: 1/5          test accuracy: 0.5064
epoch: 2/5          test accuracy: 0.5618
epoch: 3/5          test accuracy: 0.5933
epoch: 4/5          test accuracy: 0.6088
epoch: 5/5          test accuracy: 0.6187
```

In Listing 4-8, we define a training loop function named trainingLoop(epochCount:) that takes the number of epochs as argument (default epochCount is 5). We have already explained data sampling (see Section 4.2). For each batch, we perform a single training step by passing the sampled samples and labels to the trainingStep(samples:labels:) function. After each epoch, we print the statistics concerned with the model's accuracy on the validation dataset, and we also write the trained model's parameters to the checkpointDirectory directory with name as the model's type, that is, LeNet. Because both checkpoint writing and reading methods can throw an error, we use the **try** statement in a **do-catch** block.

Listing 4-9. Define a computed property to calculate accuracy of the model on a validation set

```
var testAccuracy: Float {
  let totalSamples = 10000
  var correct = 0
  for batch in dataset.validation {
    let (data, label) = (batch.data, batch.label)
    let prediction = softmax(model(data)).argmax(squeezingAxis: 1)
    for index in 0..<data.shape[0] {
      if prediction[index] == label[index] { correct += 1 }
    }
  }
  return Float(correct) / Float(totalSamples)
}
```

In Listing 4-9, we declare an only gettable computed property testAccuracy that computes the accuracy of the model on a validation set. We set the total number of samples in the validation set to 10000 and start with zero correct classifications. Iterating through all the batches in the validation set, we make the prediction and compare it against each corresponding label, conditionally adding up one to the correct variable if prediction matches label. Note that we use the argmax(squeezingAxis:) method on softmax-activated logits to get the index of the vector which contains the element with highest value (remember from Chapter 1 that each index in a one-hot encoded vector belongs to a certain class). Finally, we return the fraction of correct classifications.

After training the model, we get the training accuracy of LeNet on CIFAR-10 equal to 0.6187.

4.4.3 TrainingLoop

You might have noticed that defining the training step and loop, accuracy property, and other things makes the program a little more complicated. We can use the TrainingLoop library from the swift-models package to make our program much smaller. It is also inspired from the Keras training design. TrainingLoop is contemporarily focused on classification tasks.

Let us see TrainingLoop in action by replicating the previous program from scratch.

Listing 4-10. Training LeNet on MNIST with the TrainingLoop library

```
import Datasets
import TensorFlow
import TrainingLoop

// Configurations
let epochs = 5
let device = Device.defaultXLA

// Load CIFAR 10 dataset
let dataset = CIFAR10(batchSize: 128, on: device)

// Initialize the LeNet model
var model = LeNet()

// Initialize the optimizer
var optimizer = SGD(for: model, learningRate: 0.01, momentum: 0.9)

// Train and test the model
let trainingProgress = TrainingProgress()
var trainingLoop = TrainingLoop(
  training: dataset.training,
  validation: dataset.validation,
  optimizer: optimizer,
  lossFunction: softmaxCrossEntropy,
  callbacks: [trainingProgress.update])

try! trainingLoop.fit(&model, epochs: epochs, on: device)
```

In Listing 4-10, we have imported Datasets, TensorFlow, and TrainingLoop. We then declare configurations such as epochs set to 5 and device set to Device.defaultXLA. The dataset, model (using the LeNet structure from Listing 4-9), and optimizer are initialized as in Listing 4-9.

Then we declare the trainingProgress instance of the TrainingProgress class which tracks the statistics related to training

160

and testing such as loss and accuracy. The next variable we define is `trainingLoop` which takes training and validation sets, the optimizer, the loss function (`softmaxCrossEntropy` here), and callbacks as arguments. Then we call the `fit(_:epochs:on:)` method on `trainingLoop` by passing the model as an **inout** argument, epochs, and the `device` on which we desire the training. This executes the training process and prints the statistics in real time without you requiring to write complex functions. After the training is completed, the model is shown to perform with an accuracy of 0.5607 on the training set and 0.5625 on the validation set.

Notice that, when training with TrainingLoop, we do not require to copy `model` and `optimizer` to the `device`; the `fit(_:epochs:on:)` method handles it all for us. Another important thing to notice is that the `callbacks` argument takes an array of functions to execute during training at various events of the loop. Here, we have only passed the statistics-tracking function, but we will see how to save checkpoints by defining our own callback function!

4.5 From Scratch for Research

In this section, we implement the dense layer, swish activation function, L^1 loss function, and stochastic gradient descent optimizer. These examples demonstrate how you can implement your own layers, activation functions, loss functions, and optimizers for research or production purposes when something is not yet available right out of the box. These examples also encourage the usage of various protocols. We encourage you to read the API documentation[1] and code base[2,3,4] of TensorFlow for deeper understanding of these and many other protocols.

---

[1] www.tensorflow.org/swift/api_docs
[2] https://github.com/tensorflow/swift-apis
[3] https://github.com/tensorflow/swift-models
[4] https://github.com/tensorflow/swift

4.5.1 Layer

Defining a new neural layer is similar to how we define our own neural network. Instead of using Sequential, we conform the structure to either the Layer or Module protocol. Although, the Differentiable protocol can achieve the same behavior as we shall see in Section 5.2 when we will build linear models. For now, let us define the dense layer (see Subsection 5.3.1) by conforming our structure to the Layer protocol.

Listing 4-11. Define the dense layer

```
struct DenseLayer<Scalar: TensorFlowFloatingPoint>: Layer {
  typealias Input = Tensor<Scalar>
  typealias Output = Tensor<Scalar>

  var weight: Tensor<Scalar>
  var bias: Tensor<Scalar>

  init(inputSize: Int, outputSize: Int) {
    weight = Tensor<Scalar>(randomNormal: [inputSize, outputSize])
    bias = Tensor(zeros: [outputSize])
  }

  @differentiable
  func callAsFunction(_ input: Input) -> Output {
    matmul(input, weight) + bias
  }
}
```

The DenseLayer is a generic type whose Scalar type placeholder conforms to TensorFlowFloatingPoint, and the DenseLayer itself conforms to Layer. Then we define two type aliases, namely, Input and Output, of Tensor<Scalar> type which we use as the input and output types of our dense layer in the differentiable callAsFunction(_:) instance method. DenseLayer also has two stored properties of Tensor<Scalar>

type, namely, `weight` and `bias`, which are the parameters of this layer. The initializer of `DenseLayer` accepts the number of input and output features of the layer. This information is then used to initialize both `weight` and `bias` parameteric properties. Finally, during forward pass, `callAsFunction(_:)` accepts the input, performs affine transformation on it (i.e., matrix multiply the `input` and `weight` with the `matmul(_:_:)` function and add `bias`), and returns the output.

4.5.2 Activation Function

After having affine-transformed the input, we apply the activation function. Many activation functions transform each element of tensor, individually. The swish function (Ramachandran et al., 2017), shown in Figure 4-2, is a great example of an activation function. It is given by the following equation:

$$\text{swish}(x) = x \cdot \sigma(\beta x)$$

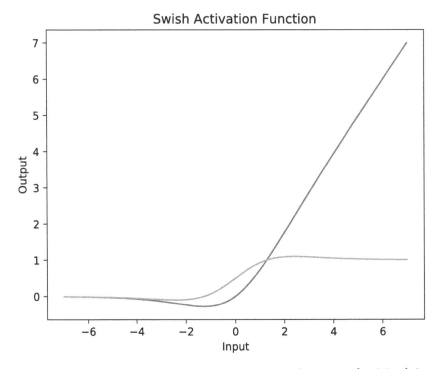

Figure 4-2. *The graph of the swish activation function (in blue) for β = 1 and its derivative (in orange)*

Here, β is a learnable or constant term. This term is usually set equal to 1. So the swish function becomes the following:

$$\mathrm{swish}(x) = x \cdot \sigma(x)$$

Listing 4-12 demonstrates how to declare your own activation function (swish activation function here).

Listing 4-12. Define the swish activation function

```
@differentiable
func swishActivation<Scalar: TensorFlowFloatingPoint>(_ input:
Tensor<Scalar>) -> Tensor<Scalar> {
  input * sigmoid(input)
}
```

Because we want our activation function `swishActivation(_:)` to be differentiable, we mark it with the `@differentiable` attribute. We declare a generic type `Scalar` conforming to `TensorFlowFloatingPoint`. This function takes the `input` argument and returns the output of `Tensor<Scalar>` type. Inside the body of `swishActivation(_:)`, we element-wise multiply the `input` with the sigmoid function–transformed `input` and return the output. We can use this activation function following any neural layer's output.

4.5.3 Loss Function

The direction for value updates of the model's parameters is guided by the gradient of loss between the neural network's prediction (also called logits) and the corresponding targets (also called labels) with respect to each parameter.

Here, we describe how to implement your own loss function in TensorFlow. We demonstrate a simple implementation of L^1 loss given by the following equation. L^1 loss computes the mean absolute error (MAE) between each element of logits and labels:

$$\frac{1}{k}\sum_{i=1}^{k}\|t_i - y_i\|$$

Here, y_i and t_i are, respectively, ith index logits and targets, and k is the number of elements in each of these vectors. The operator $\|.\|$ computes the absolute value, that is, converts the negative signs of any values of the vector into positive. The implementation of L^1 loss is demonstrated in Listing 4-13.

Listing 4-13. Define the L2 loss function

```
@differentiable(wrt: logits)
func l1Loss<Scalar: TensorFlowFloatingPoint>(
  logits: Tensor<Scalar>,
  labels: Tensor<Scalar>
) -> Tensor<Scalar> {
  abs(labels - logits).mean()
}
```

Here, the l1Loss(logits:labels:) function takes logits and labels as input arguments and returns a value of type Tensor<Scalar> where Scalar is a type placeholder that conforms to TensorFlowFloatingPoint. The body of this closure computes the difference between the corresponding elements of logits and labels, then takes the absolute value of it, and finds the mean of them.

During training, we compute the gradient of loss with respect to each parameter of the model which gives us the direction of steepest ascent. We aim to minimize the loss function, which is simply composed of the model's prediction and target, so we take small steps in the parameters space in the negative direction of the gradient. This is called gradient-based optimization, discussed in Section 5.1. Next, we see how to define our own optimizer in TensorFlow.

4.5.4 Optimizer

We can define a new optimizer by conforming the new optimizer class to the Optimizer protocol. Listing 4-14 demonstrates this by redefining the stochastic gradient descent (SGD) optimizer.

Listing 4-14. Define the stochastic gradient descent optimizer

```
class SGDOptimizer<Model: Differentiable>: Optimizer
where Model.TangentVector: VectorProtocol & ElementaryFunctions &
KeyPathIterable, Model.TangentVector.VectorSpaceScalar == Float
{
  // The learning rate
  var learningRate: Float

  init(for model: Model, learningRate: Float) {
    self.learningRate = learningRate
  }

  func update(_ model: inout Model, along direction: Model.
  TangentVector) {
    model.move(along: direction.scaled(by: -learningRate))
  }

  required init(copying other: SGDOptimizer<Model>, to device:
  Device) {
    learningRate = other.learningRate
  }
}
```

An optimizer must always be defined as a class. We define the SGDOptimizer class conforming to the Optimizer protocol. We also define a generic type Model conforming to the Differentiable protocol. Then we define some conditional conformances for Model. We say that TangentVector of Model must conform to VectorProtocol and ElementaryFunctions and must be KeyPathIterable. The ampersand sign (**&**) between each protocol composes all these protocols into a single protocol. Although this doesn't actually create any new protocol, this *protocol composition* behaves as a single protocol. This way, Model conforms to VectorProtocol (for vector operations and more), ElementaryFunctions (for arithmetic), and KeyPathIterable (for being able to iterate through its properties via KeyPath on the Model instance). Then we also require that Model's TangentVector's VectorSpaceScalar (which is basically the scalar value in the vector space, as the name implies) to be of Float type.

We declare an instance property for this class named learningRate which is the learning rate for optimization. We declare an initializer that takes model of Model type and learningRate of Float type as arguments. Here, model is only passed for the purpose of finding the type of Model and not for using it inside the optimizer. This is the intended behavior. For discussion, please refer to the GitHub issue.[5] Then the update instance method simply updates the model in the negative direction of the gradient of the loss function with respect to the model's parameters. It takes **inout** Model and along of Model.TangentVector as arguments. TangentVector stores the gradient of Model. The **inout** parameters reflect the changes back to the instance passed to the function. The move(along:) instance method on the model updates its parameters in the negative direction of the gradient after scaling it to smaller values with learningRate. We always pass the instance to **inout** parameters prefixed with the ampersand sign.

4.6 Summary

This chapter was focused on deep learning programming and introduced the TensorFlow library of S4TF. We started off with explaining how to create Tensor instances. Next, we saw how to load the dataset in TensorFlow. We also learned how to create deep learning models and

---

[5]https://github.com/tensorflow/swift-apis/issues/656

train and test them. We also created checkpoints of the model. Finally, we learned how to create the layer, activation and loss functions, and optimizer from scratch in TensorFlow for research purposes. In the next chapter, we will understand the basics of neural networks.

CHAPTER 5

Neural Networks

I like nonsense; it wakes up my brain cells.

—*Dr. Seuss*

This chapter covers the basics of neural networks, a.k.a. deep learning. We discuss various foundational topics as follows: gradient-based optimization of input and parameters of the function (Section 5.1), linear models (Section 5.2), deep and dense neural network (Section 5.3), activation functions (Section 5.4), loss functions (Section 5.5), and optimization (Section 5.6) and regularization (Section 5.7) techniques. Finally, we summarize the chapter in Section 5.8.

5.1 Gradient-Based Optimization

In this section, we introduce the concept of maxima, minima, and saddle points. Next, we introduce input and parameters optimization. Input optimization will be used to find the maxima and minima of the function. On the other hand, parameters optimization will be used to find the function itself using the available function mapping dataset. Both optimizations play important roles in deep learning and will be used throughout the book. Here, we focus on the online gradient-based learning strategy. More efficient approaches to gradient descent for large deep learning models are introduced in Section 5.6.

© Rahul Bhalley 2021
R. Bhalley, *Deep Learning with Swift for TensorFlow*,
https://doi.org/10.1007/978-1-4842-6330-3_5

We restrict ourselves to study the unconstrained optimization method because it is simple and suffices our requirement of demonstrating the deep learning methods presented in the book. Readers interested in constrained optimization may refer to Chapter 7 of (Deisenroth et al., 2020) textbook.

5.1.1 Maxima, Minima, and Saddle Points

Here, we consider a scalar function $f: \mathbb{R} \to \mathbb{R}$. The derivative of a function at a point can have three possible kinds of values: positive, negative, or zero. In the first case, when the derivative is positive at a point, then the function increases as input increases. In the second case, when the derivative is negative at a point, then the output of the function decreases as input increases. In other words, the sign of the derivative gives the direction, either negative or positive, in which the function increases when input is increased by a small amount. In the third case, when output doesn't change with any change in input, then the derivative is zero at that point.

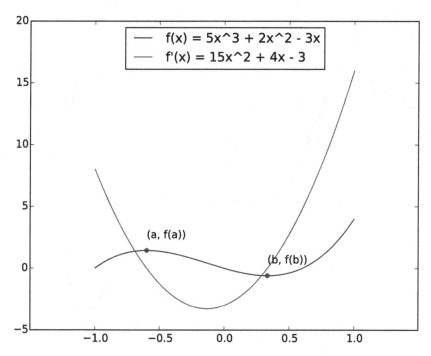

Figure 5-1. *Function described by equation f(x) = 5x³ + 2x² − 3x has one maxima and one minima. The tangent at a point on the function gives the slope of the gradient*

Figure 5-1 shows a graph of function $f(x) = 5x^3 + 2x^2 - 3x$ in blue and its derivative $f(x) = 15x^2 + 4x - 3$ in red color. The green points $(a, f(a)) = (-3/5, 1.44)$ and $(b, f(b)) = (1/3, -0.59)$ on $f(.)$ (blue line) are, respectively, maxima and minima of the function. At these points, the derivative is zero, that is, $f(a) = 0$ and $f(b) = 0$. On the horizontal axis, starting from $x = -1$, the function increases but slowly decreases until it reaches $x = a$. This can be verified by a corresponding red derivative line in the same range of input x as mentioned earlier; the derivative is first large but slowly decreases until it becomes zero at point $x = a$. This is the point where the slope (or derivative) of the function $f(.)$ becomes zero. The tangent at a point on function gives the slope of gradient.

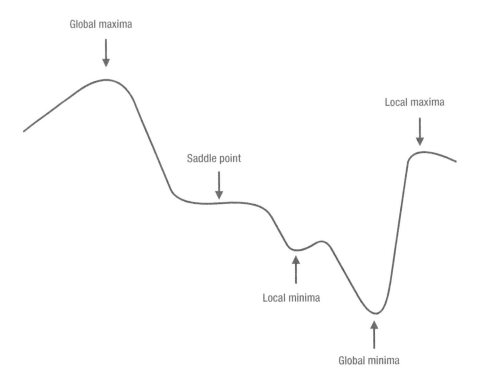

Figure 5-2. *The visualization of maxima, minima, and saddle points of an arbitrary scalar function*

Similarly, starting from $x = a$ to $x = b$, the function decreases for half a distance; and then for another half, its rate of change increases (but still negative) such that its slope starts coming closer to zero, so does the derivative value.

The function $f(.)$ has maxima at $f(a)$ because the function's outputs before and after $x = a$ are less than at point a. Formally, $f(a \pm \epsilon)$ is less than $f(x = a)$ where ϵ is a small positive number. On the other hand, the minima of the function lies at $x = b$, that is, the value $f(b)$ is minimum. Because the values $f(b \pm \epsilon)$ are larger than $f(b)$, the function $f(.)$ has minima at b. In the last case, when in a certain range of input, the output $f(x)$ remains the same, and then the derivative at these input values stays zero and satisfies the condition $f'(x \pm \epsilon) = 0$. All the points in this range are known as *saddle points*. In a nutshell, at maxima, minima, and saddle point x, the derivative of function $f(.)$ is always zero, that is, $f'(x) = 0$.

The concept of maxima, minima, and saddle points (see Figure 5-2) is not limited to only univariate functions but is also equally applicable to higher-dimensional functions, although difficult to visualize on the plane (such as a paper).

5.1.2 Input Optimization

In high school, the math problem usually encountered is as follows: find the input value(s) for which a given fixed function outputs minimum and maximum values. These values are known as the *minima* and *maxima* of a function, respectively, as discussed previously. We also know that the derivative of the function's output with respect to input describes the rate of change of output as input increases.

We can leverage the directional information of the derivative to find either the maxima or minima of a fixed function, numerically. For instance, the minima of a function can be found by iteratively updating (or optimizing) the input value with small steps in the negative direction (because the derivative gives the direction in which the function increases the most) of the derivative of output with respect to input. We can write the *gradient-based optimization* (Cauchy, 1847) equation as follows:

$$x_{(\tau+1)} \leftarrow x_{(\tau)} - \eta \nabla_{x_{(\tau)}} f \qquad (5.1)$$

We've already encountered a similar equation for updating the parameters of a function in Equation 1.8. Here, we update the value of input variable x of function f, iteratively over multiple steps. In this equation, η is a small positive number in range $(0,1]$ known as *step size* (or *learning rate*, in deep learning literature), τ represents time step such that

$x_{(\tau+1)}$ is the value of x at time step $(\tau+1)$, and $\nabla_{x_{(\tau)}} f$ is the derivative of function's f output with respect to input x at time step τ.

On the other hand, sometimes we might require to find the maxima of a function. In this case, we can simply move the input in the same direction as the derivative with small steps, described by the following equation:

$$x_{(\tau+1)} \leftarrow x_{(\tau)} + \eta \nabla_{x_{(\tau)}} f \qquad (5.2)$$

In gradient-based optimization, the η term plays a very important role. We desire to find the optimal input value following a smooth trajectory of input updates. Because the derivative usually has a large value at a point, the updates can follow an irregular trajectory exhibiting a bouncy behavior around the optimal value. To mitigate this problem, we downscale the derivative value with the η term which helps in updating the value following a smooth trajectory of updates.

In Listing 5-1, we will maximize the function $f(x) = 5x^3 + 2x^2 - 3x$.

Listing 5-1. Declare configuration variables and function $f(x) = 5x^3 + 2x^2 - 3x$ to demonstrate maxima and minima optimization

```
var x: Float = 0
let η: Float = 0.01
let maxIterations = 100

@differentiable
func f(_ x: Float) -> Float {
  return 4 * pow(x, 3) + 2 * pow(x, 2) - 3 * x
}

print("Before optimization, ", terminator: "")
print("x: \(x) and f(x): \(f(x))")
```

Output

```
Before optimization, x: 0.0 and f(x): 0.0
```

We first define the preceding function $f(x) = 5x^3 + 2x^2 - 3x$. We make it differentiable by marking it with the **@differentiable** attribute. Then the initial value of input variable x of type Float is set to 0, and step size η is defined as a Float constant set to 0.01. We can see that the input and output values of the function are zero before optimization.

Listing 5-2. Find the maxima of the function $f(x) = 5x^3 + 2x^2 - 3x$

```
// Optimization loop
for iteration in 1...maxIterations {
  /// Derivative of `f` w.r.t. `x`.

  let ∇xF = gradient(at: x, in: { x -> Float in
    return f(x)
  })
  // Optimization step: update `x` to maximize `f`.
  x += η * ∇xF
}
print("After gradient ascent, ", terminator: "")
print("input: \(x) and output: \(f(x))")
```

Output

```
After gradient ascent, input: -0.5999994 and output: 1.4399999
```

Listing 5-2 demonstrates the optimization process for finding the maxima. We iterate for maxIterations, gradually optimizing the input x. At each iteration step, we compute the derivative of function f with respect to input x and store it in constant ∇xF. The derivative is computed using the gradient(at:in:) function. The argument labels at and in take input x and a closure returning a scalar as parameters. The closure takes x as argument and returns Float computing f(x). The derivative of f with respect to x is automatically computed for us by Swift. The optimization update step for input x simply adds the derivative scaled by η to itself. We can easily verify that the optimized input value x is very close to the maxima value of function f(x) as shown in Figure 5-1.

One must be cautious when initializing the value of optimizable variables. If we initialized x at 1, then it wouldn't have been possible to find the local maxima of function $f(x)$ because its global maxima is at infinity. It is very important to note that in the case of minimization, in the context of deep learning, we actually desire to find the global minima of the function (or minima function for a given dataset), but in practice we can only find the closer local minima to it. So this function is not a very good example but still demonstrates, in simple scalar real-valued space, what might be happening to millions or billions of variables when we train large deep learning models.

Although it is as simple as applying a negative sign before step size η to compute the minima, in Listing 5-3, we take a look at the excellent design of the differentiation closures in Swift. This may also be considered as one of the motivating reasons to adopt Swift for deep learning.

Listing 5-3. Find the minima of the function $f(x) = 5x^3 + 2x^2 - 3x$

```
// Optimization loop
for _ in 1...maxIterations {
  /// Derivative of `f` w.r.t. `input`.
  let ∇xF = gradient(at: x) { x in f(x) }
  // Optimization step: update `x` to minimize `f`.
  x.move(along: ∇xF.scaled(by: -η))
}
print("After gradient descent, ", terminator: "")
print("input: \(x) and output: \(f(x))")
```

Output

```
After gradient descent, input: 0.33333316 and output:
-0.5925926
```

We first reset all the variables to initial values by executing Listing 5-1 again. Notice that much of the code in Listing 5-3 is similar to that in Listing 5-2. But we instead use a trailing closure for the in argument label in the gradient(at:in:) function. We also omit the return type information because the compiler can infer it from the context, that is, using the type of value returned when we call f(x) after the in keyword inside the closure's body. Also when the function has only one statement and it returns some value, we can omit writing the **return** keyword to make the code more readable. Furthermore, the body of the closure is just one line, so we have compressed it into a single line of code. Please see Section 3.4 for more information on functions and closures.

Finally, we use the move(along:) method on Float type. Swift's documentation description of move(along:) says, "Moves self along the given direction. In Riemannian geometry, this is equivalent to exponential map, which moves self on the geodesic surface along the given tangent vector." Every differentiable type in Swift's type system automatically gets the implementation of the move(along:) method. This method takes a value of TangentVector associated with the differentiable variable as parameter and updates the variable itself. Here, the derivative of f with respect to x is ∇xF and has type Float.TangentVector. We pass it to move(along:) where ∇xF is first scaled by negative step size -η for finding the minima of function f. After the iterative optimization of input, we finally approximate the minima of the function close to the true minima.

Next, we introduce parameters optimization and explain how it is different from and similar to input optimization.

5.1.3 Parameters Optimization

Usually, in deep learning, our aim is to optimize the differentiable function. This is done by optimizing the coefficients (also known as *parameters*) of the function instead of the input. We are also given a fixed set of training datapoints containing input and target pairs. These pairs are sampled from some unknown data-generating probability distribution. Our goal is to approximate this data-generating distribution using the available dataset. We do this by maximizing the log-likelihood (see Section 1.3) of parameters of the function and dataset, because the dataset statistically represents the data-generating distribution. In other words, we search for a function, which is a good approximation of the data-generating function, in a space of functions restricted by a set of variable parameters and the equation's structure such that for a given set of inputs, it predicts the outputs closer to their corresponding target values.

5.1.3.1 Inference

Consider the Photos app on Apple devices. The Photos app processes the images and videos on-device using deep learning models to predict objects, scenes, faces, animals, and so on and allows searching media content with text. This is called inference. Formally, the process of predicting the output (for instance, category of an image) for a given input sample (for instance, image) is known as *inference* (or *forward pass*). A little more complex example of inference is speech processing. When you speak to Siri, Google Assistant, or other voice assistants, your speech is sent to and processed on the respective company's servers (and sometimes on-device) by passing it through a sequence of deployed trained natural language processing (NLP) models including, but not limited to, speech recognition, syntax parsing, and parts of speech tagging, to make predictions. Predictions made by different models represent different things. For instance, the speech recognition model predicts the spoken sequence of words; the parts of speech tagging model tags, categorizes, or classifies different words as noun, adverbs, and so on. Interestingly, we have already seen inference in action in the preceding text. We inferred our model when we predicted a scalar output for an optimal input value in Listings 5-1, 5-2, and 5-3. See Figure 5-3 for a graph describing the inference process.

Figure 5-3. *An inference process where input x is fed to the model function f(.) to predict the output y*

But before our model is ready to make correct predictions, it must be trained by the gradient-based parameters optimization process discussed next.

5.1.3.2 Optimization

We first consider the problem statement of parameters optimization. As already discussed in the preceding text, we have a set of input and output pairs in a dataset sampled from some unknown data distribution. The fundamental goal of designing any machine learning algorithm is to approximate the true data-generating function with some parameterized density function (also known as *model*) of our choice. In other words, we desire to learn the mapping from inputs to their corresponding target values.

Let us first clarify the difference between input and parameters optimization problems. To make a clearer distinction between these problems, we use the same function $f(.)$ as a running example. In input optimization, we have a function with a fixed set of parameters, and we update the input value until we find the one for which our given function returns zero output, giving us the minima or maxima of the function. In contrast, in parameters optimization, we are given a fixed set of input and target pairs in a dataset and a parameterized function of our own choice whose coefficients can be updated. Here, our goal is to find a function that best represents the mapping of inputs and targets or, in other words, best approximates the data-generating function.

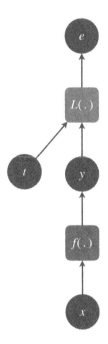

Figure 5-4. *The loss function mapping $L(y, t)$ where $y = f(x)$ and t are the prediction and target variables, respectively. The final output variable e is called error or loss which we desire to minimize*

At first glance, in analogy to the input optimization, one might consider tackling this problem by optimizing the parameters to find the minima function for a given dataset. In the minimization case, the function can be found by iteratively making the following updates till the output value emitted by our searched function is close to zero for a given dataset:

$$\theta_{(\tau+1)} \leftarrow \theta_{(\tau)} - \eta \nabla_{\theta_{(\tau)}} f \tag{5.3}$$

Here, we represent the parameters of function $f(.)$ with a Greek letter θ (called theta). If we assume our function of form $f(x) = ax^3 + bx^2 + cx$ is parameterized by coefficients a, b, and c, then $\theta = \{a, b, c\}$. The preceding equation individually updates each parameter value.

Notice that Equation 5.3 considers only inputs and not their corresponding targets. This simply means finding the function map from inputs to zero, $f: x \rightarrow 0$, whereas we desire to approximate the mapping $f: x \rightarrow t$ where x and t are input and target variables, respectively. The mapping $f: x \rightarrow 0$ is not really the desired solution because it doesn't represent the dataset mapping.

So how can we find the desired dataset mapping? To find the mapping, we instead introduce a loss function $L(f(x), t)$ in our equation to approximate the unknown data-generating function map (see Figure 5-4). The loss function is helpful in learning the mapping for our model $f(.)$, indirectly. It tells how far is our model's prediction y from the target t for a given input x. It takes the model's prediction and target values as arguments and returns a scalar value for variable e representing some notion of distance (or error) between prediction and target. We strive to minimize the error term e using its gradient information with respect to each parameter of the loss function. If we optimize our loss function to minimize this error via gradient descent technique, our predictions will gradually start coming closer to desired targets. As a result of this optimization process, we will be able to automatically find the function mapping represented by the dataset. In other words, we will be able to approximate the function that best represents the data-generating PDF, from which the given dataset was sampled, in a restricted space of functions described by the model's equation.

We simply require to compute the partial derivatives of the loss function with respect to the model's parameters and then iteratively update each of these parameters via the gradient descent process as described by Equation 5.4. This is done until the loss function emits error between the model's predictions and desired targets closer to zero for corresponding input samples given in a dataset:

$$\theta_{(\tau+1)} \leftarrow \theta_{(\tau)} - \eta \nabla_{\theta_{(\tau)}} L\left(f\left(x^{(i)}\right), t^{(i)};\theta\right) \tag{5.4}$$

Because we are dealing with a regression problem, it is appropriate to use a popular loss function called sum of squared errors described by Equation 5.5:

$$L(\mathbf{x}, \mathbf{t}; \theta) = \frac{1}{2}\sum_{i=1}^{N}\left(f\left(x^{(i)}\right) - t^{(i)}\right)^2 \tag{5.5}$$

This loss function always returns a non-negative output. The minimum value it returns is zero only when prediction is equal to target which means the prediction function completely replicates the data-generating function's mapping. Listing 5-4 shows how to compute the sum of squared errors between scalar target t and prediction y.

Listing 5-4. Sum of squared errors function

```
@differentiable
func sumOfSquaresError(_ t: Float, _ y: Float) -> Float {
  0.5 * pow(t - y, 2)
}
```

We mark sumOfSquaresError(_:_:) with the **@differentiable** attribute. Similar to Equation 5.5, we raise the difference between the target t and prediction y to the power of 2 and then halve it.

184

Let us define our data-generating function in Listing 5-5.

Listing 5-5. Data-generating function $g(x) = 5x^3 + 2x^2 - 3x$

```
/// Data generating function
func g(_ x: Float) -> Float {
  4 * powf(x, 3) + 2 * powf(x, 2) - 3 * x
}
```

We declare our model function as a structure with stored differentiable properties as shown in Listing 5-6.

Listing 5-6. Declare a model as a Function structure

```
struct Function: Differentiable {
  var a, b, c: Float
  init() {
    (a, b, c) = (1, 1, 1)
  }
  func callAsFunction(_ x: Float) -> Float {
    a * pow(x, 3) + b * pow(x, 2) - c * x
  }
}
```

When we take the partial derivative of this loss function's output *e* (called error) with respect to prediction output, then we get a simple partial derivative as follows:

$$\frac{\partial e}{\partial y} = y - t \tag{5.6}$$

If our model is a deep neural network, then this error is further backpropagated via the chain rule of differentiation with respect to previous variables and then deeper in the chain and so on. In Swift, this is done using a more general technique for computing partial derivatives called algorithmic differentiation (see Section 3.3).

Following the more meaningful problem formulation of parameters optimization via the loss function, the parameter update Equation 5.3 now changes to the following:

$$\theta = \theta - \eta \nabla_\theta L \qquad (5.7)$$

Here, L is the loss function; and similar to Equation 5.3, we update the parameters θ in Equation 5.7. Let us see parameters optimization in action in Listing 5-7.

Listing 5-7. Find the minima function having free parameters equation $f(x) = ax^3 + bx^2 - cx$ for a dataset sampled from function $g(x) = 5x^3 + 2x^2 - 3x$

```
var x: Float = 0
let η: Float = 0.01
let epochCount = 174

// Model
var f = Function()

// Dataset
let inputs = [Float](stride(from: -1, to: 1, by: 0.01))
let outputs = inputs.map{ g($0) }

print("Before optimization")
dump(f)

// Optimization loop
for _ in 1...epochCount {
  for (x, t) in zip(inputs, outputs) {
    /// Derivative of `E` w.r.t. every differentiable parameter
    of `f`.
    let ∇θE = gradient(at: f) { f -> Float in
```

```
    let y = f(x)
    let error = sumOfSquaresError(t, y)
    return error
  }
  // Optimization step: update θ to minimize `error`.
  f.move(along: ∇θE.scaled(by: -η))
}
print("After optimization")
dump(f)
```

Output

```
Before optimization
▽ ParametersOptimization.Function
  - a: 1.0
  - b: 1.0
  - c: 1.0
After optimization
▽ ParametersOptimization.Function
  - a: 4.9880642
  - b: 2.0008333
  - c: -2.9924128
```

We first define the function $g(.)$ and then sample an array of outputs corresponding to inputs in range $[-1.0, 1.0)$ where each consecutive value has a difference of 0.01, making up our dataset. Here, map(_:) is an instance method declared on the Collection protocol and takes a closure to apply on each element of the Collection instance.

Our goal is to approximate the data-generating function's mapping. To accomplish this, we first define a differentiable structure named Function containing three stored properties a, b, and c, each representing a specific coefficient of the Function instance. The design of the function to be used for approximation is described by the equation $f(x) = ax^3 + bx^2 - cx$

and has been written inside the callAsFunction(_:) method. Here, it is okay to eliminate the usage of the **@differentiable** attribute from the callAsFunction(_:) method because the structure itself conforms to the Differentiable protocol which automatically makes this function differentiable. We also declare an instance of Function with name f.

To compute the sum of squared error between prediction and target, described by Equation 5.5, we will use the function named sumOfSquaresError(_:_:) marked with the **@differentiable** attribute from Listing 5-4.

We set the epochCount constant equal to 174. To iterate by accessing corresponding input and output datapoints, we use the zip(_:_:) function in the **for-in** loop.

Inside this loop, similar to previous examples, we compute the gradient, but this time with respect to the Function's instance f. Here, passing f as argument to gradient(at:in:) means computing the partial derivative of the error function with respect to all differentiable properties of the f instance. We first predict the output and store it in immutable instance y which is then passed to the sumOfSquaresError(_:_:) function alongside target instance t. This returns the error in prediction made by our function f. After the closing brace of the gradient(at:in:) function, we get the gradient of E with respect to all coefficients a, b, and c stored in the $\nabla\theta E$ instance of type Function.TangentVector. Recall from Chapter 3 that TangentVector is an associated type of differentiable data type; this holds true for all differentiable fundamental and custom types. Finally, we utilize the gradient information stored in $\nabla\theta E$ to update the differentiable properties in the f instance. As noted earlier, this is done for 174 times which finally approximates the data-generating function g(x) closely.

By dumping the values of the f instance, we can see that its coefficients' values are very close to that of function $g(x)$. Therefore, we successfully approximated the data-generating function via parameters optimization with the help of an error function.

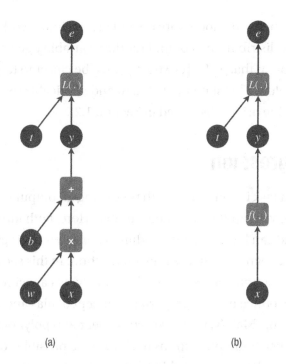

Figure 5-5. *The computational graph of the linear regression model $y = wx + b$ where we also compute the loss $e = L(y, t)$. (a) Explicit graph (showing affine transformation) and (b) implicit graph (assumes the operations from (a)). In later figures, adopting (b), we implicitly consider affine transformation. Hereafter, we will color-encode the operations in graphs*

Next, we discuss some basic linear models for tackling regression and classification problems.

5.2 Linear Models

Linear models are the simplest form of neural networks that can perform regression and classification tasks. Although they are incapable of learning highly complex dataset mapping, they do work well for simpler cases; and due to their small size, they are fast at processing the input.

189

The neural network models are essentially the framework for modeling the probability distribution of output random variable y given the input random variable x, that is, $P(y|x)$ where y must be closer to target t given the same sample x. This statement is valid and applicable to all kinds of machine learning briefly discussed in Section 1.2.

5.2.1 Regression

The regression task is concerned with predicting an output real-valued variable for a given input real-valued variable. Here, both input and output are tensors and can have any desired dimensions. Interestingly, we have already studied regression in the previous section. In this section, we will discuss various simple regression models of varying capacities which will further introduce us to an important concept of bias and variance in machine learning. Mainly, we will discuss linear and polynomial models. Bias and variance trade-off helps us to choose the possible correct capacity of the model to solve a given problem. Here, we introduce very simple regression models designed to predict scalar output.

5.2.1.1 Linear Regression

We start with the simplest model for a regression task known as the *linear model* (shown in Figure 5-5). It represents a univariate function mapping $f: \mathbb{R} \to \mathbb{R}$ between input and output real-valued scalars. As the name describes, this model learns a linear relationship between input x and output $f(x)$ scalars, and this relation geometrically represents a straight line on a plane. A linear model is given by the following equation:

$$f(x) = wx + b \tag{5.8}$$

Here, Equation 5.8 describes a straight line in two-dimensional space (or plane). In the context of machine learning, the terms w and b are, respectively, known as *weight* (or *slope*) and *bias* (or *intercept*) and are collectively called *parameters*. This bias term should not be confused with statistical bias discussed in Section 1.5.

We will fit the linear model to Equation 5.8. See Listing 5-8.

Listing 5-8. Declare a linear model

```
struct LinearModel: Differentiable {
  var w, b: Float
  init() {
    (w, b) = (1, 1)
  }
  func callAsFunction(_ x: Float) -> Float {
    w * x + b
  }
}
```

We have declared a LinearModel structure consisting of weight w and bias b terms. Next, we fit the model to samples from data-generating function $g(.)$.

Listing 5-9. Train to fit the LinearModel to samples from function $g(x)$

```
import Foundation

let η: Float = 0.01
let epochCount = 174

// Model
var model = LinearModel()

// Dataset
let inputs = [Float](stride(from: -1, to: 1, by: 0.01))
let outputs = inputs.map{ g($0) }
```

```
print("Before optimization")
dump(f)
// Optimization loop
for _ in 1...epochCount {
  for (x, t) in zip(inputs, outputs) {
    /// Derivative of `E` w.r.t. every differentiable parameter
    of `model`.
    let ∇θE = gradient(at: f) { f -> Float in
      let y = model(x)
      let error = sumOfSquaresError(t, y)
      return error
    }
    // Optimization step: update θ to minimize `error`.
    model.move(along: ∇θE.scaled(by: -η))
  }
  print("After optimization")
  dump(f)
```

Output

```
Before optimization
▽ LinearRegression.LinearModel
  - w: 1.0
  - b: 1.0
After optimization
▽ LinearRegression.LinearModel
  - w: 4.9880642
  - b: 2.0008333
```

Unfortunately, our linear model is not able to approximate the function $g(.)$ because it has only two parameters and, therefore, less capacity. Now, we resort to a higher-capacity model to learn the mapping.

5.2.1.2 Polynomial Regression

We have seen that a linear model does not learn the mapping well because the relation between inputs and targets is not linear. Because the function $g(.)$ is a polynomial of order 3, we must experiment learning the mapping using a polynomial function. The polynomial regression model (shown in Figure 5-6) also learns a mapping between scalar values, that is, $f: \mathbb{R} \rightarrow \mathbb{R}$, and is given by the following equation:

$$f(x) = \sum_{i=0}^{m} w_i x^i \qquad (5.9)$$

For $m = 3$, we get a polynomial of the same order as data function $g(.)$ which is given as follows:

$$f(x) = w_0 + w_1 x + w_2 x^2 + w_3 x^3 \qquad (5.10)$$

Here, w_0 is a bias term usually written as b. The input with bias b is always $x^0 = 1$ so we ignore showing it in the equation. We eliminate it from the model definition because it is a redundant term and partial derivative with respect to b is always zero.

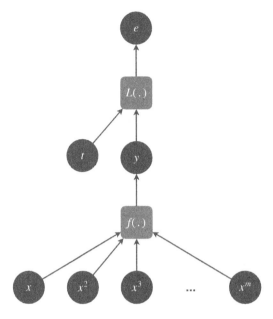

Figure 5-6. *The computational graph of the polynomial regression model* $y = \sum_{i=0}^{m} w_i x^i$ *where we also compute the loss* $e = L(y, t)$

Also note that a linear model is a special case of a polynomial model when its order is 1:

$$f(x) = b + w_1 x$$

The polynomial model has advantage over the linear model in that it can have more adaptive parameters which give it more learning capacity. This means that the model can approximate the data-generating function more accurately.

Let us declare our polynomial regression model with a flexibility of choosing an arbitrary order.

Listing 5-10. Declare a polynomial model

```swift
struct PolynomialModel: Differentiable {
  var weights: [Float]
  var bias: Float = 1
  @noDerivative var order: Int

  init(order: Int) {
    weights = Array(repeating: 1, count: order)
    self.order = order
  }

  @differentiable
  func callAsFunction(input: Float) -> Float {
    var output = bias
    for index in 0..<order {
      output += weights[index] * pow(x, Float(index))
    }
    return output
  }
}
```

We define a PolynomialModel structure containing the weights array and bias as differentiable stored properties and the order non-differentiable stored property. The differentiable callAsFunction(_:) instance method maps from Float to Float type values. Inside this method, the output local variable, initially set equal to bias, is iteratively added with a weighted input where input corresponding to each weight from the weights array is powered to index of weight, therefore giving us the result of polynomial equation. Finally, we return the output from this method.

We simply initialize the model as an instance of PolynomialModel in Listing 5-6 with order set equal to 3. And we train the model for the same epochs over the same dataset. By doing so, we are able to approximate the coefficients of data-generating function $g(.)$. This shows that the polynomial model has more capacity than the linear model and, therefore, it is able to approximate more complex data-generating distributions.

Here, we could easily make a principled guess to try out the polynomial model because we have access to the equation of data-generating function $g(.)$. But in real-world problems, we cannot actually know beforehand which model to try out first. Our only option is to train multiple models of varying capacities and choose the one which gives the lowest generalization error on a test set. A more principled approach is to study research papers that tackle the same problem as yours and try out those models on your dataset and make minor modifications to the algorithm until you get good results.

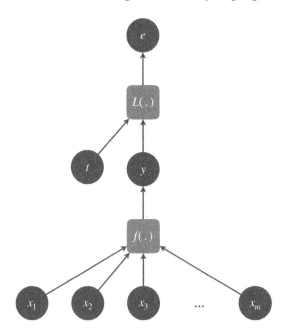

Figure 5-7. *The computational graph of the multiple regression model* $f(x) = \sum_{i=1}^{m} w_i x_i + b$ *where we also compute the loss* $e = L(y, t)$

5.2.1.3 Multiple Regression

Previously, we visited regression models where we learned a map between scalar input and target values. But sometimes the input sample in a dataset might contain multiple features, which we will represent as a vector $\mathbf{x} \in \mathbb{R}^m$, and the target has a scalar value $t \in \mathbb{R}$. The model described by multivariate function $f: \mathbb{R}^m \rightarrow \mathbb{R}$ is termed as the *multiple regression model*, and the task is known as *multiple regression* (see Figure 5-7). We write this model's equation as follows:

$$f(\mathbf{x}) = \sum_{i=1}^{m} w_i x_i + b \qquad (5.12)$$

Here, w_i is called weight and represents the importance of input variable x_i in predicting the correct output, and b is a bias term where each of these is a scalar. By representing all input variables and their corresponding weights as m-dimensional vectors $\mathbf{x} = [x_1 \ldots x_m]$ and $\mathbf{w} = [w_1 \ldots w_m]$, respectively, we can rewrite this equation more succinctly, using matrix multiplication between inputs (as a row matrix) and weights (as a column matrix) and adding a bias term. This is called *affine transformation* of input $\mathbf{x}$:

$$f(\mathbf{x}) = \mathbf{x}\mathbf{w} + b \qquad (5.13)$$

The affine transformation in Equation 5.13 may also be considered as a dense layer, as we shall see later. For now, we will study the linear models for the classification task.

5.2.2 Classification

The task of assigning a class label to an input sample is known as *classification*. We discuss two types of classification tasks, namely, binary and multiclass classification.

5.2.2.1 Binary Classification

In binary classification, we label the sample as belonging to one of the two possible classes, that is, $K = 2$. The output is a scalar value where either class is represented as 1 or 0. To restrict the predicted output in range $(0,1)$, we apply *sigmoidal function* $\sigma(.)$, also called *logistic sigmoid function* or *sigmoid function* (Han and Moraga, 1995), written as follows:

$$\sigma(x) = \frac{1}{1 + e^{-x}} \qquad (5.14)$$

where $e(.)$ is an exponential function (see Figure 3-5). The graph of the sigmoid function has an "S" shape (see Figure 5-8) nicely bounding the outputs in range $(0,1)$.

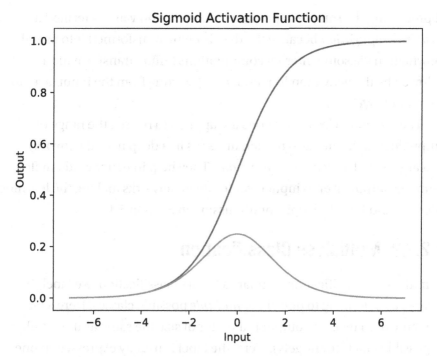

Figure 5-8. *The graph of the logistic sigmoid activation function (in blue) and its derivative (in orange)*

This binary classification model is a multivariate function $f : \mathbb{R}^m \rightarrow \{0,1\}$ and is written as follows:

$$\sigma(y) = \frac{1}{1 + e^{-(\mathbf{xw}+b)}} \tag{5.15}$$

Here, the affine-transformed input $\mathbf{x}$ produces a scalar prediction logit y (the inputs to the activation function in the output layer of the network) where $y = \mathbf{w}x + b$. Then we apply the sigmoid function element-wise on these logit units to normalize the predicted scalar's value in range $(0,1)$. Because we apply the sigmoid function on the logit of this model, we also call this model as the *sigmoidal classification* or *logistic regression* (a misnomer, but commonly used in the literature) model. The process of processing the sample to produce the prediction value is termed as *forward propagation* because the data is being transformed into useful information via some internal computations (affine transformation followed by the activation function, here) starting from the input layer to the output layer.

These element-wise functions are applied to restrict the range of output logit units and also hidden units (as in a deep neural network) and are termed as *activation functions*. They help in better gradient flow from the output layer to input layer for deep networks making the learning effective and form the topic for discussion in Section 5.4.

5.2.2.2 Multiclass Classification

In multiclass classification, similar to binary classification, we label the sample as belonging to one of the *multiple* possible classes. Here, classes are more than two. The output is a vector of size the same as the number of possible labels (or targets). Here, the label is usually expressed in one-hot encoding (also called 1-of-K coding where K is the number of classes), a representation where only a single index in a whole vector has a value of one and all others are set to zero. Each index is assumed to represent a certain class, and the index whose value is one is the class to which the sample belongs. Because we desire only one index of the label vector to be equal to 1, we use the multiclass generalization of the sigmoid function known as the softmax function written as follows:

$$\text{softmax}(\mathbf{x})_i = \frac{e^{\mathbf{x}_i}}{\sum_{j=1}^{K} e^{\mathbf{x}_j}} \tag{5.16}$$

Here, softmax is computed for the ith index element of vector $\mathbf{x}$. The numerator computes the exponential of the ith index value, and the denominator computes the sum of exponentials of all elements of the vector. Assume $y_i = \text{softmax}(\mathbf{x})_i$ and then the sum of all elements y_i, where $i = \{1,...,K\}$ and $\mathbf{y} = [y_1 \ldots y_k]$, is equal to 1. In other words, softmax normalizes the vector $\mathbf{x}$ such that the sum of its resulting vector $\mathbf{y}$'s all elements is equal to 1.

We construct a multiclass classifier by considering a vector-to-vector function $\mathbf{f} : \mathbb{R}^m \rightarrow \mathbb{R}^n$ mapping from m- to n-dimensional vectors where m and n are the number of the sample's features and target classes, respectively. For an input sample vector $\mathbf{x} \in \mathbb{R}^{1 \times m}$, we get $\hat{\mathbf{x}} = \mathbf{x}\mathbf{W} + \mathbf{b}$ where $\hat{\mathbf{x}} \in \mathbb{R}^{1 \times n}$ are logits, $\mathbf{W} \in \mathbb{R}^{m \times n}$ are weights, and $\mathbf{b} \in \mathbb{R}^{1 \times n}$ are biases. Then we apply softmax on logits $\hat{\mathbf{x}}$ to produce a vector $\mathbf{y} = \text{softmax}(\hat{\mathbf{x}})$ of normalized values for class prediction.

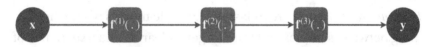

Figure 5-9. *The computational graph of the three-layer neural network describing forward propagation. The gray-colored rounded square box means arbitrary parameterized function, that is, it can be any neural layer*

Because we apply the softmax function on the logits of this model, we also call this model as the *softmax classification model, multiclass classifier,* or simply *softmax classifier.* We will see later that, similar to the softmax classifier, dense neural networks are built using matrix multiplication of input vectors (or matrix containing multiple vectors or samples) and weights, followed by addition of a bias vector and application of an activation function (not limited to only sigmoid and softmax) but for multiple layers where the output of a previous layer is input to the next layer. Here, the affine transformation $\mathbf{x}\mathbf{W} + \mathbf{b}$ is a dense or fully-connected layer operation.

5.3 Deep Neural Network

In the previous section, we visited various linear models. The limitation of those models is that they can only approximate a linear relationship between samples and targets. But in the real world, datasets are more complex in terms of correlation between sample's features and sample's features' relationship with targets. Although the softmax model attains good accuracy on small and simple datasets like MNIST, we can do better. So we resort to non-linear models like deep neural networks for help. Deep neural networks are capable of solving classification as well as regression problems.

Deep neural networks are a class of learnable models where the mapping between samples and their targets is learned via a sequence of chained multiple high-dimensional functions called *neural layers*. The word "deep" comes from the fact that there are multiple layers in a non-linear neural network. For the same reason, we call the field of studying such machine learning models as "deep learning" as opposed to "machine learning." There are various kinds of neural layers such as the dense layer (discussed next), recurrent and attention layers, the convolutional layer (discussed in Chapter 6), and others. Note that there exists a minor exception to this definition that all the hidden layers of neural networks are *not always* entirely chained starting from the input layer to the output layer, but a sequence of few hidden neural layers, called *neural blocks*, are chained, while other layers might have skip connections (see Section 6.3) to other farther layers.

Let us consider a three-layer deep neural network which can be written as $\mathbf{y} = \mathbf{f}^{(3)}(\mathbf{f}^{(2)}(\mathbf{f}^{(1)}(\mathbf{x})))$ or $\mathbf{y} = \mathbf{f}^{(3)} \circ \mathbf{f}^{(2)} \circ \mathbf{f}^{(1)}(\mathbf{x})$ (see Figure 5-9). Here, $\mathbf{x}$ is a sample features vector, and $\mathbf{y}$ is the prediction vector. We represent the neural layer as a vector function $\mathbf{f}(.)$ where the natural number in superscript is the layer's position in the sequential chain. Here, $\mathbf{f}^{(1)}(.)$, $\mathbf{f}^{(2)}(.)$, and $\mathbf{f}^{(3)}(.)$ are, respectively, *input, hidden,* and *final* (or *output*) *neural layers*. The output of the first layer $\mathbf{f}^{(1)}(.)$ returns a new features vector $\mathbf{f}^{(1)}(\mathbf{x})$

which becomes the input for the second layer $\mathbf{f}^{(2)}(.)$. The output of the second layer $\mathbf{f}^{(2)} \circ \mathbf{f}^{(1)}(\mathbf{x})$ becomes the input for the third layer $\mathbf{f}^{(3)}(.)$. Then finally the output of the third layer $\mathbf{f}^{(3)} \circ \mathbf{f}^{(2)} \circ \mathbf{f}^{(1)}(\mathbf{x})$ is the prediction vector $\mathbf{y}$.

The output of any layer can be considered as the transformation of its input features into different features represented in a new dimensions vector, for instance, the output features vector of the first layer $\mathbf{f}^{(1)}(\mathbf{x})$ is the input features vector for the second neural layer $\mathbf{f}^{(2)}(.)$. Here, we have omitted activation functions for clarity, but each layer's output follows an element-wise application of activation functions. The transformation of the input features vector to the desired output prediction vector is called *forward propagation* or *forward pass*. All the deep neural networks can be described with this methodology with an exception for skip connections.

Next, we introduce one of the simplest deep neural networks called the dense neural network.

5.3.1 Dense Neural Network

A *dense neural network*, also called *densely connected* or *fully connected neural network*, is composed of more than one sequentially connected dense layers. The softmax model discussed earlier is a special case of dense neural network having only one layer. The deep dense neural network has an input layer, multiple hidden layers, and a final layer, each being a dense layer type. The *dense layers* are simply vector-to-vector functions mapping to different dimensions in each layer with a restriction that any given layer's output dimension must match the input dimension of its succeeding layer. The output of a dense layer (shown in Figure 5-10) is computed by the affine transformation of its input features vector and then applying the activation function. The output features of a layer serve as the input features for the next layer in a sequential chain of dense neural layers. This process is continued until we compute the final layer's output predicting the result we care about.

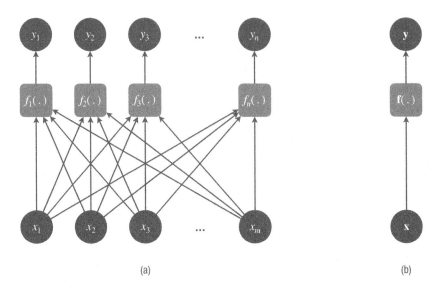

Figure 5-10. *The computational graph of the dense layer (in pink color) in (a) explicit and (b) implicit form. Here,* $y = f(x) = xW + b$ *where* $x \in \mathbb{R}^m$, $y \in \mathbb{R}^n$, $W \in \mathbb{R}^{m \times n}$, $b \in \mathbb{R}^n$, *and* $f: \mathbb{R}^m \to \mathbb{R}^n$

Let us consider an **L**-layer deep dense neural network where each of its layers' feature computation during forward pass can be described by the following equations:

$$\mathbf{z}^{(l)} = \mathbf{x}^{(l-1)} \times \mathbf{W}^{(l)} + \mathbf{b}^{(l)} \tag{5.17}$$

$$\mathbf{x}^{(l)} = \mathbf{a}^{(l)}\left(\mathbf{z}^{(l)}\right) \tag{5.18}$$

Here, $l = 1,..., L$ is the layer index. The terms $\mathbf{W}^{(l)}$ and $\mathbf{b}^{(l)}$ are the weight matrix and bias vector of the lth layer, respectively. The multiplication sign ($\times$) represents matrix multiplication. The terms $\mathbf{x}^{(l)}$, $\mathbf{z}^{(l)}$, and $\mathbf{a}^{(l)}$ are features, activations, and activation function of the lth layer, respectively. As a special case when $l = 1$, we get $\mathbf{x}^{(0)}$ which is the input sample features vector to the model. We assume all the vectors as a row matrix to make matrix multiplication possible and which makes using mini-batch samples for parallel computation possible in a later chapter.

We already know that it is straightforward to forward propagate the sample features $\mathbf{x}^{(l)}$ through a dense neural network sequentially to produce the prediction $\mathbf{y}$. This prediction is then passed through loss function $L(\mathbf{y}, \mathbf{t})$ along with targets $\mathbf{t}$ to compute a scalar error e.

The next thing is to compute the gradient of error with respect to each layer's parameters $\partial e/\partial \mathbf{W}^{(l)}$. This is done by performing the chain rule of differentiation. Swift for TensorFlow uses reverse-mode algorithmic differentiation to find partial derivatives of loss with respect to each parameter of the neural network. Also recall from Subsection 2.3.5 that the derivative with respect to any neural layer's higher-dimensional parameters can be easily expressed in Jacobian by reshaping them before applying the chain rule. This provides an efficient and general approach to compute partial derivatives in neural networks.

Next, we look at some popular activation functions.

5.4 Activation Functions

The neural networks learn to map feature and target tensors having small real-valued numbers because they meaningfully represent the task at hand. Activation functions help in maintaining the small range of values so that values don't either shrink or grow uncontrollably, or it'll defeat our purpose of predicting values in a label distribution's range. Activation functions also help in better generalization and faster convergence of the model.

Activation functions are used in hidden layers and the output layer of the network. They enforce the desired probability distribution when applied in a layer. The choice of output units' activation function is based on the task of the model, whereas the choice of hidden units' activation function impacts the training (or convergence) speed and performance of the neural network.

There has been a long research history of activation functions to find better ones. We present various important activation functions for output and hidden units of the neural network and discuss their pros and cons. Activation functions can be linear, non-linear, or even a combination of linear and non-linear functions. We mainly focus on non-linear activation functions because a neural network with linear activations can be described by a single-layer network which makes the representational capacity useless. This also destroys the aim of deep neural networks because the idea of depth is meant to help networks learn hierarchical and richer representations of datasets. This aim is achieved by using non-linear activation functions which makes the network represent a wider range of functions and, therefore, capable of learning more complex non-linear mappings.

Now we take a deeper look at various activation functions and their derivatives.

5.4.1 Sigmoid

The sigmoid function, shown in Figure 5-8, was introduced in Subsection 5.2.2 and is given by Equation 5.14. The sigmoid is a scalar function and is applied element-wise on the tensor transforming its each element, individually. It simply rescales the input's value to the range (0,1).

When the logistic sigmoid function is applied on the scalar logit, it learns a Bernoulli distribution and can be, therefore, helpful in learning to perform a binary classification task. In this case, output is a scalar value, and either of the two classes $K = 2$ can be represented by 1 or 0 as its probability being a possible class for input. In the other case, when we desire to learn multiple-class classification (when a sample belongs to more than one class), we apply sigmoid on a prediction vector. In this case, output is a vector value, and the classes are represented with index (without one-hot coding), and multiple elements can be 1.

The sigmoid function can also be used for the activation of hidden units. But it shouldn't be used in hidden layers because its derivative with respect to input values (coming from affine transformed features) for large (positive or negative) values is almost zero. Let's take a closer look at this problem.

We know that the repeated application of the chain rule of differentiation in the neural network means multiplying partial derivatives of two consecutive composite functions. Now consider multiple composite neural layer functions (dense, for instance) with sigmoid as the activation function. The gradient of sigmoid activated values with respect to affine-transformed values $\partial x^{(l)}/\partial z^{(l)}$ (which are sigmoid's input) will require to be multiplied with the Jacobian of affine-transformed values with respect to its weight parameters matrix $\partial z^{(l)}/\partial W^{(l)}$. Using the chain rule, we get the following equation:

$$\frac{\partial L}{\partial W^{(l)}} = \frac{\partial L}{\partial X^{(l)}} \cdot \frac{\partial X^{(l)}}{\partial Z^{(l)}} \cdot \frac{\partial Z^{(l)}}{\partial W^{(l)}} \tag{5.19}$$

We know that the affine transformation $z^{(l)}$ for any dense layer is the matrix multiplication of the previous layer's activation $x^{(l-1)}$ with the current layer's weight matrix $W^{(l)}$ and addition of a bias vector $b^{(l)}$. This transformation is then activated to produce the activated features vector $x^{(l)}$. This is simply a dense layer operation.

Let's take a closer look at the middle term in the preceding equation which is the gradient of activation $x^{(l)}$ vector with respect to affine-transformed vector $z^{(l)}$:

$$\frac{\partial X^{(l)}}{\partial Z^{(l)}} = \sigma'\left(X^{(l-1)} \times W^{(l)} + b^{(l)}\right) \tag{5.20}$$

Here, $\sigma'(.)$ is the derivative of the sigmoid function given by following equation and is shown in Figure 5-8:

$$\sigma'(x) = \sigma(x)(1-\sigma(x)) = \frac{e^{-x}}{(e^{-x}+1)^2} \tag{5.21}$$

Remember: We are using activations to bind the input values in a small range. This is because affine transformations can make values large. During error backpropagation, we have to pass these transformed features through derivative activation functions. When we input a large (positive or negative) value (for instance, $\mathbf{x}^{(l-1)} \times \mathbf{W}^{(l)} + \mathbf{b}^{(l)}$ in Equation 5.20) through the sigmoid derivative function $\sigma'(.)$, the output can be very close to zero (see Figure 5-8). That is, the value of activation with respect to affine-transformed $\partial\mathbf{x}^{(l)}/\partial\mathbf{z}^{(l)}$ in the chain rule when multiplied with other derivatives gives almost zero derivative of the loss scalar with respect to the weight matrix, as shown in the following:

$$\frac{\partial L}{\partial \mathbf{W}^{(l)}} = \frac{\partial L}{\partial \mathbf{X}^{(l)}} \cdot (\text{close to } 0) \cdot \frac{\partial \mathbf{Z}^{(l)}}{\partial \mathbf{W}^{(l)}} \tag{5.22}$$

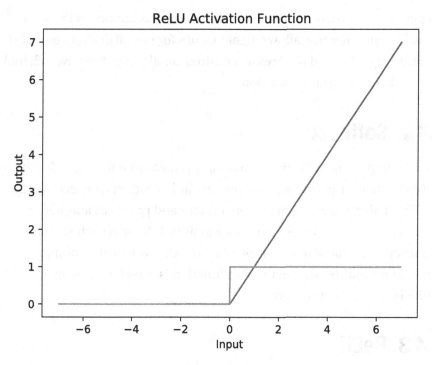

Figure 5-11. *The graph of the ReLU activation function (in blue) and its derivative (in orange)*

During training, we use the Jacobian $\partial L / \partial \mathbf{W}^{(l)}$ and gradient of $\partial L / \partial \mathbf{b}^{(l)}$ loss with respect to each layer's l parameters $\mathbf{W}$ and $\mathbf{b}$ to update their values via the gradient-based optimization technique. When the gradient of the activation function with respect to transformed features is small, the partial derivative of loss with respect to parameters is also small. This means we are barely making any updates to the parameters and, therefore, the neural network is barely learning anything! This is called the *vanishing gradient problem*. And when the network becomes deeper, this problem becomes much more severe. This is because many small values will be multiplied together along the depth. The partial derivatives with respect to parameters of layers closer to the loss function will have small values, whereas those far away from the loss function (closer to the input layer) might have zero partial derivatives! This is why it is important to use an activation function that allows higher values for partial derivatives and still binds the transformed features in a desired small range. Next, we will look at some better activation functions.

5.4.2 Softmax

Another important activation function, specifically for the logits, is the softmax function, given by Equation 5.16 and introduced in Section 5.2.

This activation function acts on a vector and produces another vector whose sum of all its elements equals to 1. It turns each element (representing a class) into a probability. In other words, the softmax function normalizes the vector. This function is used for learning a multiclass classification task.

5.4.3 ReLU

In early years of neural network research, the sigmoid function was used heavily as the activation function of hidden units, but now the trends have changed. Let us take a look at a famous activation function called *rectified linear unit* (ReLU) (Jarrett et al., 2009; Nair and Hinton, 2010; Glorot et al., 2011) given by the following equation and is shown in Figure 5-11:

$$\text{ReLU}(x) = \max(0, x) \qquad (5.23)$$

The ReLU activation acts as a linear function (whose output is equal to its input value) for input feature x in range $[0, \infty)$ but clamps the negative values to zero. This activation function is a go-to choice for hidden units. Also note that ReLU is non-differentiable at zero input. It is because its limit approaching from left (lower value by adding a very small number $h \to 0$) to zero, at zero, and approaching from right (higher value by subtracting a very small number $h \to 0$) to zero does not exist; and, therefore, the ReLU function is not continuous. (Remember a function must be continuous to be differentiable.)

In simple words, derivatives approaching from left and right, and at zero, are not equal. This makes ReLU discontinuous at zero. But in software implementation, the derivative of ReLU is intentionally set equal to zero for allowing gradient computation so that the network can learn.

But what about the solution to the gradient vanishing problem? Let us look at ReLU's derivative function:

$$\text{ReLU}'(x) = \begin{cases} 1, & \text{if } x > 0 \\ 0, & \text{if } x \leq 0 \end{cases} \tag{5.24}$$

We can see that we won't get very small derivative values for large transformed features but 1. So ReLU mitigates the gradient vanishing problem. But there is one problem with ReLU's derivative. If the transformed feature value is either zero or negative, then the gradient of ReLU with respect to that feature value will be zero. This is problematic because if many transformed feature values are zero or negative, the resulting zero partial derivative won't provide any direction to the parameters affected in the chain rule application for parameters update. This is called the *dying ReLU* or *dead ReLU* problem. Many improvements have been made to ReLU recently and are discussed next.

5.4.4 ELU

One improvement to ReLU is *exponential linear unit* (ELU), researched by (Clevert et al., 2015), shown in Figure 5-12, which has been shown to perform well for image recognition tasks. The equation for ELU is as follows:

$$\text{ELU}(x) = \begin{cases} x, & \text{if } x > 0 \\ \alpha(e^x - 1), & \text{if } x < 0 \end{cases} \tag{5.25}$$

Just like ReLU, it emits the same value if input x is greater than zero. When input is less than zero, the output value is slightly smaller than zero. This way, ELU mitigates the dead ReLU problem to some extent. The constant term α is commonly set between 0.1 and 0.3, that is, $\alpha \in [0.1, 0.3]$.

The derivative of the ELU function (shown in Figure 5-12) is as follows:

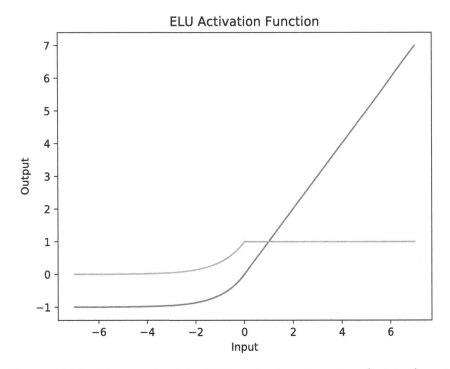

Figure 5-12. The graph of the ELU activation function (in blue) and its derivative with $\alpha = 0.2$ (in orange)

$$ELU(x) = \begin{cases} 1, & \text{if } x > 0 \\ ELU(x) + \alpha, & \text{if } x \le 0 \end{cases} \qquad (5.26)$$

We can see that for input x greater than zero, the derivative is 1. For input less than or equal to zero, the derivative is ELU of input plus α value. With this behavior, we avoid the dead ReLU problem. But a downside of ELU is that due to the introduction of exponential function e^x, ELU is a bit more computationally expensive than ReLU.

5.4.5 Leaky ReLU

The *leaky rectified linear unit* (LeakyReLU, in short) activation function (Maas et al., 2013) avoids the exponential term problem with ELU and is given by the following equation:

$$\text{LeakyReLU}(x) = \max(0, x) + \alpha \cdot \min(0, x) \tag{5.27}$$

You may either write it as follows:

$$\text{LeakyReLU}(x) = \begin{cases} x, & \text{if } x > 0 \\ \alpha x, & \text{if } x \leq 0. \end{cases} \tag{5.28}$$

The LeakyReLU sets output equal to input x if input is greater than zero. In the other case, we scale the negative input with small α term (called *negative slope*) usually set equal to 0.01:

$$\text{LeakyReLU}'(x) = \begin{cases} 1, & \text{if } x > 0 \\ \alpha, & \text{if } x \leq 0. \end{cases} \tag{5.29}$$

Looking at the derivative of LeakyReLU, we can see output is 1 if input x is less than or equal to zero and α otherwise. The derivative of LeakyReLU is linear where it is simply equal to α (or 0.01, in our choice) for zero and negative values and, therefore, avoids the dead ReLU problem.

Note that, similar to ReLU, LeakyReLU is also non-differentiable at zero but is intentionally made differentiable. Furthermore, LeakyReLU does not involve any exponential function computation like ELU, so it is way less computationally expensive.

5.4.6 SELU

All the activations discussed so far have the gradient exploding problem. With a recently introduced activation function called *scaled exponential linear unit* (Klambauer et al., 2017) (or SELU in short and shown in Figure 5-13), the vanishing and exploding gradient problems are just not possible at all (see theorems 2 and 3 in the appendix of (Klambauer et al., 2017) research! Under certain situations, when the network's parameters are initialized with the LeCun initialization technique and the network uses alpha dropout, then with SELU activations in every hidden layer, the network self-normalizes automatically. And the network can be considered to be a Gaussian distribution.

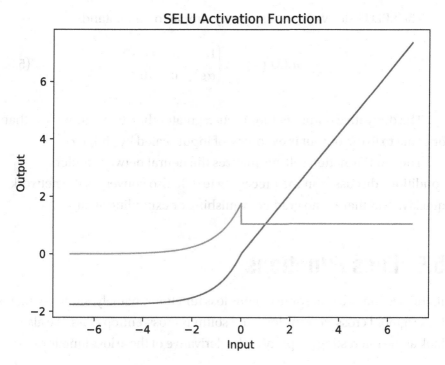

Figure 5-13. *The graph of the SELU activation function (in blue) and its derivative (in orange)*

Interestingly, the equation of SELU is easy to understand:

$$\text{SELU}(x) = \lambda \begin{cases} x, & \text{if } x > 0 \\ \alpha(e^x - 1), & \text{if } x \leq 0 \end{cases} \tag{5.30}$$

The output is the input x itself if input is greater than 0. On the other hand, if input is less than or equal to 0, then output is the exponent of input scaled by alpha α and a subtraction of alpha α from it.

What about the values of alpha α and lambda λ? The authors of (Klambauer et al., 2017) precisely calculated their values as follows and they are constant:

$$a \approx 1.6732632423543772848170429916717 \tag{5.31}$$

$$\lambda \approx 1.0507009873554804934193349852946 \tag{5.32}$$

The SELU's derivative is also pretty simple to understandL

$$\text{SELU}'(x) = \lambda \begin{cases} 1, & \text{if } x > 0 \\ \alpha e^x, & \text{if } x \leq 0 \end{cases} \qquad (5.33)$$

The derivative output is 1 for input x greater than 0. For input less than or equal to 0, the output is exponent of input scaled by alpha α.

The SELU function self-normalizes the neural network under conditions discussed in the preceding text. It also converges the network quickly. And there is no gradient vanishing or exploding at all.

5.5 Loss Functions

In this section, we visit some famous loss functions, namely, sum-of-squares loss, sigmoid cross-entropy loss, and softmax cross-entropy loss. We also look at the interesting property of the derivative of these loss functions.

5.5.1 Sum of Squares

The probability of observing a target distribution conditioned on the sample distribution is given by the following equation:

$$P(\mathbf{t}|\mathbf{x}) = \prod_{k=1}^{K} P(t_k|\mathbf{x}) \qquad (5.34)$$

For a regression task, we assume that the target distribution is a deterministic function of sample $\mathbf{x}$ with added small Gaussian noise. We will not be going into the derivation of this loss function, but following this assumption, we get the sum-of-squares loss function as follows:

$$L(\mathbf{y}, \mathbf{t}) = \frac{1}{2} \sum_{n=1}^{N} \sum_{k=1}^{K} \left(y_k^{(n)} - t_k^{(n)} \right)^2 \qquad (5.35)$$

And now if there is only one target variable, then the output is also a scalar, and the sum-of-squares loss function becomes the following:

$$L(\mathbf{y}, \mathbf{t}) = \frac{1}{2} \sum_{n=1}^{N} \left(y^{(n)} - t^{(n)} \right)^2 \tag{5.36}$$

Here, we assume the identity (or linear) activation function applied on the logit $z^{(n)}$. So the partial derivative of error with respect to logit simply turns out to be as follows:

$$\frac{\partial e}{\partial z^{(n)}} = y^{(n)} - t^{(n)} \tag{5.37}$$

Although the sum-of-squares loss function can learn a conditional mapping of target distribution given the sample distribution, it assumes that targets belong to Gaussian distribution, whereas classes representing targets are essentially binary variables which cannot be modeled with this loss function. Therefore, we resort to cross-entropy loss functions for classification tasks discussed next.

5.5.2 Sigmoid Cross-Entropy

When we perform a binary classification task, the output distribution of the neural network is represented as Bernoulli distribution by applying the sigmoid activation function. The probability of observing a class conditioned on the sample is given by the following equation:

$$P(t|\mathbf{x}) = y^t (1 - y)^{1-t} \tag{5.38}$$

The likelihood of observing the data-generating distribution with model distribution $P(t|\mathbf{x})$ is given by the following equation:

$$\mathcal{L} = \prod_{n=1}^{N} \left(y^{(n)} \right)^{t^{(n)}} \left(1 - y^{(n)} \right)^{\left(1 - t^{(n)} \right)} \tag{5.39}$$

When we take the negative logarithm of this likelihood function (5.39), we get the cross-entropy loss for two classes given by the following equation:

$$L(\mathbf{y}, \mathbf{t}) = -\ln\mathcal{L} = -\sum_{n=1}^{N} \left(t^{(n)} \ln y^{(n)} + \left(1 - t^{(n)}\right) \ln\left(1 - y^{(n)}\right) \right) \tag{5.40}$$

As described in Section 1.3, we minimize this negative log-likelihood which is equivalent to maximizing the likelihood of data distribution. Note that the total error is simply the sum of individual errors for each prediction and target pair. The derivative of error with respect to logit $z^{(n)}$ for the nth pattern (or sample) turns out to be as follows:

$$\frac{\partial e}{\partial z^{(n)}} = y^{(n)} - t^{(n)} \tag{5.41}$$

Next, we look at softmax cross-entropy which allows us to model multinomial distribution of outputs for a multiclass classification task.

5.5.3 Softmax Cross-Entropy

When we perform a multiclass classification task, the output distribution of the neural network is represented as Multinoulli distribution by applying the softmax activation function (see Equation 5.16). The probability of observing a class conditioned on the sample is given by the following equation:

$$P\left(\mathbf{t}^{(n)}\middle|\mathbf{x}^{(n)}\right) = \prod_{k=1}^{K} \left(y_k^{(n)}\right)^{t_k^{(n)}} \tag{5.42}$$

The likelihood of observing the data-generating distribution with model distribution $P(\mathbf{t}^{(n)}|\mathbf{x}^{(n)})$ is given by the following equation:

$$\mathcal{L} = \prod_{n=1}^{N} P\left(\mathbf{t}^{(n)}\middle|\mathbf{x}^{(n)}\right) = \prod_{n=1}^{N} \prod_{k=1}^{K} \left(y_k^{(n)}\right)^{t_k^{(n)}} \tag{5.43}$$

When we take the negative logarithm of the likelihood function, we get the cross-entropy loss for multiple classes given by the following equation:

$$L(\mathbf{y}, \mathbf{t}) = -\ln \mathcal{L} = -\sum_{n=1}^{N} \sum_{k=1}^{K} t_k^{(n)} \ln y_k^{(n)} \tag{5.44}$$

As described in Section 1.3, we minimize this negative log-likelihood which is equivalent to maximizing the likelihood of data distribution. Note that here total error is simply the sum of individual errors over each class in pairs of prediction and target vectors. The derivative of error with respect to logit $z^{(n)}$ for the nth pattern (or sample) and kth class turns out to be as follows:

$$\frac{\partial e}{\partial z_k^{(n)}} = y_k^{(n)} - t_k^{(n)} \tag{5.45}$$

Notice that the choice of activation and loss functions pair very well that the partial derivatives of sum-of-squares, sigmoid, and softmax cross-entropy losses with respect to their respective logits take the same form.

Now we take a deeper look at the most commonly used optimization techniques to train the neural networks.

5.6 Optimization

There are two types of optimization, namely, unconstrained (gradient based; we focus on this) and constrained (convex optimization). Our aim is to find the global minima of the function to generalize better to unseen datapoints, but for non-convex functions, it's difficult to find the global minima. So, in deep learning, we try to find the local minima as close as possible to the global minima (whose exact value is unknown). In the case of convex functions, there exists only one minima, that is, local minima is equal to the desired global minima, but these functions are less expressive.

5.6.1 Gradient Descent

The training of parameterized models is performed by maximizing the likelihood function. This requires us to modify the parameters of the model so as to mimic the data-generating distribution. We do so by updating the parameter values by using the gradient information of loss with respect to these parameters and performing the gradient descent, as discussed next.

5.6.1.1 Batch Gradient Descent

When we consider the whole dataset for computing the gradient of loss with respect to the model and use it further to update the parameters, then this approach is called *batch gradient descent*. It approximates the truest gradient of error between predictions and targets with respect to the model to descend.

For dataset $\mathbb{D} = \{(\mathbf{x}^{(i)}, \mathbf{t}^{(i)})\}$, the loss with respect to the parameters vector θ is given by L. And the gradient of scalar loss L with respect to the parameters θ at time step τ is given as $\nabla_{\theta_{(\tau)}} L$. This gradient can then be used to compute an update for parameters at next time step $\theta_{(\tau + 1)}$ with the following gradient descent equation:

$$\theta_{(\tau+1)} \leftarrow \theta_{(\tau)} - \eta \nabla_{\theta_{(\tau)}} L(\mathbb{D};\theta) \tag{5.46}$$

This computes the derivative for all datapoints in a dataset with respect to all the parameters at each time step of parameters update. This is highly computationally expensive because in practice the size of a dataset can range from gigabytes to even petabytes. And because of memory constraints in physical devices (CPU, GPU, and TPU in the context of deep learning), all the data cannot be loaded in memory. To address this issue, there are two approaches to compute the gradient approximating the whole dataset, namely, online gradient descent and stochastic gradient descent, described next.

5.6.1.2 Online Gradient Descent

In practice, real-world datasets are very large in size. And computing the gradient of loss over the whole dataset at each training step can be highly compute demanding. But one can choose to use error information of only a single datapoint to compute gradients which can be used for updating the parameters of a model. Doing this repeatedly for each datapoint in a dataset can improve the overall performance of a model. This approach is called *online gradient descent* and was presented in Section 5.1.

Online gradient descent is useful for real-world applications where datapoints coming in streams can be used for improving learning systems (Bishop, 2006). This technique can work for generative modeling, but for supervised learning, its label must be known ahead of time. In the case of semi-supervised learning, the prediction by the model can be used as target for an unseen input datapoint which can, hopefully, improve the model's performance.

Denoting loss for ith datapoint $\mathbf{x}^{(i)}$ as $\boldsymbol{L}^{(i)}$ gives the gradient of loss with respect to the parameters θ at time step τ as $\nabla_{\theta_{(\tau)}} L^{(i)}$. This gradient can then be used to compute an update for parameters at next time step $\theta_{(\tau+1)}$ with the following gradient descent equation:

$$\theta_{(\tau+1)} \leftarrow \theta_{(\tau)} - \eta \nabla_{\theta_{(\tau)}} L\left(\mathbf{x}^{(i)}, \mathbf{t}^{(i)}; \theta\right) \tag{5.47}$$

Here, $\eta \in (0,1]$ is a small non-zero positive *step size* also famously known as *learning rate*. Since the gradient values can be large, the learning rate is used to control the size of update steps taken. Furthermore, the loss function's gradient gives the direction in which the scalar output value of the loss function increases the most. Conversely, the negative gradient gives the direction in which L decreases the most. Since we want the error between prediction and target values to be close to zero, we achieve this by taking small steps in the negative direction of the gradient. This is the gradient descent algorithm given by Equation 5.47.

5.6.1.3 Stochastic Gradient Descent

Stochastic gradient descent (SGD), also called *mini-batch gradient descent*, takes a radical approach to compute gradients by incorporating the best of both worlds. It computes the gradient of a small set of examples. Because a small sample of datapoints statistically describe the dataset itself, its gradients are also roughly similar to approximating the whole dataset's gradient.

For a set of m mini-batch samples (usually ranging from 10 to 256 in count), the stochastic gradient descent computes the partial derivatives for m samples $\mathbb{D}^{(i:i+m)}$. This gives the following mini-batch stochastic gradient descent update step:

$$\theta_{(\tau+1)} \leftarrow \theta_{(\tau)} - \eta \nabla_{\theta_{(\tau)}} L\left(\mathbf{x}^{(i:i+m)}, \mathbf{t}^{(i:i+m)}; \theta\right) \tag{5.48}$$

Here, the gradient is computed for m samples from the dataset $\mathbb{D}$ with respect to the parameters of the model which is then used to update its parameters. Although we have sampled a subset of samples in a sequence, in practice, we prefer to sample them randomly to invoke stochasticity while training. This also causes a regularizing effect in the model.

The stochastic gradient descent technique also converges the model faster than and performs close to the batch gradient descent technique. The techniques described next follow the same idea of gradient descent but introduce some modifications to it for faster and better convergence.

5.6.2 Momentum

Learning with SGD can be slow. Setting the learning rate too low can slow down the learning process or might even trap the loss function in the local minima. On the other hand, a high learning rate although gets us faster to lower loss, but it might keep the low loss value oscillate around the optima and might even diverge the training.

Momentum accelerates the learning by taking the average of past gradients into account. This way it also dampens the oscillations:

$$v_{(\tau)} = \gamma v_{(\tau-1)} + \eta \nabla_{\theta_{(\tau)}} L \tag{5.49}$$

The update is as follows:

$$\theta_{(\tau+1)} \leftarrow \theta_{(\tau)} - v_{(\tau)} \tag{5.50}$$

The value of momentum term γ is usually chosen from a set of values $\{0.5, 0.9, 0.999\}$.

Next, we look at some regularization techniques to generalize deep neural networks.

5.7 Regularization

Deep neural networks are prone to overfit the model in various cases such as less number of training samples, large number of parameters, and others. This prevents the model from generalizing well to unseen samples. But we can apply regularization to the different components of the machine learning algorithm such as dataset, architecture, loss function, and optimization method. *Regularization* is any modification made to the data, model, loss function, or optimizer so as to reduce the model's generalization error. We will discuss various strategies to regularize the model by making changes in different parts of the algorithm.

5.7.1 Dataset

We know the dataset serves as experience to the model for learning. So the dataset should exhibit a good statistical description of data we want to perform well on, that is, unseen datapoints. Here, we discuss two techniques to make this possible.

5.7.1.1 Data Augmentation

Because deep neural networks have a large number of learnable parameters, the model can easily fine-tune itself to the training set (if it is small in size) and, therefore, overfit. The simplest way to generalize the model is to train it on a very large dataset. But, in practice, it is difficult to obtain a large labeled dataset. Instead of looking for more data samples, we can augment the dataset by appending a modified version of available samples to the same dataset. In the case of an image dataset, we can apply the following transformation to each sample (even multiple times with stochasticity), cropping with random sizes, flipping horizontally and vertically with some probability, and varying the contrast, brightness, and other configurations of image datapoints. (Krizhevsky et al., 2017) showed that data augmentation helps in regularizing deep neural networks (for an image classification task, in their case).

5.7.1.2 Adversarial Training

The state-of-the-art neural networks are known to perform as good as and, in some cases, even better than humans, for instance, identifying the object in an image. Although these neural networks are powerful and generalize well to unseen samples, still, they are susceptible to highly engineered datapoints (Szegedy et al., 2013) called adversarial examples. We have already briefly understood the idea of adversarial examples in Subsection 1.6.2. In order to make the neural network more robust to unseen samples, we can generate and add adversarial samples to the training set. Training the model on adversarial examples, called *adversarial training*, helps in regularizing the neural networks and, therefore, increases the model's performance on the test set.

We briefly mention a single pro and con of adversarial samples. At the time of writing, Google search uses image captcha contacting adversarial samples and requires the human to classify the image. This is done to prevent an automated program from accessing the website iteratively which might overload the servers. A negative use case of adversarial examples is to create the adversarial samples of road signs that look fine to humans but fool the convolutional networks (which process the image stream from a self-driving car's front camera). In this scenario, the adversarial examples can be fatal, for instance, if the sign board is meant for signaling the driver to slow down because the road is being constructed, but the car understands it as speed limit as 60 mph, so then it is highly probable that an accident will occur.

5.7.2 Architecture

The learning component of a machine learning algorithm is the model. The model is very much vulnerable to overfit the dataset. To prevent this problem, we present two techniques to regularize the model.

5.7.2.1 Units Dropout

The simplest way to achieve good accuracy on any test set is by training on an ensemble of models and evaluating each test sample with each of the models, the predictions of which are averaged (separately for each test sample). (Szegedy et al., 2015) won the ILSVRC competition with an ensemble of six models. But training and inferencing many neural network models become impractical for real-world applications.

A simpler technique that can learn an exponential number of models by just training one model is dropout. The *dropout* (Srivastava et al., 2014) technique simply shuts down multiple activation units of a layer with some probability defined before training. This is usually done by element-wise multiplying a binary mask whose values are randomly sampled from Bernoulli distribution with a probability p where $p \in [0,1]$. In practice, we usually apply dropout for a hidden layer and set the value of p either 0.5 or 0.8. Dropout can be thought of as learning an ensemble of models with just a single model in a memory- and computationally efficient way.

5.7.2.2 Knowledge Distillation

Another way to circumvent the problem of having to use an ensemble of models for highly accurate prediction is to use the knowledge distillation technique. The idea of *knowledge distillation* is to transfer the knowledge of a cumbersome model (bulky or an ensemble of models) into a single small model. (Hinton et al., 2015) showed that it is possible to have good classification accuracy gains in a small model if the cumbersome model exhibits good generalization.

When the small model is trained on the same dataset as the cumbersome model independently, it has decent performance (less than the cumbersome model). But when it is trained with the same training technique (optimizer and other hyper-parameters) using the predictions of the cumbersome model as soft targets, it outperforms the previous small model. This shows that a small model is less capable of learning the dataset mapping accurately by itself from scratch than learning the mapping by using the knowledge of a generalized cumbersome model. The loss function used in knowledge transfer by a small model includes minimizing (a) the error between soft targets predicted by the cumbersome model and predictions of small model and (b) the error between true targets and predictions of the small model for a given sample.

Knowledge distillation is good for practical applications in production because it helps in training a model quickly which has less inference time, therefore low latency in production, and a lightweight, better-performing model.

5.7.3 Loss Function

The loss function plays an important role in training the model. It defines the objective for the learning algorithm to achieve. But we can enforce some constraints on the loss function to cause a regularizing effect to the model.

5.7.3.1 Norm Penalties

We usually train models with a large number of parameters. In practice, a model's parameters might finely tune themselves (i.e., overfit) to the training dataset for correct predictions. If you look closely at the individual parameters, you'll notice that values have become very large in positive and negative directions, which is usually the reason of overfitting. This problem can be prevented by regularizing the model by enforcing some constraints on the size of the model's parameters in the loss function. There are mainly two norm penalties used in deep learning, namely, L^1 and L^2 norm penalties.

The L^1 norm penalty term added to loss function is written as follows:

$$\overline{L}(\mathbf{x};\theta) = L(\mathbf{x};\theta) + \|\mathbf{w}\|_1 \tag{5.51}$$

Here, $\|\mathbf{w}\|_1$ is the L^1 norm of weight parameters which is added to the original loss function $L(\mathbf{x};\theta)$ to give rise to the modified loss function $\overline{L}(\mathbf{x};\theta)$. The term $\|\mathbf{w}\|_1 = \sum_i |w_i|$ is the sum of absolute values of individual weights. Another norm penalty of great interest to the community is the L^2 norm penalty which we have already discussed in Subsection 1.4.5. Please refer to it for details and also see Subsection 2.1.4 for details on the importance of each of these norms.

5.7.4 Optimization

It is important to note that optimization can also cause the model to overfit if the model is trained for a long time. We can make modifications to the optimization technique to mitigate the overfitting problem in the model.

5.7.4.1 Early Stopping

Neural networks with a large number of parameters are capable of overfitting to the training dataset. When we train the model, the validation error also decreases with the decrease in the training error. But after iterating through a number of epochs, the validation error might start increasing, therefore worsening our model's performance. The best-known, reliable, and easiest method to prevent this problem is to store a set of parameters after every time there is a decrease in validation error and return the parameters of the model with the lowest validation error when the training termination condition is met. This technique is known as *early stopping*. One may also terminate the training process when the validation error doesn't decrease further for a predefined number of iteration steps.

5.7.4.2 Gradient Clipping

We know that when the gradient vanishes or explodes, then the model is unable to learn and, therefore, cannot perform well on unseen samples and is less generalized. In Section 5.4, we looked at some activation functions that can help in mitigating gradient vanishing and exploding problems. Here, we look at a simpler technique to mitigate this problem without any modifications to the model's architecture. We can regularize the optimization process by performing some modifications to the gradient vector before taking the optimization step.

Contemporarily, most famously used techniques for clipping the gradients by the deep learning community were introduced by (Mikolov et al., 2012) and (Pascanu et al., 2013). Note that both techniques are known to yield similar results.

The first approach (Mikolov et al., 2012) is to *clip (or clamp, bound) the gradient* of all parameters in a mini-batch and then perform the optimization step. The second approach (Pascanu et al., 2013) is to *clip the norm of gradient* (see Equation 5.52) and then perform the optimization step:

$$\nabla_\theta L \leftarrow \frac{\nabla_\theta L \cdot v}{\|\nabla_\theta L\|}, \text{if } \|\nabla_\theta L\| > v \tag{5.52}$$

Here, v is called the norm threshold, and $\nabla_\theta L$ is the gradient of loss with respect to the parameters of model. The norm is usually chosen to be Euclidean norm, and if it is greater than the threshold, we perform the gradient norm clipping, whereas the vanilla gradient clipping is applied without any conditions. In the second approach, you can think of updating the gradient by first normalizing it (i.e., dividing it with the gradient vector's length from origin via Euclidean norm) and then scaling it with the gradient threshold term v.

5.7.4.3 Learning Rate Dropout

Adaptive learning rate–based optimizers are known to converge the loss function quickly to the local minima, but they usually get stuck in saddle points and make the optimization difficult. The vanilla stochastic gradient descent with momentum is known to find a good local minima and is less prone to getting stuck at saddle points but is very slow at converging the loss function. But we would like to have speedy convergence to a good local minima without compromising either. This can be achieved by using learning rate dropout (LRD) (Lin et al., 2019) on adaptive learning rate–based optimizers.

The idea of *learning rate dropout* is similar to units dropout discussed in the preceding text. We simply drop a set of learning rates from a sample of parameters per layer with probability p. This is achieved by applying Hadamard product between a binary mask (sampled from Bernoulli distribution) and the learning rate for each parameter in that layer.

The learning rate dropout helps in finding new stochastic paths for the loss function to descend along making the convergence more robust to saddle points and poor local minima.

5.8 Summary

In this chapter, we studied various concepts related to neural networks starting from fundamentals and finishing with advanced topics. We first understood the differences between input and parameters optimizations. We studied various linear models concerned with the regression task (i.e., linear, polynomial, and multiple regression models) and classification task (i.e., binary and multiclass classification models). Then we understood deep neural networks or more specifically dense neural networks. Then we visited various activation functions and analyzed them. We also looked at three commonly used loss functions. Then we focused on different gradient-based optimization techniques and regularization techniques.

We will now study convolutional neural networks in the next chapter which are specially designed for solving the computer vision problems with deep learning.

CHAPTER 6

Computer Vision

All models are wrong, but some are useful.[1]

—*George Box*

In this chapter, we will understand the role of deep learning in computer vision tasks. In Section 6.1, we discuss a special neural network, called convolutional neural network, designed to solve computer vision problems. It has some major advantages (Section 6.2) over dense neural networks discussed in Chapter 5. We introduce a technique for mitigating the gradient vanishing problem (Section 6.3). In Section 6.4, we implement a deep convolutional neural network to perform an image classification task. Finally, we conclude the chapter and book in Section 6.5.

6.1 Convolutional Neural Network

In this section, we discuss an important class of neural networks known as convolutional neural networks (LeCun et al., 1989). Convolutional neural networks, also called convolutional networks or simply ConvNet, were invented to process grid-like data having some spatially local informative features. For example, in a 2D image, small patches in different locations might contain a ball, face, and other things. A 1D time series data such as speech might contain phonetic sounds in different time frame segments.

---

[1]Quoted from (Box, 1976).

© Rahul Bhalley 2021
R. Bhalley, *Deep Learning with Swift for TensorFlow*,
https://doi.org/10.1007/978-1-4842-6330-3_6

Convolutional networks learn many small parameters tensors called filters which are helpful for extracting basic features. In the context of an image, features include edges, curves, object shapes, color gradients, and so on, whereas in the context of an audio waveform, the basic features of speech might include phones, intonations, timbre, and so on.

We entered the deep neural network regime, in Chapter 5, by introducing dense neural networks. A dense network-based image classifier is suitable for image data with small dimension size, say 784-dimensions from MNIST dataset. But when the input image size increases, then the number of parameters in the dense network grows very quickly. We have seen that parameters in the dense layer are connections from every unit in the previous layer (m units) to every unit in the current layer (n units). Here, the total number of connections from the previous to the current layer is $m \times n$. If we increase the capacity of the layer by increasing either of the layer's units, then the number of parameters increases very quickly. For example, consider an image of dimensions $32 \times 32 \times 3$ which has 3,072 features (pixel values) in total. Now, if the first layer has 1,024 feature units, then the total number of parameters is $(3{,}072 \times 1{,}024) + 1{,}024$ (additional 1,024 are biases) $= 3{,}146{,}752$. For now, this seems like a manageable number of parameters from the memory viewpoint. But if we consider an image of a reasonable size $224 \times 224 \times 3$, then the number of parameters quickly reaches around 154 millions, or precisely 154,141,696, and this is just the first layer! This is the intrinsic nature of the dense layer that does not let the dense neural networks to scale with large input dimension sizes and large numbers of features in hidden activations. It becomes difficult to use dense networks in real-world computer vision applications because, in practice, the image datapoint is usually large in size. The convolution layer circumvents these problems by its intrinsic design (Section 6.2) which motivates us to use convolutional networks over dense networks to process data of large dimension sizes.

Unlike matrix multiplication in the dense layer, the convolution layer uses a mathematical operation called convolution which gave these networks the name convolutional neural networks. This simple operation is what makes convolutional networks so unique from other neural networks in deep learning literature. In general, a neural network is called a convolutional network if at least one layer in the network uses a convolution operation (Goodfellow et al., 2016). Based on current research trends in deep learning, this definition might not always help in classifying the network because the whole network might be composed of different kinds of neural layers. For example, networks such as LSTNet (Lai et al., 2018) and Tacotron 2 (Shen et al., 2018) contain both convolution and recurrent layers which confuses the classification of these networks as either recurrent networks or convolutional networks following this definition. On the other hand, attention mechanism is used in dense networks (Vaswani et al., 2017) and even convolutional networks (Parmar et al., 2018; Li et al., 2019). We emphasize that a better description of the network is that it is composed of certain blocks (containing few neural layer instances of either homogeneous or heterogeneous types) instead of naming a neural network based on a single-layer operation. If a neural network uses same operation in each layer we might name that neural network prefixed by that operation such as convolutional neural network, recurrent neural network, and so on.

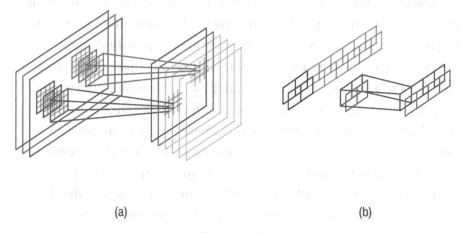

(a)   (b)

Figure 6-1. *Abstract diagrammatic view of the convolution operation on (a) an RGB image and (b) two-channel stereo audio tensors*

Both features and kernel tensors have the same depth dimension size but different spatial dimension sizes where the kernel is spatially smaller. Each kernel produces a single map of features with depth dimension size 1 (shown in shades of green for (a) where gray ones are created by other filters and light green for (b)). In (b) blue features are overlapped to produce a green output scalar feature, whereas in (a) checkerboard kernels are applied on input features to produce scalar features forming a rectangular shape when fully convolved.

In the following text, we explain various layers used in the convolutional network and approaches to downsample and upsample the dimensions of datapoints.

6.1.1 Convolution Layer

The basic requirement for a layer to be called a *convolutional layer* is the application of the convolution operation. We start by explaining the convolution operation in simple words (without mathematical complexity) along with the hyper-parameters involved, and then we present the formula to calculate output dimension sizes.

The convolution operation is a function of two tensors with different spatial but the same depth dimension sizes. The convolution operation begins by overlapping a spatially small portion of the *features* tensor with a *filter* tensor (also called *kernel* or *parameters*). Since the depth of both tensors is the same, the filter overlaps all the feature values within its spatial dimensions along the whole depth of the features tensor (see Figure 6-1). Then we apply the Hadamard product between these overlapping values to produce a new temporary tensor with dimension sizes the same as those of the filter. Now we sum all the values in this temporary tensor to output a scalar value. This is equivalent to the dot product operation between filter and input features tensors overlap. We then stride (or move) the same filter spatially on the features tensor to overlap another set of values. (In the context of an image, stride of (1, 2) will move the filter on the x axis by 1 pixel value and y axis by 2 pixel values, one direction at a time. But in practice, the filter is usually stridden by same amount in all axes). Now we again take dot product of filter tensor and the overlapped values of features tensor to generate another scalar number. This process is repeated until the filter has stridden the whole features tensor, once. This produces a feature map of depth dimension size 1. We will soon learn how to compute its spatial dimension sizes. This is called the *convolution operation*. In other words, convolution is an iterative application of the dot product between the features tensor overlapped by filter tensor by striding the filter until the whole features tensor is traversed once. See Figures 6-2 and 6-3 for concrete examples of the convolution operation on audio and image datapoints, respectively.

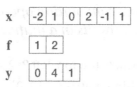

Figure 6-2. *Example of the convolution operation between input **x** and filter **f** vectors which results in a vector **y***

Here, the filter first performs the dot product with values at 0th and 1st indexes of input and produces 0 at the 0th index of the output vector. Then the filter strides by two steps to the right and again performs the dot product with overlapping input values and produces 4 at the 1st index of output. And the same process is repeated for the remaining values of input.

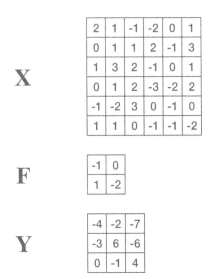

X

F

Y

Figure 6-3. *Example of the convolution operation between input* **X** *and filter* **F** *matrices which results in a matrix* **Y**

Here, filter first dot products the top-left 2x2 square matrix and produces scalar in the resulting matrix (at (0, 0) index). Then the filter strides by two steps in either the x or y axis and again performs the dot product. This process is repeated until it convolves the whole input matrix.

Since the idea of deep learning is to learn useful representation of complex patterns in data, we don't use only one filter in convolution but multiple of them. If each filter produces a single feature map, then n filters, each applying one convolution operation on the features tensor, produce n feature maps, corresponding to each filter. These feature maps are stacked along the depth dimension to create an output features tensor. The depth dimension size of the output features tensor is equal to the number of filters in the convolution layer.

Note that, mathematically speaking, a convolution operation involves only one filter and an input tensor. But in the context of deep learning, a convolution layer has one features tensor and may have multiple filters where the convolution operation is applied between the features tensor and each filter separately, to produce a new features tensor of depth dimension size the same as the number of filters.

6.1.2 Dimensions Calculation

Now we know how a convolution operation works. Here, we will discuss the calculation of output dimension sizes of the new features tensor when a filter convolves on a given features tensor.

Let us begin by assuming an arbitrary input features tensor $T \in \mathbb{R}^{a \times b \times c \times d}$ where a, b, c, and d are dimension sizes. The application of the convolution operation on input tensor T produces another features tensor $T' \in \mathbb{R}^{a' \times b' \times c' \times d'}$ where a', b', c', and d' are the corresponding output dimension sizes of those of the input features tensor.

Because the choice of features tensor is arbitrary, one may choose to replace it with a 2D audio tensor, 3D image tensor, or others with certain dimension sizes. To prevent confusions, we will assume an image tensor $I \in \mathbb{R}^{h \times w \times c}$ and audio matrix $\mathbf{A} \in \mathbb{R}^{t \times c}$ instead of arbitrary tensor T, to more concretely understand the calculation of output tensor dimension sizes. Here, h, w, c, and t are, respectively, height, width, channel (or depth), and time dimension sizes.

Let there be two filters $F_I \in \mathbb{R}^{f_h \times f_w \times c}$ and $F_A \in \mathbb{R}^{f_t \times c}$ for image I and audio A tensors, respectively, where F_I is a 3 rank tensor, $\mathbf{F}_A$ is a 2 rank tensor (or matrix), and channel c has separate values for image and audio. Here, f_h and f_w are filter sizes corresponding to height h and width w dimension sizes of image tensor I. In the case of audio tensor A, f_t is the filter size along time dimension t. Let us also consider other hyper-parameters of the convolution operation such as stride size s, zero-padding size p, and dilation factor d. (Don't worry; these are explained later.) So, with all the required terms defined, the output features tensor dimension size is calculated using the following formula:

$$o = \frac{\left(i + 2p - \left(d(f-1)+1\right)\right)}{s} + 1 \tag{6.1}$$

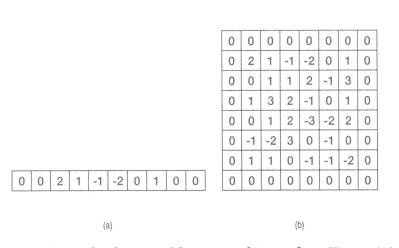

(a)   (b)

Figure 6-4. *Example of zero-padding around inputs from Figures 6-2 and 6-3. Here, (a) has a zero-padding of 2 and (b) has a zero-padding of 1*

Here, i is the input dimension size of the tensor's desired axis, and o is its corresponding output dimension size. It can be any dimension of input tensor, for instance, h, w, or t, in our case. We also specify the filter size with f which, in our case, can be either f_h, f_w, or f_t. Other variables (or hyper-parameters) that impact the output dimension size are strides s, padding size p, and dilation d. Let us get familiar with these hyper-parameters before understanding the calculation of output dimension sizes.

6.1.2.1 Stride

The stride s is the movement step of the filter in the allowed (spatial or temporal) directions (one at a time) on the input features tensor. In the context of an image, if stride is 2, the filter moves in allowed directions (x and y axes) by 2 pixel values and then dot products the overlap. Similarly, in temporal data such as audio, the filter with stride 16 will move temporally (in the x axis) by 16 samples and take a dot product between the overlaps. So *stride* is the movement step size of the filter on the tensor.

6.1.2.2 Padding

Another hyper-parameter called *padding* (or *zero-padding*) is a boundary of zero values around a features tensor's spatial or temporal dimensions along all the depth channels. The padding p is a positive integer value and is shown in Figure 6-4.

6.1.2.3 Dilation

In 2015, (Yu and Koltun, 2015) introduced a new hyper-parameter for the convolution layer called *dilation* (also known as *à trous convolution* or *convolution with holes*). The features tensor produced by convolution without dilation has a small receptive field of the previous layer. The *receptive field* is the number of features in any previous layer that are responsible for the prediction of a specific feature unit (see Figure 6-5). To increase the receptive field, we will need to increase the filter size (or number of parameter values in the filter). But one of the goals of introducing convolution layers is to reduce the memory footprint. This is where dilated convolution comes to mitigate the excess memory allocation problem. By using *dilation in filters*, we can increase the receptive field of features tensors without increasing the number of parameters in the filter. To increase the receptive field while keeping the same number of parameter values, we simply distance the parameter values by $d \in Z^+$ dilations. Normally, a filter has one dilation; and when we increase the dilation, the receptive field (between the corresponding layer and distant layers along network depth) increases. See Figure 6-6 for examples of dilated convolution. Also note that apart from the memory footprint, the dilation had many successes over past years on various tasks such as image segmentation (Yu and Koltun, 2015), raw audio waveform modeling (Oord et al., 2016a), memory efficiency and dampening of vanishing and exploding gradient problems in recurrent neural networks (Chang et al., 2017), and keyword spotting (Coucke et al., 2019), just to name a few.

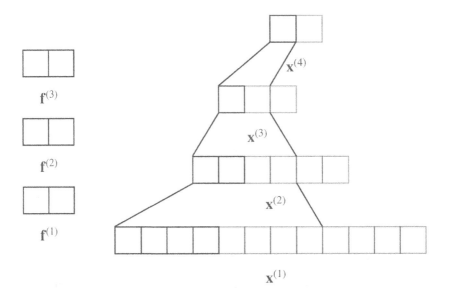

Figure 6-5. *Receptive field in a three-layer 1D convolutional network*

All the filters are 2D vectors and are applied with stride of 1 on data. Here, the receptive field of the shaded last layer's $\mathbf{x}^{(4)}$ feature unit is 2 for $\mathbf{x}^{(3)}$, 4 for $\mathbf{x}^{(2)}$, and 8 for $\mathbf{x}^{(1)}$.

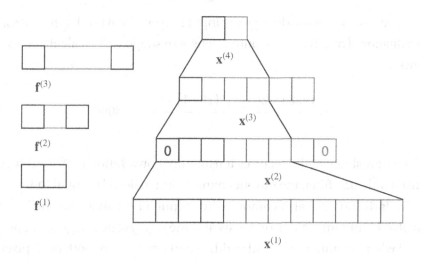

Figure 6-6. *Receptive field in a three-layer 1D dilated convolutional network*

Here, $\mathbf{f}^{(1)}$, $\mathbf{f}^{(2)}$, and $\mathbf{f}^{(3)}$ have dilation of 1, 2, and 4, respectively, and are 2D vectors. (The light-colored region in filters shows dilation and is just an empty space in which the overlapped region of input is not dot product with.) All the filters are applied with stride of 1 on data. We zero-pad with 1 unit in $\mathbf{x}^{(2)}$ to prevent heavy resolution reduction in $\mathbf{x}^{(3)}$. Here, the receptive field of the shaded last layer's $\mathbf{x}^{(4)}$ feature unit is 4 for $\mathbf{x}^{(3)}$, 6 for $\mathbf{x}^{(2)}$, and 12 for $\mathbf{x}^{(1)}$. Notice the exponential increase in the receptive field in corresponding layers of the non-dilated convolutional network. Dilation of kernels effectively increases the receptive field without increasing the memory requirement.

6.1.2.4 Examples

Let us see a simple example of an audio tensor where its shape is $\mathbb{R}^{16384 \times 2}$ where channels c are 2 and temporal length t is 16,384. This is a two-channel audio (or stereo audio) with 16,384 samples (one datapoint contains 16,384 scalar amplitude values). If we convolve it with a filter matrix $\mathbf{F}$ of shape

$\mathbb{R}^{16 \times 2}$, stride s of 4, zero-padding p the input tensor with 6 border thickness, and a dilation d of 1, we get an output tensor of shape $\mathbb{R}^{4096 \times 1}$ calculated as follows:

$$t' = \frac{16384 + 2(6) - (1(16-1)+1)}{4} + 1 = 4096$$

The new shape of the features tensor after convolution is $\mathbb{R}^{4096 \times 1}$. Since we used only one filter, the output channel dimension c' is equal to 1.

Similarly, one can also compute the output tensor shape for the convolved input image tensor. Let us assume a grayscale image of shape $\mathbb{R}^{28 \times 28 \times 1}$ where channel c is 1 and width w and height h are both of 28 pixels. The values of filter (f_h, f_w), stride s, zero-padding p, and dilation d are (5, 5), 1, 0, and 1, respectively. Following this configuration, the convolution operation produces the output width w' and height h' dimension sizes equal to 24:

$$w' = \frac{28 + 2(0) - (1(5-1)+1)}{1} + 1 = 24$$

In both these examples, the setting of dilation to 1 is the same as the normal convolution operation (which, by default, sets dilation equal to 1).

Note that you should use only those filter dimension sizes which impact the certain feature dimension size. For instance, it's appropriate to use f_w and w in this formula, together, to calculate w' because the value of f_w impacts the tensor's width dimension size w and not h. A meaningless usage of this formula would be trying to calculate h' when f_w and h are arguments to this formula.

In recent deep learning models, the encoder network in an auto-encoder and the discriminator network in generative adversarial networks usually use a convolution of filter size $\mathbb{R}^{4 \times 4}$, stride (2, 2), and padding 1. This decreases the dimension size by a factor of 2. For instance, an image of dimension $\mathbb{R}^{1024 \times 1024 \times c}$ with specified configuration gets downsampled to $\mathbb{R}^{512 \times 512 \times c'}$ size. Interestingly, when the decoder network in an auto-encoder and the generator network in generative adversarial networks use these same hyper-parameters for transposed convolution operation, we get an output features tensor of double dimension size. That is, if an image has dimensions $\mathbb{R}^{512 \times 512 \times c}$, then after applying this transposed convolution, we get a features tensor of $\mathbb{R}^{1024 \times 1024 \times c'}$ size.

In practice, a filter of size $\mathbb{R}^{2 \times 2}$ is also very commonly used. Particularly in vision models, usually the usage of larger filter sizes and strides leads to degradation in performance. Notably, some recent researches (Lin et al., 2013; Szegedy et al., 2014; Iandola et al., 2016; Oord et al., 2016a,b,c; Springenberg et al., 2014) also use $\mathbb{R}^{1 \times 1}$ filter size. This might seem weird at first, but it lets the network learn deeper representation without changing spatial dimension sizes. And also having multiple $\mathbb{R}^{1 \times 1}$ filters produces multiple output feature maps, therefore a features tensor.

Also note that, as a rule of thumb, when constructing a convolutional network for a classification task, a simple idea is to increase the depth dimension size and correspondingly decrease the spatial dimension sizes. After reaching a layer with a low number of feature units, reshape the convolved features tensor into a flat tensor which is then passed through a mini dense network. This trend has been prevalent in deep learning literature (Krizhevsky et al., 2017; Simonyan and Zisserman, 2014; Szegedy et al., 2015, 2016; Iandola et al., 2016; Tan and Le, 2019).

6.1.3 Pooling Layer

Another important layer commonly used in convolutional networks is the pooling layer. The role of the *pooling layer* is to reduce all the dimension sizes, except depth dimension size, of the features tensor. Pooling further reduces the computational requirement for a convolution operation in the following layer because its input is now a smaller features tensor. We have already used the pooling operation in our tiny image classifier in Listing 4-3.

Any pooling function takes a pool size (also called pooling window), strides, and zero-padding as its arguments. Using these arguments, the pooling function summarizes all the scalar values in a small bound (defined by a pooling window) of the features tensor with a single scalar value. The pooling function operates individually on each depth index of the features tensor which reduces the temporal, spatial, or spatiotemporal dimension sizes leaving the depth dimension size unchanged. Here, pool size is only used to determine the position of scalar values on the features tensor to pool.

In deep learning literature, we encounter various pooling operations. But here we discuss the most commonly used pooling operations, namely, max pooling and average pooling.

We know that the pool function summarizes the scalar values in position (described by a pool window) on the features tensor, in every depth dimension individually, to a single scalar number. In the case of the *max pool function*, the value of the pooled number is simply the maximum value in the pool window. The *average pool function* computes the scalar value by taking the average of all the numbers in the pool window. Just as the filter convolves over the features tensor, the pool window moves on the features tensor by a given stride value to determine the position of values to pool.

The following formula computes the dimension size of the output features tensor when a pooling function is applied on the input features tensor:

$$o = \frac{(i - f) + 2p}{s} + 1 \tag{6.2}$$

Here, i and o are the input and output dimension sizes. In the context of image features tensor $I \in \mathbb{R}^{h \times w \times c}$, i can be either width w or height h, whereas for audio features matrix $A \in \mathbb{R}^{t \times c}$, i is time t. Other arguments f, s, and p represent pool window size, stride of the pooling window, and zero-padding around the features tensor. Notice that this formula is similar to Equation 6.1, but there is no dilation argument that calculates the output dimension size when the convolution operation is applied.

Pooling is a constant function and, therefore, cannot be differentiated because there are no tunable parameters associated with it, with respect to which loss gradient could be obtained. (Zeiler and Fergus, 2012) did propose a differentiable pooling function to benefit learning from pooling operations. But it did not grow to too much popularity and has been rarely used in practice. Interestingly, (Springenberg et al., 2014) found that similar accuracy could be achieved by replacing the pooling operation with the large-stride convolution operation in convolutional networks. This approach makes the network fully convolutional and architecturally simple. A possible reason for fully convolutional networks being better than using the pool operation is that when the features tensor is downsampled (spatially) with the pool operation, some information loss occurs, whereas the convolution layer can learn to retain the information important for a task when downsampling the features tensor.

6.1.4 Upsampling

We have seen that the convolution layer downsamples the spatial size of the features tensor. This is useful when the network's output size is desired to be smaller than the input size. Most common examples of this are image classification (Krizhevsky et al., 2017), object detection (Redmon et al., 2016; Redmon and Farhadi, 2017, 2018; Girshick et al., 2014; Girshick, 2015), and audio classification (Hershey et al., 2017). However, there are situations when we require the output size to be larger than the input features tensor. Such tasks include generative modeling (Vincent et al., 2008; Radford et al., 2015) and activation feature map visualization (Zeiler and Fergus, 2014).

The upsampling of a datapoint can be achieved through the application of various upsampling layers, for instance, bicubic, nearest neighbor, and other interpolations followed by convolution (Dong et al., 2014; Kim et al., 2016) or transposed convolution (Zeiler et al., 2010).

6.1.4.1 Transposed Convolution Layer

The *transposed convolution*, also known as *fractionally strided convolution* or *deconvolution* (a misnomer), learns its own set of parameters while upsampling the features tensor. It enlarges the features tensor spatially where, just like convolution, the output depth dimension size depends on the number of filters used. The transposed convolution operation can be thought of as a reverse application of the convolution operation using the same arguments (filters, stride, padding, and dilation) which spatially upsamples the features tensor instead of downsampling it. The transposed convolution also has same properties as the convolution layer, namely, sparse connectivity, parameter sharing, and translation equivariance, discussed in Section 6.2.

Given the shape of image tensor $I \in \mathbb{R}^{h \times w \times c}$, filter $f \in \mathbb{R}^{f_h \times f_w \times c}$, and hyper-parameters, namely, strides s and padding p, we can compute the output features tensor dimension, for the transposed convolution operation, with the following formula:

$$o = s(i-1) + f - 2p \qquad (6.3)$$

Here, i and o denote the input and output features tensor's dimension sizes. Consider an image tensor of shape $\mathbb{R}^{128 \times 128 \times 3}$ and a transposed convolution operation with hyper-parameters filter size $\mathbb{R}^{6 \times 6 \times 3}$, strides of $(2, 2)$, and zero-padding of 1. When this filter is applied to the transposed convolution operation, we get an output tensor of shape $\mathbb{R}^{256 \times 256 \times 1}$. Akin to the formula in Equation 6.2, any output dimension size of an input tensor can be computed correctly when this formula is used appropriately.

6.1.4.2 Checkerboard Artifact Removal

The transposed convolution has been successfully used for image superresolution (Shi et al., 2016a) and image generation (Radford et al., 2015). But if the hyper-parameters of transposed convolution are not set correctly, it may produce checkerboard artifacts in generated data such as audio (Donahue et al., 2018) or image (Odena et al., 2016). The checkerboard artifact in images is observed as irregular brightly colored pixels, whereas in raw audio it can be interpreted as noise.

A finding by (Odena et al., 2016) suggests that using a simple upsampling operation following the convolution operation completely mitigates the checkerboard artifact problem. Although transposed convolution has more representation capacity (Shi et al., 2016b) than the upsample operation following the convolution approach, better performance is gained by the latter. The results are astounding because the checkerboard artifacts are completely eliminated in generated datapoints. Following this work the researchers can focus solely on improving the generative models that generate real-valued datapoints.

6.2 Prominent Features

It's interesting to note that convolutional networks can process tensors of arbitrary dimension sizes. There are many other important features of convolutional networks. In this section, we discuss such features and see how convolutional networks are a better choice than dense networks for various deep learning tasks, mainly related to computer vision.

6.2.1 Local Connectivity

The densely connected layers, discussed in Chapter 5, apply matrix multiplication between a parameters-containing matrix and an input feature vector (can be viewed as a matrix) to produce an output feature vector. In this case, each neuron in the output feature vector is connected to every neuron in the input feature vector. This makes the layer very dense but also unscalable to larger input tensors and model capacity (from the memory viewpoint) as discussed in Section 6.1.

The convolutional layer takes a radical approach to compute the output tensor. It considers the input features tensor and parameters tensor (called kernel or filter) which have a very small size in comparison to that of the input tensor. When a dot product is applied between the filter and input tensor, a single neuron of output tensor is produced. In other words, the output tensor's certain single neuron is connected to only a small contiguous portion of the input tensor. This is called the *receptive field* of the output tensor's neuron. In contrast, in the case of the dense layer, each output tensor neuron is connected to every neuron in the input tensor. The approach of convolution makes the connectivity in the convolutional layer sparse (or local). This also speeds up the computation.

Also note that the receptive field is usually very small between closer layers. But when the network is made deeper, the receptive field of neurons in layers farther from the input layer becomes larger.

6.2.2 Parameter Sharing

In the convolutional layer, the same kernel is repeatedly used in different locations of the input tensor to compute the output tensor. That is, a same set of parameters are shared across different locations of input. These parameters are also called *tied parameters* because the value of parameters at any location of the input is dependent on the value of same parameters in a different location. In contrast, a set of parameters in the dense layer connects an output unit to every input neuron. And every output neuron has its own separate parameters set connected to the same input neurons. This, in turn, increases the memory requirement. Moreover, such dense connection also makes it inefficient to compute output. On the other hand, all output neurons in the convolution layer have a same small set of parameters connected to contiguous input neurons. These parameters are reused in different locations of the input tensor to compute each output scalar value (dot product between the filter and input tensor overlap). The small size of parameters and sharing across different input tensor locations make the computation faster and memory efficient.

Although real-world images are large in spatial dimension sizes in comparison to the filter, the filter can automatically learn to detect (or activate certain neurons in the output tensor) basic features in input such as edges, contrast, color gradients, and so on. Convolutions when used in a raw audio waveform can learn the representation of features such as timbre, intonations, phonetic sounds, and so on. This becomes possible due to tied parameters because the fundamental patterns are similar in the whole spatial dimensions of data and can be detected in different locations using the same parameters.

6.2.3 Translation Equivariance

Due to parameter sharing, as a side effect, the convolution layer is also translation equivariant. If input is translated by some pixel values in either the x or y axis and follows the convolution operation, then the resulting tensor will be the same to the case when convolution follows the same translation operation. For instance, assume a function $f(.)$ that translates an input tensor by 5 pixels along the y axis and another function $g(.)$ that applies convolution. Now, due to the translation equivariance property, when either of these functions follows the other, the resulting tensor will be the same $f(g(x)) = g(f(x))$.

Consider recognizing a spoken word in a raw audio waveform x with convolutional neural network $f(.)$. Let us assume that a word "hello" appears from 2 to 3 seconds. So the word will be transcribed $f(x)$ in this time frame segment. Then we translate the $g(f(x))$ transcribed output to 5-6 seconds with translation function $g(.)$. This translation says that the word is recognized between 5 and 6 seconds. In the other case, say we translate the "hello" sound to time frame segment of 5-6 seconds of audio waveforms $g(x)$ and then apply convolution $f(g(x))$. Now the word will be transcribed within the time frame segment of 5-6 seconds. That means $f(g(x)) = g(f(x))$ and the convolution operation is translation equivariant.

Similarly, in the case of an image, the result of translating the image along a desired axis by some pixels and applying convolution will be the same as if we applied convolution followed by the translation function. This shows translation equivariance exhibited by convolution remains valid for different input feature dimension sizes (for data like audio or image) and their corresponding filter sizes.

Note that convolutions are not translation equivariant to all kinds of translations such as scaling, rotations, warping, and so on. Some researches (Jaderberg et al., 2015; Sabour et al., 2017; Zhang, 2019) have contributed to eliminate this problem in convolutional networks.

6.3 Shortcut Connection

We have discussed that deep neural networks with non-linear activations are capable of learning highly complex dataset mappings. Next, you might guess that adding more layers to the network would help in increasing its performance (say, accuracy). However, this is true in theory, but in practice, this is not as easy as it seems, that is, stacking up multiple layers. As discussed in Section 5.4, deeper networks suffer from the gradient vanishing problem. And surprisingly, it is so severe that the deeper the network, the more the degradation of its performance, whereas the layers closer to the logits layer have large gradients and learn fast. In contrast, layers closer to the input layer have smaller (vanishing) gradients and, therefore, learn slowly; and some might even stop learning at all.

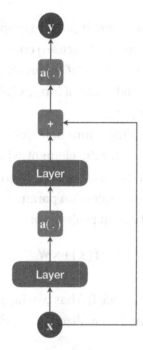

Figure 6-7. *A residual connection for a two-layer neural block*

The choice of layer operations is arbitrary. The first layer processes the input **x** and activates it with **a**(.), whereas the second layer first predicts the output and adds it to the input to this neural block, that is, forms a shortcut connection and then applies the activation to generate the output **y**.

But we would like to use deeper networks for better performance. So how can we circumvent this problem? One solution is to use the residual learning framework (He et al., 2016). Let us understand this framework from the equation that describes it:

$$\mathbf{y} = \mathbf{f}(\mathbf{x}) + \mathbf{x} \tag{6.4}$$

In Equation 6.4, the $\mathbf{x}$ and $\mathbf{y}$ are input and output variables. Here, $\mathbf{f}(.)$ is a neural block (or composite function) containing more than one neural layer (usually two). The *shortcut connection*, also called *residual connection*, is formed by the addition of input $\mathbf{x}$ (also called *residual* here) of neural block $\mathbf{f}(.)$ to its output $\mathbf{y}$.

From Equation 6.4, the dimensions of intermediate output $\mathbf{f}(\mathbf{x})$ must be equal to those of its input $\mathbf{x}$ for the element-wise addition to be a valid operation. When this is not the case, we simply project the input $\mathbf{x}$ to the same dimensions as $\mathbf{f}(\mathbf{x})$ with projection parameters $\mathbf{W}_s$ as follows where the subscript s stands for shortcut projection:

$$\mathbf{y} = \mathbf{f}(\mathbf{x}) + \mathbf{x}\mathbf{W}_s \tag{6.5}$$

In the case when neural block $\mathbf{f}(.)$ has two layers, then the Equation 6.4 can be written as follows and is visualized in Figure 6-7:

$$\mathbf{y} = \mathbf{f}^{(2)}\left(\mathbf{f}^{(1)}(\mathbf{x})\right) + \mathbf{X} \tag{6.6}$$

The type of neural layers in a neural block for residual connection is an arbitrary choice and is based on the task to be performed. Now if we choose all neural layers as dense layer operations, then we can rewrite Equation 6.4 as follows:

$$\mathbf{y} = \mathbf{a}^{(2)}\left(\mathbf{W}^{(2)}\left(\mathbf{a}^{(1)}\left(\mathbf{W}^{(1)}\mathbf{x}\right)\right) + \mathbf{X}\right) \tag{6.7}$$

Here, the terms $\mathbf{x}$, $\mathbf{W}$, and $\mathbf{a}(.)$ are input vector, weight matrix, and activation function, respectively. The superscript index in round brackets signifies the layer to which these elements belong. We have omitted the bias terms for simplicity. Note that, in any shortcut connection, the input to the neural block is added to the output of the last (nonactivated) layer of the block which then follows the activation function of that last layer.

Next, we will build our own residual convolutional network and train it to perform an image recognition task.

6.4 Image Recognition

In this section, we will build a deep convolutional neural network, called residual network (or ResNet) (He et al., 2016), to perform an image recognition task on toy dataset. ResNet was the one to introduce the idea of residual connections discussed in the previous section. There are various ResNet architectures based on the number of layers (such as 18, 34, 50, 101, and 152 layers). We build an 18-layer deep residual network and train it on the CIFAR-10 dataset and see if our ResNet performs better than LeNet we previously trained in Chapter 4. In reality, researchers also usually train large convolutional networks on the ImageNet dataset because learning its underlying mapping is tough as there are nearly 1.2 million images belonging to 1000 categories.

A sidenote: Although highway connections (Srivastava et al., 2015) were invented earlier, they did not see much success because later the residual connections outperformed them in terms of speed, effective deeper model training (with experimental verification of up to 1000 layers), and being a simple and parameterless operation.

Now we look at the architecture of the ResNet18 model which has essentially 18 convolutional layers. A residual block is composed of two sequences of convolution and batch normalization layers which we will denote as ConvBN, for brevity. The input to the residual block is passed through the first ConvBN block followed by the activation function (ReLU, in our case). Next, this intermediate output is passed through another ConvBN block whose output is added to the residual block's input and follows an activation operation. For the residual addition to be possible, the output's dimensions of the second `ConvBN` block must be same as the residual's input's dimensions. In other words, the input filters to the first convolutional layer must be equal to the output filters of the second convolutional layer. If this is not the case, we downsample the residual input by a factor of 2 and match its number of filters (which is usually twice as the input's filters) to those of the second `ConvBN` block's output via a separate convolutional layer named `projection`.

Before programming the residual block, let us import some libraries.

Listing 6-1. Import libraries

```
import Dispatch
import Foundation

import Datasets
import TensorFlow
import TrainingLoop

import PythonKit
let np = Python.import("numpy")
```

The next thing to do is declare some configuration constants such as image sample channels for the network, number of classes in the CIFAR-10 dataset, number of epochs to train the model for, and mini-batch size of samples, and some type aliases for convenience and initialize the device on which every training-related operation will execute.

Listing 6-2. Initialize configuration properties, device, and type aliases for the ResNet18 model and load the CIFAR-10 dataset

```
let inChannels: Int = 3
let classCount = 10
let epochCount = 25
let batchSize = 128
```

```
let device = Device.defaultXLA

typealias TFloat = Tensor<Float>
typealias Input = Tensor<Float>
typealias Output = Tensor<Float>

let imagenetteDataset = Imagenette(batchSize: batchSize,
inputSize: .resized320, outputSize: imageSize, on: device)
```

The input channels accepted by the network are three, the CIFAR-10 dataset has image size of $\mathbb{R}^{32\times32\times3}$ dimensions, the number of classes the network can predict is set to 10, the network will experience the dataset 50 times, and each sample will be a batch of 128 images and the batch dimensions will be $\mathbb{R}^{128\times32\times32\times3}$. We set the device to the XLA backend, and the default device will be selected automatically, that is, hardware accelerator if one is selected (described next) but CPU otherwise.

If you're programming on Google Colaboratory, you may choose the hardware accelerator as either GPU or TPU by following *Runtime ➤ Change runtime type* in the menu bar, then selecting either device from the *Hardware accelerator* dropdown in a pop-up menu, and clicking the *Save* button. Now the device will be automatically set to GPU or TPU accelerator with the XLA backend, and ResNet18 will train on the selected accelerator. In my experiments, I selected GPU.

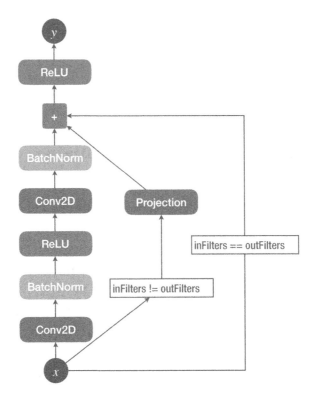

Figure 6-8. *The detailed architecture of the residual convolutional block*

The input goes through convolutional and batch normalization layers, ReLU activation, and another sequence of convolutional and batch normalization layers. This output is added to the residual input which is then activated with ReLU giving the final output of the residual block. The residual input is first projected (or downsampled) to the same dimensions (i.e., half of those of the input) and channels as the output of the second batch normalization layer (i.e., twice as those of the input), but if the channels and dimensions are same, then it is passed to the residual connection as it is.

Now we will program the ConvBN block in Listing 6-3.

Listing 6-3. Program a convolutional and batch normalization layers block

```
struct ConvBN: Layer {
  var conv: Conv2D<Float>
  var norm: BatchNorm<Float>

  init(
    filterShape: (Int, Int, Int, Int),
    strides: (Int, Int) = (1, 1),
    padding: Padding = .same
  ) {
    conv = Conv2D(filterShape: filterShape, strides: strides,
    padding: padding, useBias: false)
    norm = BatchNorm(featureCount: filterShape.3, momentum: 0.1,
    epsilon: 1e-5)
  }

  @differentiable
  func callAsFunction(_ input: Input) -> Output {
    input.sequenced(through: conv, norm)
  }
}
```

Let us start by looking at the initialization of the Conv2D instance named conv which takes filterShape, strides, and padding as arguments. The first argument, filterShape, is a tuple of four Int values where the first, second, third, and fourth values stand for height of kernel, width of kernel, depth of kernel (i.e., filters of the input feature map), and number of kernels (i.e., desired number of the output feature map's filters or depth dimension size, respectively). The second argument, strides, is a tuple of two Int values which at first and second indexes means the steps to take in the height (i.e., vertical) and width (i.e., horizontal) direction, respectively, before applying the convolution operation. The third argument is padding of Padding enumeration type which we have already discussed. In TensorFlow, we don't require to calculate the zero padding and put it in the layer such as convolution or pooling. We can set padding as either .valid or .same. The difference between these is that .same applies zero padding around input (if required) to produce output of the same spatial or temporal dimensions as input, whereas .valid does not apply any zero padding around input and the spatial or temporal dimensions of output may or may not be same as those of input. But in our code examples, we will mostly use the .same case of Padding enumeration. Finally, we don't use the bias term in our conv instance and set the useBias argument equal to **false**.

Next, notice that the batch normalization layer norm takes the featureCount argument equal to the number of output filters of convolutional layer conv. We also set the momentum and epsilon of norm equal to 0.1 and 0.00001, respectively.

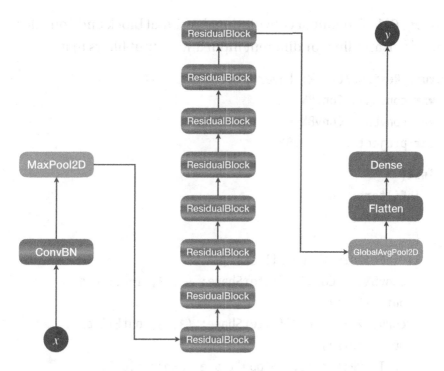

Figure 6-9. *The detailed architecture of the residual convolutional network with 18 layers*

The input $x \in \mathbb{R}^{b \times 224 \times 224 \times 3}$ goes through convolutional and batch normalization layers and ReLU activation followed by a max pool operation. Here, b is the mini-batch size. The output is then passed through a sequence of eight residual blocks whose output goes through a global average pooling operation, flatten layer (to turn a multiple-dimensional tensor into a batched vector), and a dense layer which produces the logits vector $y \in \mathbb{R}^{b \times 10}$.

Now we will program the residual block, shown in Figure 6-8, in Listing 6-4.

Listing 6-4. Program a convolutional residual block and consider the downsampling for different input and output filters to it

```
struct ResidualBlock: Layer {
  var convBN1: ConvBN
  var convBN2: ConvBN
  var projection: ConvBN

  init(
    inFilters: Int,
    outFilters: Int
  ) {
    if inFilters == outFilters {
      convBN1 = ConvBN(filterShape: (3, 3, inFilters,
      outFilters))
      convBN2 = ConvBN(filterShape: (3, 3, outFilters,
      outFilters))
      // In this case, we don't use `projection`.
      projection = ConvBN(filterShape: (1, 1, 1, 1))
    } else {
      convBN1 = ConvBN(filterShape: (3, 3, inFilters,
      outFilters), strides: (2, 2))
      convBN2 = ConvBN(filterShape: (3, 3, outFilters,
      outFilters), strides: (1, 1))
      projection = ConvBN(filterShape: (1, 1, inFilters,
      outFilters), strides: (2, 2))
    }
  }
}
```

```
@differentiable
func callAsFunction(_ input: Input) -> Output {
  let residual = convBN1.conv.filter.shape[2] != convBN2.
  conv.filter.shape[3] ? projection(input) : input
  let convBN1Output = relu(convBN1(input))
  let convBN2Output = relu(convBN2(convBN1Output) + residual)
  return convBN2Output
  }
}
```

The residual block is the basic building block of ResNet models. See Figure 6-8 for visualization and explanation of the residual block. In Listing 6-4, the residual block structure named ResidualBlock has three stored properties, namely, projection, convBN1, and convBN2 of type ConvBN. In its initializer, it accepts the first two Int arguments, namely, inFilters and outFilters. When initializing layers, we check if inFilters and outFilters are equal. If this is true, then we set the kernels' height and width equal to 3 units each for both convBN1 and convBN2. The input channels of convBN1 and convBN2 are set equal to inFilters and outFilters, and the output channels of both are set equal to outFilters.

Also the strides of both layers is (1, 1) by default. In this case, because padding is .same and strides is (1, 1) by default, the input and output features dimensions will be same; therefore, we don't require to project the input, and we initialize the projection instance to a default value.

When the inFilters and outFilters of ResidualBlock are not the same, we set the strides of convBN1 equal to (2, 2), while the other arguments are the same for both convBN1 and convBN2 as in the previous case. With this strides value of convBN1, the spatial dimensions of input features will be halved. So we set all the arguments of the projection instance the same as those of convBN1 to project the input to the same dimensions as the convBN1 and convBN2 sequence will project.

During the forward pass in the callAsFunction(_:) method, we first
set the residual input equal to the projected input if the input and output
filters of two ConvBN sequences are not the same but equal to input itself
otherwise. Then we apply convBN1 and activate it with relu, run through
convBN2, add the residual input, and activate it with relu to return the
output of the residual block.

Listing 6-5 shows the ResNet18 model structure. The ResNet18 model
is visualized in Figure 6-9.

Listing 6-5. Define the residual convolutional network with 18 layers

```
struct ResNet18: Layer {
  var initialConvBNBlock = Sequential {
    ConvBN(filterShape: (7, 7, inChannels, 64), strides: (2, 2))
    MaxPool2D<Float>(poolSize: (3, 3), strides: (2, 2),
    padding: .same)
  }
  var block1 = Sequential {
    ResidualBlock(inFilters: 64, outFilters: 64)
    ResidualBlock(inFilters: 64, outFilters: 64)
  }
  var block2 = Sequential {
    ResidualBlock(inFilters: 64,  outFilters: 128)
    ResidualBlock(inFilters: 128, outFilters: 128)
  }
  var block3 = Sequential {
    ResidualBlock(inFilters: 128, outFilters: 256)
    ResidualBlock(inFilters: 256, outFilters: 256)
  }
```

```
var block4 = Sequential {
  ResidualBlock(inFilters: 256, outFilters: 512)
  ResidualBlock(inFilters: 512, outFilters: 512)
}
var globalAvgPool = GlobalAvgPool2D<Float>()
var flatten = Flatten<Float>()
var classifier: Dense<Float>

init(classCount: Int) {
  classifier = Dense(inputSize: 512, outputSize: classCount)
}

@differentiable
func callAsFunction(_ input: Input) -> Output {
  let initialConvBNOutput = maxPool(relu(initialConvBN(input)
  ))
  let convFeatures = initialConvBNOutput.sequenced(through:
  block1, block2, block3, block4)
  let logits = convFeatures.sequenced(through: globalAvgPool,
  flatten, classifier)
  return logits
 }
}
```

As shown in Figure 6-9, this structure has four blocks each containing two ResidualBlocks. There are also initialConvBN and maxPool properties that performing convolution and batch normalization and a max pool operation. There is an average pooling property named globalAvgPool and a flatten property of type Flatten. Finally, we have a classifier property of Dense type for predicting the logits. In forward pass, the input tensor is passed through initialConvBN, relu, maxPool, block1, block2, block3, and block4. The output is convolved features of the input image which is then pooled, flattened (i.e., reshaped into a batched vector), and passed through the classifier layer for prediction.

Next, we hack into the Layer protocol to implement the reading and writing checkpoint methods with NumPy arrays.

Listing 6-6. Implement custom checkpoint reading and writing methods on the Layer protocol using the NumPy library with Python interoperability

```
extension Layer {
  public func writeCheckpoint(to file: String) throws {
    var parameters = Array<PythonObject>()
    for keyPath in self.recursivelyAllWritableKeyPaths(to: TFloat.
    self) {
      parameters.append(self[keyPath: keyPath].makeNumpyArray())
    }
    np.save(file, np.array(parameters))
  }

  public mutating func readCheckpoint(from file: String) throws {
    let parameters = np.load(file)
    for (index, keyPath) in self.recursivelyAllWritableKeyPaths
    (to: TFloat.self).enumerated() {

      self[keyPath: keyPath] = TFloat(numpy: parameters[index])!
    }
  }
}
```

We declare two instance methods on the Layer protocol which are automatically made available to all the types conforming to it, namely, writeCheckpoint(to:) and readCheckpoint(from:). The checkpoint writing method declares a parameters array of PythonObject type. Then we iterate through all the properties of Tensor<Float> type via KeyPath that can be written to. We append each property to the parameters array after converting the TFloat instance to NumPy array by calling the makeNumpyArray() method. After the loop, we save the NumPy array typecasted parameters to the file location.

In the checkpoint reading method, we load the checkpoint file. Then we recursively iterate over all the writable KeyPaths pointing to TFloat type and set the Layer-conforming instance's properties at keyPath keyPath equal to the NumPy loaded parameters from the file at the index by forced unwrapping. This way we load the parameters in our Layer-conforming instance.

Next, we define a function writeCheckpoint(_:event:) to save checkpoints after the ending of each epoch during training. We will pass it to the callbacks argument in an array. The callbacks takes an array of functions to call based on a specific event during training.

Listing 6-7. Define a function to automatically write checkpoint during training

```
func writeCheckpoint<L: TrainingLoopProtocol>(_ loop: inout L,
event: TrainingLoopEvent) throws {
  DispatchQueue.global(qos: .userInitiated).async {
    switch event {
    case .epochEnd:
      do {
        try preTrainingModel.writeCheckpoint(to: "ResNet18.npy")
      } catch {
        print(error)
      }
    default: break
    }
  }
}
```

In Listing 6-7, we define a function writeCheckpoint(_:event:) whose placeholder type L conforms to TrainingLoopProtocol, and it takes two arguments: loop of type **inout** L and event of TrainingLoopEvent type. This function can throw an error. If you want to define your function for other custom tasks during training by passing to callbacks, you should use the same arguments and define custom functionality inside the function's body.

Inside the body, we have a **switch** statement enclosed in DispatchQueue for using another thread to perform this task (you might not need to write this statement, but I had some problem with code execution). The **switch** statement compares the event parameters to various cases. Because we want to save checkpoints at the end of each epoch, we try to write the checkpoint when event is equal to .epochEnd case. There are many other cases of event available that you can leverage to customize the training loop.

Listing 6-8. Initialize the model and optimizer, and train the model

```
// Initialize the model and optimizer
var model = ResNet18(classCount: classCount)
var optimizer = SGD(for: model, learningRate: 0.1, momentum: 0.9)

// Training setup
let trainingProgress = TrainingProgress()
var trainingLoop = TrainingLoop(
  training: dataset.training,
  validation: dataset.validation,
  optimizer: optimizer,
  lossFunction: softmaxCrossEntropy,
  callbacks: [trainingProgress.update, writeCheckpoint])

// Train the model
try! trainingLoop.fit(&model, epochs: epochs, on: device)
```

In Listing 6-8, we have initialized the `model` with `ResNet18` having `classCount` classes for prediction. The optimizer `optimizer` is initialized with stochastic gradient descent optimizer having a learning rate of `0.1` and momentum set equal to `0.9`. Then `TrainingProgress` and `TrainingLoop` instances `trainingProgress` and `trainingLoop` are initialized, respectively. The `trainingLoop` is initialized with `datasets` for `training` and `validation`, the optimizer is set equal to `optimizer`, the loss function is set as `softmaxCrossEntropy`, and `callbacks` is an array containing the update method `trainingProgress.update` and `writeCheckpoint` function.

Finally, we train the `model` and achieve image classification accuracy on training and validation sets 0.9960 and 0.7305, respectively. Our ResNet18 model performs better than the small LeNet trained on the same dataset (see Chapter 4) which had accuracy on training and validation sets equal to only 0.5607 and 0.5625, respectively.

6.5 Conclusion

In this chapter, we studied that convolutional neural networks are great for tackling computer vision problems and have many advantages over dense networks. We also studied a technique to mitigate the gradient vanishing problem. Finally, we trained a deep convolutional network to classify images which performed better than a smaller convolutional network signaling that deep non-linear models are better than the shallow ones.

This book introduced the deep learning subject with Swift for TensorFlow. But we only scratched the surface of the deep learning field, and there is a lot more to know! I hope you enjoyed understanding and programming deep learning in the Swift language. Until next time...

References

Abadi, M., Barham, P., Chen, J., Chen, Z., Davis, A., Dean, J., Devin, M., Ghemawat, S., Irving, G., Isard, M., Kudlur, M., Levenberg, J., Monga, R., Moore, S., Murray, D., Steiner, B., Tucker, P., Vasudevan, V., Warden, P., Wicke, M., Yu, Y., and Zhang, X. (2016). TensorFlow: A system for large-scale machine learning. In *OSDI*.

Akaike, H. (1973). Information theory and an extension of the maximum likelihood principle.

OpenAI, Akkaya, I., Andrychowicz, M., Chociej, M., Litwin, M., McGrew, B., Petron, A., Paino, A., Plappert, M., Powell, G., Ribas, R., Schneider, J., Tezak, N., Tworek, J., Welinder, P., Weng, L., Yuan, Q., Zaremba, W., and Zhang, L. (2019). Solving Rubik's Cube with a Robot Hand. *arXiv preprint arXiv:1910.07113.*

Al-Rfou, R., Alain, G., Almahairi, A., Angermüller, C., Bahdanau, D., Ballas, N., Bastien, F., Bayer, J., Belikov, A., Belopolsky, A., Bengio, Y., Bergeron, A., Bergstra, J., Bisson, V., Snyder, J.B., Bouchard, N., Boulanger-Lewandowski, N., Bouthillier, X., Brébisson, A.D., Breuleux, O., Carrier, P.L., Cho, K., Chorowski, J., Christiano, P.F., Cooijmans, T., Côté, M., Côté, M., Courville, A.C., Dauphin, Y., Delalleau, O., Demouth, J., Desjardins, G., Dieleman, S., Dinh, L., Ducoffe, M., Dumoulin, V., Kahou, S., Erhan, D., Fan, Z., Firat, O., Germain, M., Glorot, X., Goodfellow, I.J., Graham, M., Gülçehre, Ç., Hamel, P., Harlouchet, I., Heng, J., Hidasi, B., Honari, S., Jain, A., Jean, S., Jia, K., Korobov, M., Kulkarni, V., Lamb, A., Lamblin, P., Larsen, E., Laurent, C., Lee, S., Lefrançois, S., Lemieux, S., Léonard, N., Lin, Z., Livezey, J.A., Lorenz, C., Lowin, J., Ma, Q., Manzagol, P., Mastropietro, O., McGibbon, R., Memisevic, R., Merrienboer, B.V., Michalski, V., Mirza, M., Orlandi, A., Pal, C., Pascanu, R., Pezeshki, M., Raffel, C., Renshaw, D.,

© Rahul Bhalley 2021
R. Bhalley, *Deep Learning with Swift for TensorFlow*,
https://doi.org/10.1007/978-1-4842-6330-3

REFERENCES

Rocklin, M., Romero, A., Roth, M., Sadowski, P., Salvatier, J., Savard, F., Schlüter, J., Schulman, J., Schwartz, G., Serban, I., Serdyuk, D., Shabanian, S., Simon, É., Spieckermann, S., Subramanyam, S., Sygnowski, J., Tanguay, J., Tulder, G.V., Turian, J.P., Urban, S., Vincent, P., Visin, F., Vries, H.D., Warde-Farley, D., Webb, D.J., Willson, M., Xu, K., Xue, L., Yao, L., Zhang, S., and Zhang, Y. (2016). Theano: A Python framework for fast computation of mathematical expressions. *arXiv preprint arXiv:1605.02688.*

Aleksandrowicz, G., Alexander, T., Barkoutsos, P., Bello, L., Ben-Haim, Y., Bucher, D., Cabrera-Hernández, F., Carballo-Franquis, J., Chen, A., Chen, C., et al. (2019). Qiskit: An open-source framework for quantum computing. Retrieved online at http://reu.cct.lsu.edu/documents/2019-presentations/Siddiqui.pdf.

Baydin, A.G., Pearlmutter, B.A., Radul, A., and Siskind, J. (2017). Automatic differentiation in machine learning: a survey. *The Journal of Machine Learning Research*, 18(1):5595–5637.

Bellman, R. E. (2015). *Adaptive Control Processes: A Guided Tour.* Princeton University Press.

Bengio, Y., Lamblin, P., Popovici, D., and Larochelle, H. (2007). Greedy layer-wise training of deep networks. In *Advances in Neural Information Processing Systems*, pages 153–160.

Bergholm, V., Izaac, J., Schuld, M., Gogolin, C., and Killoran, N. (2018). PennyLane: Automatic differentiation of hybrid quantum-classical computations. *arXiv preprint arXiv:1811.04968.*

Bezanson, J., Edelman, A., Karpinski, S., and Shah, V. B. (2017). Julia: A fresh approach to numerical computing. *SIAM Review*, 59(1):65–98.

Bezanson, J., Karpinski, S., Shah, V. B., and Edelman, A. (2012). Julia: A fast dynamic language for technical computing. *arXiv preprint arXiv:1209.5145.*

Bischof, C. H., Bücker, H. M., Rasch, A., Slusanschi, E., and Lang, B. (2007). Automatic differentiation of the general-purpose computational fluid dynamics package fluent.

Bishop, C. M. (1995). *Neural Networks for Pattern Recognition*. Oxford University Press.

Bishop, C. M. (2006). *Pattern Recognition and Machine Learning*. Springer.

Bottou, L. (1998). Online learning and stochastic approximations. *On-line learning in neural networks*, 17(9):142.

Box, G. E. (1976). Science and statistics. *Journal of the American Statistical Association*, 71(356):791–799.

Buitinck, L., Louppe, G., Blondel, M., Pedregosa, F., Mueller, A., Grisel, O., Niculae, V., Prettenhofer, P., Gramfort, A., Grobler, J., Layton, R., VanderPlas, J., Joly, A., Holt, B., and Varoquaux, G. (2013). API design for machine learning software: experiences from the scikit-learn project. *arXiv preprint arXiv:1309.0238*.

Carter, S., Armstrong, Z., Schubert, L., Johnson, I., and Olah, C. (2019). Exploring neural networks with activation atlases. *Distill*.

Casanova, D., Sharp, R. S., Final, M., Christianson, B., and Symonds, P. (2000). Application of automatic differentiation to race car performance optimisation, automatic differentiation of algorithms: from simulation to optimization.

Cauchy, A. (1847). Méthode générale pour la résolution des systemes d'équations simultanées. *Comp. Rend. Sci. Paris*, 25(1847):536–538.

Chang, S., Zhang, Y., Han, W., Yu, M., Guo, X., Tan, W., Cui, X., Witbrock, M., Hasegawa-Johnson, M. A., and Huang, T. S. (2017). Dilated recurrent neural networks. In *Advances in Neural Information Processing Systems*, pages 77–87.

Chapelle, O., Schölkopf, B., and Zien, A. (2006). *Semi-Supervised Learning*. The MIT Press.

Chollet, F. et al. (2015). Keras. https://github.com/fchollet/keras.

Clevert, D.-A., Unterthiner, T., and Hochreiter, S. (2015). Fast and accurate deep network learning by exponential linear units (ELUs). *arXiv preprint arXiv:1511.07289*.

REFERENCES

Corliss, G. F. (1988). Applications of differentiation arithmetic. In *Reliability in Computing*, pages 127–148. Elsevier.

Coucke, A., Chlieh, M., Gisselbrecht, T., Leroy, D., Poumeyrol, M., and Lavril, T. (2019). Efficient keyword spotting using dilated convolutions and gating. In *ICASSP 2019-2019 IEEE International Conference on Acoustics, Speech and Signal Processing (ICASSP)*, pages 6351–6355. IEEE.

Deisenroth, M. P., Faisal, A. A., and Ong, C. S. (2020). *Mathematics for Machine Learning*. Cambridge University Press.

Donahue, C., McAuley, J., and Puckette, M. (2018). Adversarial audio synthesis.

Dong, C., Loy, C. C., He, K., and Tang, X. (2014). Learning a deep convolutional network for image super-resolution. In *European conference on computer vision*, pages 184–199. Springer. *arXiv preprint arXiv:1802.04208*.

Forth, S. A. and Evans, T. P. (2002). Aerofoil optimisation via ad of a multigrid cell-vertex Euler flow solver. In *Automatic differentiation of algorithms*, pages 153–160. Springer.

Girshick, R. (2015). Fast R-CNN. In *Proceedings of the IEEE international conference on computer vision*, pages 1440–1448.

Girshick, R., Donahue, J., Darrell, T., and Malik, J. (2014). Rich feature hierarchies for accurate object detection and semantic segmentation. In *Proceedings of the IEEE conference on computer vision and pattern recognition*, pages 580–587.

Glorot, X., Bordes, A., and Bengio, Y. (2011). Deep sparse rectifier neural networks. In *Proceedings of the fourteenth international conference on artificial intelligence and statistics*, pages 315–323.

Goodfellow, I., Bengio, Y., Courville, A., and Bengio, Y. (2016). *Deep learning, Volume 1*. MIT Press Cambridge.

Goodfellow, I., Pouget-Abadie, J., Mirza, M., Xu, B., Warde-Farley, D., Ozair, S., Courville, A., and Bengio, Y. (2014). Generative adversarial nets. In *Advances in neural information processing systems*, pages 2672–2680.

Grabmeier, J. and Kaltofen, E. (2003). *Computer Algebra Handbook: Foundations, Applications, Systems.* Springer Science & Business Media.

Griewank, A. and Walther, A. (2008). *Evaluating derivatives: principles and techniques of algorithmic differentiation.* SIAM.

Han, J. and Moraga, C. (1995). The influence of the sigmoid function parameters on the speed of backpropagation learning. In *International Workshop on Artificial Neural Networks,* pages 195–201. Springer.

Harris, C., Millman, K. J., Walt, S., Gommers, R., Virtanen, P., Cournapeau, D., Wieser, E., Taylor, J., Berg, S., Smith, N. J., Kern, R., Picus, M., Hoyer, S., Kerkwijk, M., Brett, M., Haldane, A., del R'io, J. F., Wiebe, M., Peterson, P., G'erard-Marchant, P., Sheppard, K., Reddy, T., Weckesser, W., Abbasi, H., Gohlke, C., and Oliphant, T. E. (2020). Array programming with NumPy. *Nature,* 585 7825:357–362.

He, K., Zhang, X., Ren, S., and Sun, J. (2016). Deep residual learning for image recognition. In *Proceedings of the IEEE conference on computer vision and pattern recognition,* pages 770–778.

Heideman, M. T., Johnson, D. H., and Burrus, C. S. (1985). Gauss and the history of the fast Fourier transform. *Archive for history of exact sciences,* 34(3):265–277.

Hershey, S., Chaudhuri, S., Ellis, D. P., Gemmeke, J. F., Jansen, A., Moore, R. C., Plakal, M., Platt, D., Saurous, R. A., Seybold, B., et al. (2017). CNN architectures for large-scale audio classification. In *2017 IEEE international conference on acoustics, speech and signal processing (ICASSP),* pages 131–135. IEEE.

Hinton, G., Vinyals, O., and Dean, J. (2015). Distilling the knowledge in a neural network. *arXiv preprint arXiv:1503.02531.*

Hinton, G. E., Osindero, S., and Teh, Y.-W. (2006). A fast learning algorithm for deep belief nets. *Neural computation,* 18(7):1527–1554.

Hoerl, A. E. and Kennard, R. W. (1970). Ridge regression: Biased estimation for nonorthogonal problems. *Technometrics,* 12(1):55–67.

REFERENCES

Iandola, F. N., Han, S., Moskewicz, M. W., Ashraf, K., Dally, W. J., and Keutzer, K. (2016). Squeezenet: Alexnet-level accuracy with 50x fewer parameters and <0.5mb model size. *arXiv preprint arXiv:1602.07360.*

Jaderberg, M., Simonyan, K., Zisserman, A., and Kavukcuoglu, K. (2015). Spatial transformer networks. In *Advances in neural information processing systems*, pages 2017–2025.

Jarrett, K., Kavukcuoglu, K., Ranzato, M., and LeCun, Y. (2009). What is the best multi-stage architecture for object recognition? In *2009 IEEE 12th international conference on computer vision*, pages 2146–2153. IEEE.

Jerrell, M. E. (1997). Automatic differentiation and interval arithmetic for estimation of disequilibrium models. *Computational Economics*, 10(3):295–316.

Kim, J., Kwon Lee, J., and Mu Lee, K. (2016). Deeply-recursive convolutional network for image super-resolution. In *Proceedings of the IEEE conference on computer vision and pattern recognition*, pages 1637–1645.

Klambauer, G., Unterthiner, T., Mayr, A., and Hochreiter, S. (2017). Self-normalizing neural networks. In *Advances in neural information processing systems*, pages 971–980.

Krizhevsky, A., Sutskever, I., and Hinton, G. E. (2017). ImageNet classification with deep convolutional neural networks. *Communications of the ACM*, 60(6):84–90.

Kutz, J. N. (2017). Deep learning in fluid dynamics. *Journal of Fluid Mechanics*, 814:1–4.

Lai, G., Chang, W.-C., Yang, Y., and Liu, H. (2018). Modeling long-and short-term temporal patterns with deep neural networks. In *The 41st International ACM SIGIR Conference on Research & Development in Information Retrieval*, pages 95–104.

Lattner, C. and Pienaar, J. (2019). MLIR primer: A compiler infrastructure for the end of Moore's law.

Lattner, C., Pienaar, J., Amini, M., Bondhugula, U., Riddle, R., Cohen, A., Shpeisman, T., Davis, A., Vasilache, N., and Zinenko, O. (2020). MLIR: A compiler infrastructure for the end of Moore's law. *arXiv preprint arXiv:2002.11054*.

LeCun, Y. (1998). The MNIST database of handwritten digits. http://yann.lecun.com/exdb/mnist.

LeCun, Y., Bengio, Y., and Hinton, G. E. (2015). Deep learning. *Nature*, 521(7553):436–444.

LeCun, Y., Boser, B., Denker, J. S., Henderson, D., Howard, R. E., Hubbard, W., and Jackel, L. D. (1989). Backpropagation applied to handwritten zip code recognition. *Neural computation*, 1(4):541–551.

LeCun, Y., Bottou, L., Bengio, Y., and Haffner, P. (1998). Gradient-based learning applied to document recognition. *Proceedings of the IEEE*, 86(11):2278–2324.

Li, Y., Kaiser, L., Bengio, S., and Si, S. (2019). Area attention. In *International Conference on Machine Learning*, pages 3846–3855. PMLR.

Lin, H., Zeng, W., Ding, X., Huang, Y., Huang, C., and Paisley, J. (2019). Learning rate dropout. *arXiv preprint arXiv:1912.00144*.

Lin, M., Chen, Q., and Yan, S. (2013). Network in network. *arXiv preprint arXiv:1312.4400*.

Maas, A. L., Hannun, A. Y., and Ng, A. Y. (2013). Rectifier nonlinearities improve neural network acoustic models. In *Proc. icml*, volume 30, page 3.

Maclaurin, D. (2016). *Modeling, inference and optimization with composable differentiable procedures*. PhD thesis.

Maclaurin, D., Duvenaud, D., and Adams, R. P. (2015). Autograd: Effortless gradients in NumPy. In *ICML 2015 AutoML Workshop*, volume 238, page 5.

McCorduck, P. (2004). *Machines who think: A personal inquiry into the history and prospects of artificial intelligence*. CRC Press.

Mikolov, T. et al. (2012). Statistical language models based on neural networks. *Presentation at Google, Mountain View, 2nd April*, 80:26.

Mitchell, T. M. (1997). *Machine Learning*. McGraw-Hill, New York.

Mnih, V., Kavukcuoglu, K., Silver, D., Rusu, A.A., Veness, J., Bellemare, M.G., Graves, A., Riedmiller, M.A., Fidjeland, A.K., Ostrovski, G., Petersen, S., Beattie, C., Sadik, A., Antonoglou, I., King, H., Kumaran, D., Wierstra, D., Legg, S., and Hassabis, D. (2015). Human-level control through deep reinforcement learning. *Nature*, 518, 529-533.

Müller, J.-D. and Cusdin, P. (2005). On the performance of discrete adjoint CFD codes using automatic differentiation. *International journal for numerical methods in fluids*, 47(8–9):939–945.

Murphy, K. P. (2012). *Machine Learning: A Probabilistic Perspective*. MIT Press.

Nair, V. and Hinton, G. E. (2010). Rectified linear units improve restricted Boltzmann machines. In *ICML*.

Nakamoto, S. (2008). Bitcoin: A peer-to-peer electronic cash system. Retrieved online at `https://bitcoin.org/bitcoin.pdf`.

Ng, A. (2019). Machine Learning Yearning: Technical strategy for AI engineers in the era of deep learning. Retrieved online at `https://www.mlyearning.org`.

Odena, A., Dumoulin, V., and Olah, C. (2016). Deconvolution and checkerboard artifacts. *Distill*, 1(10):e3.

Olah, C., Mordvintsev, A., and Schubert, L. (2017). Feature visualization. *Distill*, 2(11):e7.

Olah, C., Satyanarayan, A., Johnson, I., Carter, S., Schubert, L., Ye, K., and Mordvintsev, A. (2018). The building blocks of interpretability. *Distill*, 3(3):e10.

Oord, A. v. d., Dieleman, S., Zen, H., Simonyan, K., Vinyals, O., Graves, A., Kalchbrenner, N., Senior, A., and Kavukcuoglu, K. (2016a). Wavenet: A generative model for raw audio. *arXiv preprint arXiv:1609.03499*.

Oord, A. v. d., Kalchbrenner, N., Espeholt, L., Kavukcuoglu, K., Vinyals, O., and Graves, A., (2016b). Conditional image generation with PixelCNN decoders. In *Advances in neural information processing systems*, pages 4790–4798.

Oord, A. v. d., Kalchbrenner, N., and Kavukcuoglu, K. (2016c). Pixel recurrent neural networks. *arXiv preprint arXiv:1601.06759*.

Parmar, N., Vaswani, A., Uszkoreit, J., Kaiser, Ł., Shazeer, N., Ku, A., and Tran, D. (2018). Image transformer. *arXiv preprint arXiv:1802.05751*.

Pascanu, R., Mikolov, T., and Bengio, Y. (2013). On the difficulty of training recurrent neural networks. In *International conference on machine learning*, pages 1310–1318.

Paszke, A., Gross, S., Chintala, S., Chanan, G., Yang, E., Devito, Z., Lin, Z., Desmaison, A., Antiga, L., and Lerer, A. (2017). Automatic differentiation in PyTorch.

Paszke, A., Gross, S., Massa, F., Lerer, A., Bradbury, J., Chanan, G., Killeen, T., Lin, Z., Gimelshein, N., Antiga, L., Desmaison, A., Köpf, A., Yang, E., DeVito, Z., Raison, M., Tejani, A., Chilamkurthy, S., Steiner, B., Fang, L., Bai, J., and Chintala, S. (2019). PyTorch: An imperative style, high-performance deep learning library. *arXiv preprint arXiv:1912.01703*.

Preskill, J. (2018). Quantum computing in the NISQ era and beyond. *Quantum*, 2:79.

Radford, A., Metz, L., and Chintala, S. (2015). Unsupervised representation learning with deep convolutional generative adversarial networks. *arXiv preprint arXiv:1511.06434*.

Raina, R., Madhavan, A., and Ng, A. Y. (2009). Large-scale deep unsupervised learning using graphics processors. In *Proceedings of the 26th annual international conference on machine learning*, pages 873–880.

Ramachandran, P., Zoph, B., and Le, Q. V. (2017). Searching for activation functions. *arXiv preprint arXiv:1710.05941*.

Ranzato, M., Poultney, C., Chopra, S., and Cun, Y. L. (2007). Efficient learning of sparse representations with an energy-based model. In *Advances in neural information processing systems*, pages 1137–1144.

Redmon, J., Divvala, S., Girshick, R., and Farhadi, A. (2016). You only look once: Unified, real-time object detection. In *Proceedings of the IEEE conference on computer vision and pattern recognition*, pages 779–788.

Redmon, J. and Farhadi, A. (2017). Yolo9000: better, faster, stronger. In *Proceedings of the IEEE conference on computer vision and pattern recognition*, pages 7263–7271.

REFERENCES

Redmon, J. and Farhadi, A. (2018). Yolov3: An incremental improvement. *arXiv preprint arXiv:1804.02767.*

Rumelhart, D. E., Hinton, G. E., and Williams, R. J. (1986). Learning representations by back-propagating errors. *Nature*, 323(6088):533–536.

Russakovsky, O., Deng, J., Su, H., Krause, J., Satheesh, S., Ma, S., Huang, Z., Karpathy, A., Khosla, A., Bernstein, M., et al. (2015). ImageNet large scale visual recognition challenge. *International journal of computer vision*, 115(3):211–252.

Russell, S. and Norvig, P. (2002). *Artificial Intelligence: A Modern Approach.* Pearson.

Sabour, S., Frosst, N., and Hinton, G. E. (2017). Dynamic routing between capsules. In *Advances in neural information processing systems*, pages 3856–3866.

Schulman, J., Wolski, F., Dhariwal, P., Radford, A., and Klimov, O. (2017). Proximal policy optimization algorithms. *arXiv preprint arXiv:1707.06347.*

Sharma, A. S. and Bhalley, R. (2016). ASR—a real-time speech recognition on portable devices. In *2016 2nd International Conference on Advances in Computing, Communication, & Automation (ICACCA) (Fall)*, pages 1–4. IEEE.

Shen, J., Pang, R., Weiss, R. J., Schuster, M., Jaitly, N., Yang, Z., Chen, Z., Zhang, Y., Wang, Y., Skerrv-Ryan, R., Saurous, R.A., Agiomyrgiannakis, Y., and Wu, Y. (2018). Natural TTS synthesis by conditioning WaveNet on mel spectrogram predictions. In *2018 IEEE International Conference on Acoustics, Speech and Signal Processing (ICASSP)*, pages 4779–4783. IEEE.

Shi, W., Caballero, J., Huszár, F., Totz, J., Aitken, A. P., Bishop, R., Rueckert, D., and Wang, Z. (2016a). Real-time single image and video super-resolution using an efficient sub-pixel convolutional neural network. In *Proceedings of the IEEE conference on computer vision and pattern recognition*, pages 1874–1883.

Shi, W., Caballero, J., Theis, L., Huszar, F., Aitken, A., Ledig, C., and Wang, Z. (2016b). Is the deconvolution layer the same as a convolutional layer? *arXiv preprint arXiv:1609.07009*.

Simonyan, K. and Zisserman, A. (2014). Very deep convolutional networks for large-scale image recognition. *arXiv preprint arXiv:1409.1556*.

Springenberg, J. T., Dosovitskiy, A., Brox, T., and Riedmiller, M. (2014). Striving for simplicity: The all convolutional net. *arXiv preprint arXiv:1412.6806*.

Srivastava, N., Hinton, G., Krizhevsky, A., Sutskever, I., and Salakhutdinov, R. (2014). Dropout: a simple way to prevent neural networks from overfitting. *The journal of machine learning research*, 15(1):1929–1958.

Srivastava, R. K., Greff, K., and Schmidhuber, J. (2015). Highway networks. *arXiv preprint arXiv:1505.00387*.

Sutton, R. S. and Barto, A. G. (2018). *Reinforcement Learning: An Introduction*. The MIT Press.

Szegedy, C., Liu, W., Jia, Y., Sermanet, P., Reed, S., Anguelov, D., Erhan, D., Vanhoucke, V., and Rabinovich, A. (2015). Going deeper with convolutions. In *Proceedings of the IEEE conference on computer vision and pattern recognition*, pages 1–9.

Szegedy, C., Reed, S., Erhan, D., Anguelov, D., and Ioffe, S. (2014). Scalable high-quality object detection. *arXiv preprint arXiv:1412.1441*.

Szegedy, C., Vanhoucke, V., Ioffe, S., Shlens, J., and Wojna, Z. (2016). Rethinking the inception architecture for computer vision. In *Proceedings of the IEEE conference on computer vision and pattern recognition*, pages 2818–2826.

Szegedy, C., Zaremba, W., Sutskever, I., Bruna, J., Erhan, D., Goodfellow, I., and Fergus, R. (2013). Intriguing properties of neural networks. *arXiv preprint arXiv:1312.6199*.

Tan, M. and Le, Q. V. (2019). EfficientNet: Rethinking model scaling for convolutional neural networks. *arXiv preprint arXiv:1905.11946*.

Taylor, M., Purdy, S., breznak, Surpur, C., Marshall, A., Ragazzi, D., Ahmad, S., numenta ci, Malta, A., Weinberger, P. C., Akhila, Lewis, M., Crowder, R., Borgne, M. L., Simons, Y. C., McCall, R. J., Scheinkman, L., Eric, M., Song, U., keithcom, Romano, N., Bolliger, S., vitaly krugl, Bridgewater, J., Danforth, I., Weiss, J., Silver, T., Ray, D., and zuhaagha (2018). NuPIC: Numenta platform for intelligent computing. https://github.com/numenta/nupic.

Theodoridis, S. and Koutroumbas, K. (2009). *Pattern Recognition*. Academic Press.

Thomas, J. P., Dowell, E. H., and Hall, K. C. (2010). Using automatic differentiation to create a nonlinear reduced-order-model aerodynamic solver. *AIAA journal*, 48(1):19–24.

Turing, A. M. (1936). On computable numbers, with an application to the entscheidungsproblem. *Journal of Math*, 58(345–363):5.

Vaswani, A., Shazeer, N., Parmar, N., Uszkoreit, J., Jones, L., Gomez, A. N., Kaiser, Ł., and Polosukhin, I. (2017). Attention is all you need. In *Advances in neural information processing systems*, pages 5998–6008.

Verma, A. (2000). An introduction to automatic differentiation. *Current Science*, pages 804–807.

Vincent, P., Larochelle, H., Bengio, Y., and Manzagol, P.-A. (2008). Extracting and composing robust features with denoising autoencoders. In *Proceedings of the 25th international conference on Machine learning*, pages 1096–1103.

Walther, A. (2007). Automatic differentiation of explicit Runge-Kutta methods for optimal control. *Computational Optimization and Applications*, 36(1):83–108.

Wei, R., Zheng, D., Rasi, M., and Chrzaszcz, B. (2018). Differentiable programming manifesto. https://github.com/apple/swift/blob/main/docs/DifferentiableProgramming.md.

Yu, F. and Koltun, V. (2015). Multi-scale context aggregation by dilated convolutions. *arXiv preprint arXiv:1511.07122*.

Zeiler, M. D. and Fergus, R. (2012). Differentiable pooling for hierarchical feature learning. *arXiv preprint arXiv:1207.0151.*

Zeiler, M. D. and Fergus, R. (2014). Visualizing and understanding convolutional networks. In *European conference on computer vision,* pages 818–833. Springer.

Zeiler, M. D., Krishnan, D., Taylor, G. W., and Fergus, R. (2010). Deconvolutional networks. In *2010 IEEE Computer Society Conference on computer vision and pattern recognition,* pages 2528–2535. IEEE.

Zeller, C. (2011). CUDA C/C++ basics. *NVIDIA Coporation.*

Zhang, R. (2019). Making convolutional networks shift-invariant again. *arXiv preprint arXiv:1904.11486.*

Zhu, C., Byrd, R., Lu, P., and Nocedal, J. (1994). L-BFGS-B, Fortran subroutine for large-scale bound constrained optimization. *Department of Electrical Engineering and Computer Science, Northwestern University, IL, USA.*

Index

A

Accumulation modes, 75–77
Activation functions, 163, 165
    leaky ReLU, 213, 214
    ReLU, 210–213
    SELU, 214–216
    sigmoid function, 206–210
    softmax, 210
Adversarial training, 224, 225
Algorithmic differentiation (AD),
    75, 82
    accumulation modes
      forward mode, 77–80
      reverse mode, 80–82
    implementation approaches
      operator overloading, 82–85
      SCT, 85, 86
    programming approaches
      algorithmic
        differentiation, 75
      manual differentiation, 73
      numerical differentiation, 74
      symbolic differentiation, 74
Amazon Web Services (AWS), 70
Array, 89, 90, 93, 98, 104, 117,
    118, 124
Artificial intelligence (AI), 1, 3, 4
Augmented reality (AR), 2

B

Backward pass, 80, 82
Batches, 149–151, 159
Batch gradient descent, 220, 222
Batch normalization
    layers block, 257
Bayesian inference, 14
Bayes rule, 52
Bias, 28, 29
Binary classification, 198–200,
    206, 217
Binary matrix operations, 41–44
Break statement, 98, 150

C

case keyword, 106
Central processing unit (CPU), 34
Chain rule of probability, 50–52
Checkpointable protocol, 154, 155
Classification, 154, 159, 189,
    197–201, 206, 210, 217, 218,
    224, 226, 230, 231, 233, 243,
    245, 267
Closure expressions, 100, 103,
    104, 134
Composite function, 54, 65
Conditional probability, 48, 49

© Rahul Bhalley 2021
R. Bhalley, *Deep Learning with Swift for TensorFlow*,
https://doi.org/10.1007/978-1-4842-6330-3

D

Printed in the United States
By Bookmasters